Music of
the Gilded Age

Music of the Gilded Age

John Ogasapian
and N. Lee Orr

American History through Music
David J. Brinkman, Series Editor

GREENWOOD PRESS
Westport, Connecticut • London

Library of Congress Cataloging-in-Publication Data

Ogasapian, John.
  Music of the gilded age / John Ogasapian and N. Lee Orr.
      p. cm. — (American history through music)
  Includes bibliographical references (p.   ) and index.
  ISBN-13: 978–0–313–33552–5 (alk. paper)
  ISBN-10: 0–313–33552–4 (alk. paper)
  1. Music—Social aspects—United States—History—19th century.   I.
Orr, N. Lee, 1949–   II. Title.
  ML3917.U6O44   2007
  780.973'09034—dc22   2007000419

British Library Cataloguing in Publication Data is available.

Library of Congress Catalog Card Number: 2007000419
ISBN-13: 978–0–313–33552–5
ISBN-10: 0–313–33552–4

First published in 2007

Greenwood Press, 88 Post Road West, Westport, CT 06881
An imprint of Greenwood Publishing Group, Inc.
www.greenwood.com

Printed in the United States of America

The paper used in this book complies with the
Permanent Paper Standard issued by the National
Information Standards Organization (Z39.48–1984).

10 9 8 7 6 5 4 3 2 1

For John

Contents

Series Foreword

The elements of music are well known. They include melody, rhythm, harmony, form, and texture. Music, though, has infinite variety. Exploring this variety in the music of specific time periods, such as the Colonial and Revolutionary periods, the Roaring Twenties, and the Counterculture Era, is the purpose of the "American History through Music" series. The authors of each volume describe the music in terms of its basic elements, but more important, they focus on how the social, economic, political, technological, and religious influences shaped the music of that particular time. Each volume in the series describes not only the music of a particular era but the ways in which the music reflected societal concerns. For these purposes, music is defined inclusively; this series considers such diverse musical genres as classical, folk, jazz, rock, religious, and theater music, as each of these genres serves as both reflections of society and as illustrations of how music influences society.

Perhaps the most important conclusion that readers will draw from this series is that music does not exist independently of society. Listeners have enjoyed music throughout time for its aesthetic qualities, but music has also been used to convey emotions and ideas. It has been used to enhance patriotic rituals and to maintain order in social and religious ceremonies. The "American History through Music" series attempts to put these and other uses of music in an historical context. For instance, how did music serve as entertainment during the Great Depression? How did the music of the Civil War contribute to the stability of the Union—and to the Confederacy? Answers to these and other questions show that music is not just a part of society; music *is* society.

The authors of "American History through Music" present essays based in sound scholarship, written for the lay reader. In addition to discussing important genres and approaches to music, each volume profiles the composers and performers whose music defines their era, describes the musical instruments and technological innovations that influenced the musical world, and provides a glossary of important terms and a bibliography of recommended readings. This information will help students and other interested readers understand the colorful and complex mosaics of musical history.

David J. Brinkman
University of Wyoming

Acknowledgments

My dear colleague and beloved friend John Ogasapian began this book and had completed about half of it (chapters one, two, three, and much of four, as well as the timeline and further reading) before he died from pancreatic cancer in July 2005. I was quite honored when his wife Nancy and Greenwood Press asked me to complete it, a project that has been a joy and a pleasure. John was not only a first-rate scholar but one of the wittiest, most insightful people I knew, whose dry comments could pierce puffery and pretense more immediately and cleverly than anyone. He also had a great heart. John, we all miss you.

I also want to note my deep appreciation for the eagle-eyed, no-nonsense readings my friend Judi Caldwell provided. The book is better for it. And my editor, Debra Adams from Greenwood Press, has been gracious, supportive, and forgiving throughout these months.

N. Lee Orr

Introduction

After the close of the Civil War in 1865, the American economic engine roared to life, transforming the country from an agrarian society of isolated communities into an urban and industrial colossus, opening what would be popularly known as the Gilded Age. Resolutely announcing this new period was the great Centennial Exhibition, set to open on May 10, 1876 in Philadelphia. The Exhibition was to celebrate a number of important events: it would close the country's first century and open the new one; it would also symbolize the healing of the painful divisions left by the Civil War; it honored the enormous technological progress that the nineteenth century had made, especially the new inventions promising a brighter future for humankind—the Corliss engine, the Bell telephone, and the Otis elevator—and finally, the Exhibition announced to the world the coming of age of America, which appeared to many would become the *American* century.

Wednesday, May 10, in Philadelphia dawned with mostly sunny skies. Rain seemed imminent but held off until afternoon. Within an hour of the 9 A.M. opening, as the bells of Independence Hall announced the opening of the festivities, more than 100,000 people had entered to marvel at the work of Chief Engineer and Architect H. J. Schwarzmann, who had overnight transformed 285 acres of fields, swamps, and ravines on the Schuylkill River into a wondrous display.[1] As the gates opened, the throng streamed in and hastened to the plaza between Memorial and Main Halls to watch the colorful opening ceremonies. The first visitors soon found themselves pressed by the crowds in the rear. A "fierce conflict" broke out between the police trying to maintain order and this "most extraordinary mass of human beings," a *New York Times* correspondent reported in the paper the next day; the correspondent had surveyed the melee safely from a perch on one of the turrets on the roof of Main. The frenzy died down slightly when Theodore Thomas, resplendent in his top hat and brandishing his baton like a field marshal, gave the downbeat for the music to begin. Across the crowd from the musicians in front of Memorial Hall stood the round grandstand for the celebrities. The arrival of the dignitaries brought more excitement as celebrated war heroes like Generals Sherman and Sheridan and Admiral Porter filed past. Next came the Brazilian Emperor Dom Pedro and his empress, making their way to the seats of honor. As other representatives from other nations paraded by, the 150 players performed 12 national airs representing some of the countries present. Finally, as Thomas launched into "Hail to the Chief" President Grant and members of his cabinet filed to the grandstand.

Just after 11 A. M., the *Centennial Inauguration March* by Richard Wagner was played. Long anticipated, dearly bought for $5,000, and marred by Wagner's dishonest machinations, the work made little effect, evaporating in the morning air. Next, the Methodist Bishop Matthew Simpson delivered a 1,100-word sermon, disguised as a prayer. At its conclusion, the 1,000-voice chorus sang the patriotic and majestic *Centennial Hymn* by John Greenleaf Whittier, set to music by John Knowles Paine, and accompanied by the orchestra and the new Roosevelt Organ in the Main Hall. Concluding the main musical portion was the *Centennial Mediation of Columbia* by Dudley Buck, already one of the most well-known American composers. By the time the Exhibition closed in mid-November, 9,910,966 people had passed through its mechanical, automatic-counting turnstiles.

The Gilded Age was in full swing. During the next 30 years the United States would become the most productive nation in history. By 1890, the value of its industrial output almost equaled the total of Britain, France, and Germany. At the same time, the railroads were binding the far-flung continent ever closer together. Nearly every American citizen lived within throwing distance of a passing freight or passenger train. In 1865, the rail network encompassed nearly 35,000 miles; by 1900 it had grown to almost 200,000 miles. The country also saw an astonishing population growth, from 35,701,000 in 1865 to 77,584,000 in 1901, most of which occurred in cities. In 1860, only one American in six lived in a community of at least 8,000 people; by 1900, one in three did so. The telegraph, telephone, and rotary printing press further solidified all of this growth, which brought about an immediacy of communication never before seen in human history.

These industrial and demographic developments transformed American life from a farm economy, rural in orientation, to a modern, urbanized society. Accelerating this trend were the waves of more than 16 million immigrants, most of whom poured into the cities, and all of whom radically altered the social construction of American life. New tensions and problems quickly arose. Native urbanites viewed the influx of rural and foreign residents with alarm, and the new city dwellers found themselves adrift from their traditional social support systems, languages, and customs. Foreign born, or native American, many urban dwellers found the harsh market urban economy disorienting. Soon, unemployment, poverty, prostitution, and crime began to take their toll.[2]

This new urban ruling class consisted mainly of northeastern, middle-income, Whig-Republican educated men and women, which Mark Twain and Charles Dudley Warner satirized in 1873 in *The Gilded Age*. One of few works of literature that named an entire period, the work relentlessly caricatures the gaudy excesses of a new class of wealthy industrialists, financiers, and politicians. They derived the title from Shakespeare's *King John*, in which King John is dissuaded from a second, unnecessary coronation with the observation that "To gild refined gold, to paint the lily,/ ... Is wasteful and ridiculous excess."

Seeking to address this disturbing social crisis precipitated by all the change, leading thinkers and commentators turned to High Art as a means to harmonize the growing social tension, as well as to provide moral guidance. This new urban ruling class had grown alarmed at what they saw as a moral deterioration of the social fabric. In an attempt to maintain social cohesion, they worked arduously to humanize the harsh effects of the emerging capitalist-industrialist order. They constructed a Victorian society marked by genteel modes of expression; strong pressure for personal and social conformity to a bourgeois world view; feminine sentimentality; faith in technological progress; an emotional, optimistic religiosity dominated by secular modes of expression; vigorous denial of social ills; and American Triumphalism.

These cultural leaders felt—indeed, earnestly hoped, that a sacralized culture would offer the edifying uplift needed to ameliorate these problems and improve the moral character of society. These comforting, unquestioned social mores were seen as offering some sense of value and order to a society that found its faith assaulted from all sides and its inner life rationalized by the modern world. Quickly, these moral judgments pervaded literature, art, politics, indeed all of American life.

These values found expression in High Culture (including classical music) in the 1870s as the Gilded Age dawned. This was the decade when literature, art, and music finally assumed the unassailable, sacralized authority they would hold for more than a century. The rapid increase of wealth accelerated the establishment of the key official institutions of High Culture in the early postbellum years: immense Beaux Arts concert halls, private universities and music conservatories, resplendent museums, magnificent churches with glorious pipe organs, and vast new Renaissance-style libraries. In 1865, the Oberlin Conservatory was established, followed two years later by the Boston and Cincinnati Conservatories, the New England Conservatory—all still operating—and the Academy of Music in Chicago, and in 1868 by the Peabody Conservatory. The 1870s saw the founding of the Illinois Conservatory of Music in 1871, the Northwestern School of Music in 1873, and the Cincinnati College of Music in 1878. The two Boston schools had been in existence for nearly 20 years before Jeanette Meyer Thurber (1850–1946) spearheaded the creation of New York's National Conservatory in 1885 and almost 40 years before the Institute of Musical Art, antecedent of that city's famed Juilliard school, opened in 1905.

This furious industrialization dramatically expanded America's economic situation after the Civil War, and along with it the musical situation. New York was the seat of wealth, but a number of other cities weren't far behind. When John Jacob Astor died in New York in 1848, his $20 million estate was the largest thus far seen in America. Even as late as 1855, there were only 19 millionaires in that city, the wealthiest of whom was William B. Astor, John Jacob's son, whose net worth was estimated at $20 million. The wave of unbridled industrial growth, national expansion, and unregulated commerce during the postbellum years enabled Astor, as well as Cornelius and William Henry Vanderbilt, Andrew Carnegie, John D. Rockefeller and a number of others, to accumulate fortunes in the hundreds of millions. By 1913, the $68 million left by J. Pierrepont Morgan would raise eyebrows only among his fellow robber barons. "And to think," John D. Rockefeller, Sr., was said to have remarked, "he isn't even a rich man."[3]

With their newly acquired wealth, America's emerging plutocracy looked to the European aristocracy as an example for their behavior and lifestyle. But there were two significant differences between the Americans and their European models. First, the aristocratic families of Europe, being accustomed over generations to culture and art patronage, possessed a relaxed and self-assured sense of elegance. Lacking such deep roots, Americans sought self-consciously to impress and overawe. They built opulent and expensive houses in the form of Italian palazzi, French châteaux, and English manor houses; they then proceeded to fill them with an extravaganza of European furniture and artworks. Second, although the male half of Europe's aristocracy enjoyed complete leisure, living off income from their estates, indulging their patronage of the arts along with their womenfolk, American men of wealth were mostly preoccupied with their business affairs, content to leave the social and cultural matters to their wives and sisters. As a result, American artistic and cultural patronage, like organized religion, became predominantly the provenance of women. To be sure, some men developed a genuine enthusiasm for music and the arts; J. P. Morgan, for instance, accumulated a spectacular art collection. But most of the plutocrats and their families affected no more interest than they imagined as appropriate to their image of affluence and social status. Indeed, most wealthy women tended to view concerts and the opera as obligatory social appearances rather than aesthetic pleasures. Young women were carefully guided through a procession of teas, balls, musicales, concerts, opera, and church services under the watchful eye of a chaperone. Everything was choreographed, with no time or space for experimentation. At the same time, the middle-class American gentry asserted their class-based moral and cultural values, which expressed the American bourgeoisie's yearning for cultural refinement and taste—middle-class taste—which emulated upper-class taste, which in turn looked to Europe for validation, most immediately to our British heritage.

To clearly demarcate themselves from the masses, proper middle- and upper-class Americans turned to European culture, meaning concert music and opera, nearly always German music and Italian and French opera. This music gradually abandoned its dependence on the marketplace for support and turned to this wealthy elite. To affirm their good taste, minstrel shows; variety acts; and burlesque, mass entertainment were shunned as low class. As the eminent conductor Walter Damrosch put it, music "was carefully introduced and nurtured by an aristocratic and cultural community.... Its original impulse sprang more strongly from the head than the heart."[4] Cultured music aimed to uplift the spirit and purify the morals, whereas popular music embraced the sensual and was seen as corrupting and contaminating.

If Gilded Age New York with its theaters and opera was America's performance capital, Boston was generally conceded to be the nation's intellectual capital, in music as in other arts and sciences. Even before the Civil War culture had become synonymous with Boston—Beacon Street, Cambridge, and Concord. Indeed, seeking instant musical status, late nineteenth-century Cincinnati music lovers took to calling it the "Boston of the West." Boston became the home of America's most prestigious music periodical between 1852 and 1881, *Dwight's Journal of Music,* which was printed and distributed by the Boston publishing house, Oliver Ditson Co. Editorial control was tightly exercised by its founder, John Sullivan Dwight (1813–1893), whose aesthetic philosophy of idealism stemmed from his early involvement with New England's transcendentalist movement.

And finally, the preeminent school of American composers during and after the Gilded Age grew up in Boston. This cluster of talent, including such figures as George Whitefield Chadwick and Edward MacDowell, first formed in the 1870s around Harvard's first professor of music, John Knowles Paine, and established the city as a center of American musical creativity. Numbered among the chain of Boston composers stretching unbroken to the present were three superbly talented women: Mabel Daniels (1878–1971), the even longer-lived Margaret Ruthven Lang (1867–1972), and arguably the most brilliant of the whole group, Amy Marcy Cheney Beach.

On the other hand, Boston's musical journalism, educational institutions, and even its composers did not make for a distinctively American music so much as an outpost of European music in America. For years Dwight had advocated German romantic styles and classical forms as a universal model of good music against the New York critic and composer William Henry Fry, who argued just as tirelessly for an indigenous American musical style. As it turned out, Fry was neither sufficiently gifted as a composer nor sufficiently long-lived to carry his point against Dwight. By the end of the Civil War, Fry was in his grave, and his music all but forgotten. Not until Antonin Dvořák stirred the American consciousness in the early 1890s did composers even consider embracing a distinctively American musical rhetoric.

By the opening of the Gilded Age, traveling pianists had changed the way music was presented and received in America. Through much of the antebellum period music was considered as much entertainment as art. Into mid-century, concert etiquette, if one can call it that, resembled more a rowdy evening at the tavern than a serious, respected artistic event. Audiences for the touring pianists of the 1840s, such as Leopold De Meyer and Henri Herz, were often disorderly and raucous; patrons would loudly shout out their dislike of a piece or leap up and insist a favorite be repeated. By the time the concert pianists and singers resumed touring after the Civil War, music was increasingly viewed as sacralized, something to be solemnly heard and edified by. The popular programs of the 1840s and 1850s of mostly operatic fantasies composed by the performers gave way to the already canonic literature of Bach, Beethoven, Chopin, Mendelssohn, and Schumann. In this way, music was no longer expected to simply entertain and compete in a noisy economic competitive arena, but to offer a deep aesthetic experience, dwelling above the fray of the marketplace.

Popular music came of age during the Gilded Age, with its attendant institutions, dependent on the market for its support. Central here were the varied types of staged musics, from bawdy burlesque, rising all the way up in status to operettas. The rise of Tin Pan Alley also produced a vibrant, driving market for popular music, fueled first by sheet music, then by recordings, and finally by radio. From mid-century on these musical activities were carefully aligned with a strict social code. Amusements in general stratified along lines of class, sex, and race. After mid-century in New York, mixed-class theaters and entertainments that had prevailed began to separate themselves out for various social classes. The milestone for this process was the Astor Place riot of 1849 in which the lower-class supporters of American actor Edwin Forrest protested vehemently against Charles Macready, the British thespian. The riot turned ugly and troops were forced to intervene; a number of people died. Theaters after mid-century increasingly abandoned the democratic houses of earlier times, where the working classes watched with the affluent set. Certain types of amusements and music were considered too fast, scandalous, and lower class, especially for women. Strict class and gender conformity replaced democratic mass entertainment. Each sex, class, and race had its particular entertainment and entertainment spaces and were expected to remain in its exclusive sphere.[5] The popular spaces for minstrelsy, variety, and burlesque soon became off-limits to respectable society; and new theaters arose comfortably tailored to genteel entertainment devoid of lewd dancing, suggestive lyrics, and indecorous costumes. Theaters presenting bawdy acts came to be attended by lower-class and male audiences.

Recreational dancing also withdrew to the private sphere during the post-bellum decades. Earlier it was generally reserved for private functions such as formal balls. Public dance halls drew mainly men and lower-class women where illicit behavior was tolerated if not condoned. The public dance hall had emerged from the nineteenth-century saloon and never shed its decadent, morally repugnant associations, which respectable women avoided. The concert saloon had developed as an urban entertainment space during the 1840s and 1850s and gave way to the new social dance crazes after the turn of the century. San Francisco's Barbary Coast in 1910 had more than 300 in a six-block radius, and Chicago's South Side boasted more than 285. New York's Tenderloin (Sixth Avenue between Twenty-fourth and Fortieth streets) and Bowery, St. Louis's Warehouse District, and the French Quarter in New Orleans also had their red-light areas. The women seen in these places were either prostitutes or considered prostitutes.

Finally, it was during the Gilded Age that African Americans and their music first made deep inroads into white, middle-class experience. By the end of the period, the new ragtime and then jazz would impact popular white music immeasurably. After Emancipation, Northern white culture essentially turned its back on black people; and Southern leaders began a gradual segregation of blacks and whites, which effectively banished black people from white public spaces. Black districts had their own saloons, dance halls, and brothels, where sensual dancing, ragtime, and jazz emerged, mingling the rhythmic energy of recently emancipated blacks with the popular music of white America. These new musics, with their infectious rhythms, invigorating dancing, and sexually charged atmosphere, were associated with blacks and kept off respectable stages until the advent of ragtime began dissolving the firm boundaries between proper songs and dances and naughty entertainment. As ragtime gradually spread north and east during the 1890s, it soon infiltrated white music, finally making it to Broadway at the close of the century. Its appearance in the songs of Tin Pan Alley would signal the end of Gilded Age gentility and restraint, ushering in the Jazz Age.

The story of American musical life during the Gilded Age is the story of how all of these institutions and styles emerged, stratified, and assumed the shape they largely hold today. What has changed significantly since then is the fluidity and routine intersection between popular and elite culture into the first years of the new century. Only rarely were the two musical worlds seen as in conflict. Both vocalists and instrumentalists routinely switched between elevated, sacralized music such as opera and oratorio one week and revue or Broadway the next, factoring it all in. Americans were as likely to recognize a tune from *Rigoletto* as "After the Ball." Many of the brightest stars in musical comedy got their start in vaudeville, or even on more unseemly stages. One of the stars of the popular music circuit, Louis Moreau Gottschalk, composed what became a favorite hymntune still found in numerous hymnals. World-class opera singers gained a wide and broad popular audience by making some of the first mass-selling records. And church organists often played opera arias for preludes and postludes. This book tells the story of the emergence, development, cross-fertilization, and stabilization of these institutions and their music, and how they became part of the American experience.

Orchestras and Concert Music

Through most of its history, European concert music was directly supported and patronized by the aristocracy or the church. Noble households, royal courts, and ecclesiastical establishments employed the best and most successful musicians, concerning themselves little with public tastes. Whatever the venue, performances were patronized by aristocratic audiences, the leisured rich, or high-level clerics.

With no aristocracy and few leisured rich before 1870, America had no resources or time to support anything but the most modest and amateur musical activity. A handful of families and individuals enjoyed comfortable incomes from inherited wealth; however, no American before the Civil War had anything like the disposable income of the least significant central European princeling, and few if any were inclined to underwrite the losses a European-style orchestra would inevitably sustain in America.

Consequently, in the years before the Civil War, American music at all levels served as a pastime rather than an art, and the rare professional musicians had to appeal to a sufficiently large portion of the public to support themselves. Although there was increasing interest in continental European music during the early nineteenth century, and concert programs contained movements by Weber, Mozart, Handel, and other masters of the period, musical culture as a whole remained populist, largely amateur, and essentially entrepreneurial. The most popular ensembles were bands, usually consisting of brass instruments played by amateurs, performing not only marches and patriotic medleys, but also operatic airs and even symphonic movements.

Orchestras were usually assembled as needed from available professionals and proficient amateurs, to accompany choral performances and touring opera companies. The few semipermanent groups, from small theatre ensembles to Louis Jullien's touring orchestra of highly skilled professionals, played much of the same varied repertoire as bands; indeed, the terms *orchestra* and *band* were often used interchangeably. Professionals and serious amateurs might come together to play symphonic literature for their own pleasure, but public concerts of such repertoire seldom if ever paid for themselves. The oldest orchestra still in existence, the New York Philharmonic, was founded in 1842 as a cooperative. Players were elected to membership, paid annual dues, and divided the proceeds of concerts after expenses had been paid. A subsidiary "associate" membership allowed nonplayers to pay dues and attend rehearsals. Not until 1909 was it reorganized as the professional orchestra it is today.

By then, the Philharmonic's structure was a pronounced anachronism. The newly rich and their new-found support and patronage enabled the establishment and maintenance of resident symphony orchestras in America's major cities by the turn of the twentieth century. The predominantly German conductors and orchestra players, no longer feeling the need to appeal to the broadest possible mix of audience tastes to survive, moved away from the customary assortment of marches, patriotic airs, and dances alongside operatic airs and the occasional symphonic movement or overture. Instead, they programmed what they viewed as the best in symphonic music, primarily the work of German composers. In the process, that repertoire acquired an almost religious aura for the musically cultured, especially the music of Beethoven, and by the 1880s and 1890s, that of Wagner. American musicians like John Knowles Paine, who studied in Germany, returned as ardent exponents of German musical romanticism.

MUSIC AS ART AND CULTURE

In the spring of 1869, the eminent Boston bandmaster Patrick S. Gilmore (1829–1892) organized his Peace Jubilee, a five-day music festival commemorating the end of the Civil War. Gilmore boldly enlisted financial support and cooperation from a cross section of Boston's social, financial, political, and musical leaders, all but ignored by Boston's reigning music critic, John Sullivan Dwight (1813–1893), and his influential biweekly periodical, *Dwight's Journal of Music*. A three-and-a-half acre, 50,000-seat coliseum was built on land only recently reclaimed from the waters of the Back Bay, at what is now Copley

Square. A 10,000-voice chorus, made up of singers from New England and New York, and as far away as Ohio and Illinois, as well as 7,000 schoolchildren, were trained by Julius Eichberg (1824–1893), director of the Boston Conservatory and Eben Tourjée (1831–1891), director of the New England Conservatory. Although neither the fashionable Harvard Musical Association nor the Handel and Haydn Society was officially involved, Carl Zerrahn (1826–1909), who was conductor of both organizations, organized and rehearsed the orchestra of nearly 500 players. The highly regarded Norwegian violin virtuoso, Ole Bull (1810–1880), acted as concertmaster. An additional ensemble of 600 wind players from area bands completed the instrumental forces.

Gilmore's Peace Jubilee ran from Tuesday, June 15, through Saturday, July 9. Dwight had been dubious about the whole idea; however, he attended the concerts and in the afterglow of the affair, the June 19, 1869, issue of his *Journal* enthused "We can only say that the success of Tuesday was in the main glorious and inspiring. The vast audience were greatly stirred and delighted." The other concerts enjoyed similar success, ending with a children's program on Saturday. Gilmore shared the conductor's podium with Zerrahn, and President Grant and several other dignitaries made an appearance. The week's music varied, from operatic excerpts and symphonic movements to hymns and patriotic songs. Especially notable among the latter group was a notorious performance of "The Star-Spangled Banner" by the massed chorus and instrumentalists, with a battery of cannon fired electrically from the platform at the appropriate moments.

Works by such composers as Mozart, Beethoven, Rossini, Meyerbeer, Schubert, and Wagner, as well as John Knowles Paine (1839–1906) of Harvard were heard. Without a doubt, however, the high point of the Jubilee was a rendition of Verdi's "Anvil Chorus" from Act II of *Il Trovatore* featuring a hundred firemen, uniformed in helmets and red shirts, beating on real anvils with their sledge hammers. The firemen marched in, two abreast, sledge hammers over their shoulders, and took their places at the hundred anvils arranged along each side of the stage. Although the correspondent from *Dwight's* remarked at the "queer and toylike sound, jingle of sleigh bells, rather than the honest Vulcan *ring*," the audience loved it, and the firemen, having withdrawn in formation, were marched back in to encore the piece. Indeed, in a subsequent program, the President requested, and was obliged with, yet another encore of the "Anvil Chorus" and some patriotic tunes in place of the complete performance of Schubert's C-Major Symphony that had been scheduled.[1]

The Peace Jubilee was neither the first nor the last musical extravaganza to be mounted in America; indeed, such concert series, or music festivals, are still a tradition in many American cities. Boston, for instance, had a festival as early as 1856, when the Handel and Haydn Society offered a weeklong series including Haydn's *The Seasons,* Mendelssohn's *Elijah,* and Handel's *Messiah* with a chorus of 600 and orchestra of 78. In 1865, the Society produced another festival, this time with a chorus of 700 and orchestra of 100; and in 1868, the Handel and Haydn mounted what was to have been the first of a series of triennial festivals. As it turned out, the event was eclipsed by Gilmore's Jubilee the next year and the even larger World Peace Jubilee of 1872.

Nevertheless, Gilmore's 1869 triumph stands as a sort of benchmark separating the concert culture of the antebellum and Civil War era from that of the Gilded Age that followed. Although the 1869 Peace Jubilee would not be Gilmore's last such festival, he never quite managed to repeat its success. He tried a two-week World Peace Jubilee in Boston in 1872 to commemorate the end of the Franco-Prussian War. Gilmore assembled an international company of some 17,000 singers, 1,500 instrumentalists, and the Viennese composer, Johann Strauss, conducting them in his popular "Blue Danube Waltz." But the World Peace Jubilee garnered a disappointing response, especially considering the effort Gilmore had expended. Perhaps, with their own bloody conflict so fresh in memory, Americans cared little about celebrating the end of a European war in which few if any felt any personal stake.

More to the point, both concert programming and the very image of concert music were changing under the influence of such men as the critic John Sullivan Dwight in Boston and the conductor Theodore Thomas in New York. Dwight, in his *Journal,* and Thomas, with his professional orchestra, which first toured in 1869, were slowly establishing a core repertory, hallowed by tradition, of masterworks by such composers as Mozart, Haydn, Beethoven, and the German Romantics, works written specifically for orchestra and conceived as High Art rather than entertainment. Gilmore's mix of hymns, patriotic songs, opera overtures, flannel-clad firemen, and so on, represented pre-Civil War concert programming.[2]

After the Civil War, European concert music in such works as Beethoven, Mozart, and Haydn and later the "modern" music of Wagner, acquired the status of High Art, as distinct from such ephemeral pieces of entertainment as marches, dances, and song medleys. The word *sacralization* has come into more-or-less common use to signify the regard in which late nineteenth-century audiences came to hold such Art music. As this process of cultural sacralization set apart musical works as High Culture and Art, conductors—and increasingly their audiences—were less and less inclined to juxtapose them on concert programs with pieces of a lighter, more popular nature. Art music was not expected to earn its own way by bowing to the crass demands of the marketplace.

Writing in Boston's *Atlantic Monthly* for July 1872, William F. Apthorp observed that the use of a term like *Jubilee* attracted people who might not attend a concert but were drawn by the promise of a spectacle, and once there, they would have a chance to hear real music they might not otherwise have heard. Apthorp pointed out, however, that such performances themselves were "so vaguely imperfect and ineffective that little if any real good can be hoped from their making its acquaintance in such a manner." If the 1869 Peace Jubilee marked the passing of an era when such events would be taken at all seriously by sophisticated musicians and audiences, it would also be one of the last times when celebrated musicians like Eichner, Tourjée, and Zerrahn would be willing to share concert billing with anvil-playing firemen.

The idea of certain pieces of music as High Culture and Art, rather than simply entertainment, probably has its roots in German idealism. In any case, it was fostered in America by immigrant German professional musicians, beginning with those who came to America as refugees from the political upheavals of 1848. Economic necessity had forced them to take on the usual array of activities required of American musicians: teaching, dance orchestras, theater bands, and so on. They also organized small orchestras to play fine symphonic repertoire, like the Germania Society, formed in 1848; however, they quickly discovered that their audiences expected the usual potpourri of patriotic airs and dances, and would tolerate only small doses of symphonic music.

Things changed after the Civil War. Both population and wealth shifted to the cities, industrialists and investors began accumulating great fortunes, and a self-conscious and aspiring aristocracy of these newly super-rich began to underwrite the establishment and maintenance of permanent professional orchestras. By the 1870s and 1880s, their patronage enabled those orchestras, the majority of whose players and conductors were German-born and trained, to structure programs and select repertoire with little concern about populist appeal to a broad base of ticket buyers.

As it turned out, however, there were some unintended consequences. Even as symphonic Art music established itself as the mainstay of the orchestral repertoire, the public mind came to perceive it as the music of a sophisticated elite, rather than the democratic mix of people who made up audiences before the Civil War. John Sullivan Dwight, whose younger days were spent as a Unitarian minister and Transcendentalist and who had long preached the sacralization of art music, had at the same time and just as ardently preached its value as spiritual nourishment and edification for all classes, not just an elite. And in fact, Art music, like other artifacts of High Culture, did acquire a following among the educated and even some enthusiasts among the common folk. By and large, however, attendance at symphonic concerts was associated in the public mind with the wealthy upper class.

The issue of music as High Art as opposed to entertainment, and High Culture as opposed to mass culture, could sometimes be a matter of performance context. An overture programmed along with the set of dances, popular marches, or a patriotic medley might be perceived as mass culture and entertainment. That same overture appearing in the company of other symphonic music would acquire the sacralized status of Art and High Culture. Similarly, popular versions of a given opera in English translation coexisted with elite versions in the original language.

Opera occupied a gray area in the view of John Sullivan Dwight, among others. Dwight himself was fond of Bellini's operatic music, though not Donizetti's; of Rossini's and even Verdi's operas, though not altogether of Wagner's. As true Art, however, Dwight considered opera, like programmatic music that purported to tell a story or depict an object, songs, and pieces that drew attention to the performers technical virtuosity, to be intrinsically inferior to purely objective, intellectual, and self-referential instrumental music of German and Austrian composers. The highest and purest art lay in the symphonic works of Haydn, Mozart, Mendelssohn, and most of all Beethoven. The musically naive might be attracted by the melodies of Bellini or Rossini, but as their taste matured, they should and would graduate to an appreciation for the absolute music of the German symphonists, this "highest flower of art," in the words of German conductor Theodore Thomas. Not all musical sophisticates of the time agreed with Dwight; as we shall see in the next chapter, his New York journalistic counterpart and contemporary, William Henry Fry (1813–1864), was an advocate both for opera and for the development of a distinctively American Art music unencumbered by German influence. However, Dwight, with his biweekly *Journal* was by far the more influential.[3]

Patrick S. Gilmore left Boston in 1873 to organize yet another festival in Chicago commemorating its recovery from the great fire of 1871. He then moved to New York City as conductor of the 22nd Regiment Band, which he honed to a high standard of precision and musicianship. Gilmore was a fine musician, but his perspective was practical and old-fashioned. As had long been his custom, he continued to program symphonic and operatic excerpts alongside patriotic medleys, marches, dances, and other popular fare. His band performed at the Philadelphia Centennial Exposition of 1876 (also attended by President Grant and his cabinet) and the St. Louis Exposition of 1892, where Gilmore died unexpectedly. Bands like Gilmore's maintained their popularity through the late nineteenth century, declining gradually during the twentieth. By the late 1870s, however, they had largely ceased to be of much interest either to sophisticated concert audiences or to serious musicians. As the American pianist William Mason saw it at the turn of the twentieth century, "Enormous progress in the art and science of music has been made in America since I began my studies in Germany in the year 1849."[4]

ORCHESTRAS

During the Gilded Age, the symphony orchestra became the *sine qua non* for high Art, an institution that embodied the highest cultural authority, even if its wealthy and other supporters were not always passionately invested, knowledgeable, or even interested in its music. The sacralization of music in postbellum America was directly connected with the founding and spread of symphony orchestras.

Nearly all of the major symphony orchestras in the United States today were established between 1860 and 1920, and only three—the Cleveland Orchestra (1918), the Detroit Symphony Orchestra (1919), and the Philharmonic Society of Los Angeles (1919)—were founded in the afterglow of the Gilded Age. Some eastern cities such as New York, Boston, and Philadelphia had orchestral ensembles before mid-century, but only the New York Philharmonic survived as a viable orchestral institution. Other major orchestras followed in the 1880s: the Boston Symphony Orchestra (1881), the Chicago Symphony Orchestra (1891), the Cincinnati Symphony Orchestra (1895), the Philadelphia Orchestra (1900), the Minneapolis Symphony Orchestra (1903), and the St. Louis Symphony Orchestra (1907).

Aside from earlier groups of professionals and skilled amateurs who came together to accompany touring opera companies or oratorio performances, or to present a concert or set of concerts followed by dancing, the handful of earlier orchestras in America, from Charleston's St. Cecilia Society in the 1760s to Gottlieb Graupner's Philharmonic Society of 1810 in Boston, to the New York Philharmonic in 1842, had been cooperative ventures. The Philharmonic had been formed by a group of New York musicians headed by Ureli Corelli Hill (1802–1875), who became the orchestra's first conductor, as a means of generating some income in hard economic times. Membership was limited to 70 professionals who were elected to membership and paid dues. They chose their conductor by vote, gave a few concerts each year often preceded by open rehearsals, and divided the meager profits after expenses had been paid.[5]

Perhaps the best such cooperative group was the Germania Society, formed by 25 professional musicians, refugees from the political upheavals in Central Europe. The small orchestra performed in England before emigrating to New York in the late summer of 1848. From 1849 on, the Germania Society made its base in Boston, touring the United States and Canada, often in the company of such soloists as the violinist Ole Bull, sopranos Jenny Lind and Henriette Sontag, or the pianist Alfred Jaëll.

By the time it finally disbanded in 1854, the Germania Society had set a standard of musicianship, style, and precision for American orchestras and introduced its audiences to fine music by Beethoven, Mendelssohn, Liszt, and even the early Wagner overtures, *Rienzi* and *Tannhaüser*. But its approximately 900 concerts had also included the medleys, dances, and arrangements of popular airs, along with the novelties beloved by audiences of the era. One favorite piece was a "Railroad Galop" that featured a miniature steam engine running around the stage. The ensemble's flautist, Carl Zerrahn, continued to influence Boston's musical life as conductor both of the Harvard Musical Association and the Handel and Haydn Society. Zerrahn, as previously noted, shared conducting duties with Patrick S. Gilmore during the 1869 Peace Jubilee.[6]

During the Germania Society's last year of activity, yet another orchestra from Europe was touring the United States under the direction of Louis Antoine Jullien (1812–1860). Jullien had conducted and composed dance music in Paris and then moved to England in 1838. He formed his own orchestra and presented a series of popular "Promenade Concerts" for British audiences. In 1853, he arrived in New York along with 27 of his best players. To this core he added 60 of the best American musicians he could find, gave a series of New York concerts, and then set out to tour the country.

Jullien himself was a mix of musical virtues and vices. There can be no doubt he was a capable musician. John Sullivan Dwight was impressed with the quality of his orchestra, and the hypercritical Theodore Thomas, who played in Jullien's orchestra, called him "the musical charlatan of all ages, who, nevertheless exerted some useful influence upon orchestral music." In short, Jullien was both a capable conductor and a showman who was not above feeding his audiences' appetite for novelty. He conducted from a red-and-gilt podium with an elaborate thronelike chair in which he ensconced himself between numbers. His programs contained music by Beethoven, invariably conducted by Jullien in white gloves and with a special jeweled baton, as well as new music by American composers such as William Henry Fry (1813–1864). He would also include such pieces as the "Firemen's Quadrille," at the climax of which flames would be seen to break out and a company of firemen would rush into the hall to extinguish the blaze. The audience often had to be calmed and reassured that the "conflagration" was a part of the show. His New York farewell in May 1854, given at the Crystal Palace, included a "Grand Musical Congress," staged by P. T. Barnum.[7]

THEODORE THOMAS, NEW YORK, AND CHICAGO

Among Jullien's musicians was a headstrong young violinist of German birth who almost single-handedly established the symphony orchestra as an icon of American High Culture by the end of the nineteenth century. Theodore Thomas (1835–1905) came to New York with his family in 1845, already a precocious and accomplished violinist. By the time he was 15 years old, he had begun touring on his own, riding from town to town on horseback, acting as his own manager, making his own advertising posters billing himself as "Master T. T.," and even taking tickets at the door before going on stage to perform. He quickly entered the freelance music world of New York, joining the orchestras of the Astor Place Opera House in 1847 and the Academy of Music in 1854. That same year he was elected a member of the New York Philharmonic. Thomas also played chamber music with William Mason beginning in 1855. As Mason recalled, Thomas quickly became the leader of the group. "His dominating influence was felt and acknowledged by us all." Thomas also had a flair for good programming that would stand him in good stead in later years. In its May 1, 1858 issue, *Dwight's Journal* praised Thomas's playing of the Bach unaccompanied chaconne from memory, no mean feat for a violinist. His interpretation, it was reported, was "faithful and artistic" with "Artlove and reverence; he never plays any but good music ... [S]uch men are and ought to be missionaries of Art in this country."[8]

In April 1859, Thomas conducted Donizetti's *La Favorite* at the Academy of Music. In December 1860, he was summoned from his nearby home on E. 12th St. to take the podium at the Academy again. Either the regular conductor had suddenly become ill or—more likely—had refused to go on unless he was paid in advance, the opera company having run short of money. It is not clear why Thomas was called or how the performance went. He was turning more and more to conducting. On May 12, 1862, he directed an orchestral concert at Irving Hall in New York, opening the program with the Overture to Wagner's *The Flying Dutchman*. In the fall, he recruited an orchestra of the best musicians from New York and Brooklyn for a series of 10 weekly concerts, programming music by Beethoven, Haydn, and Wagner. That year he was also elected co-conductor of the Brooklyn Philharmonic Society.[9]

In 1864, Thomas formed his own orchestra of 40 select players. From that point on, he gave up playing the violin and devoted his energies to conducting. His first season of concerts in Irving Hall, termed Symphonic Soirées and featuring music by Beethoven, Schumann, Liszt, and Wagner, was a modest financial success and earned him notice in *Dwight's*. He also began a series of summer outdoor "pops" concerts that would continue for the next 10 years or so, playing polkas, waltzes, and occasionally slipping in a symphonic movement. Thomas increased the size of his orchestra to 60. Meanwhile, he was elected sole conductor of the Brooklyn Philharmonic in 1866, a post that paid him a modest but steady salary of $2,500 a year. The next year, he traveled to Europe to observe and study orchestras. In 1869, he was at last ready to embark on the missionary activity Dwight had envisioned for him a decade before. Having guaranteed his players employment at an adequate salary for the season and rehearsed them daily to a high level of precision, Thomas took his orchestra on the first of its tours, evidently underwritten by the piano manufacturer, William Steinway, who advised representatives: "We take great pleasure in informing you that Mr. THEODORE THOMAS, with his Grand Orchestra, has commenced his Concert Tour at Boston, and will visit the larger cities of the United States."[10]

Over the next 20 years, until it finally broke up in the fall of 1888, the Theodore Thomas Orchestra traveled to cities and towns across the United States and in Canada, described as "The Thomas Highway." From series in major cities such as Boston, Chicago, St. Louis, and Cincinnati, to single concerts in small towns, and eventually to the far West, the players spent their days on trains, their nights in different hotels, and six or seven evenings each week playing Beethoven, Weber, Liszt, and Wagner in theaters, concert halls, and churches, often to people who had never before heard an orchestra, and who were not always willing to listen quietly to German masters. At the same time, neither concerts nor orchestra had outside funding; Thomas had to depend on audiences and ticket sales, a somewhat precarious proposition. Yearly budgets were balanced and the players provided with extra employment by the ongoing summer series of popular outdoor concerts in New York's Central Park, and from 1877 to 1888 in Chicago.[11]

Thomas persevered with a steely will and gradually his efforts bore fruit. He faced down prima donnas like the soprano Adelina Patti, insisted on programming good music over objections from audiences and the press, and ultimately prevailed. In 1872, the Russian pianist Anton Rubinstein, himself conductor of the Czar's Imperial Orchestra in St. Petersburg , who was touring America and had performed with Thomas's orchestra, wrote his sponsor, the piano manufacturer William Steinway, that it was "the greatest and finest orchestra in the world." In April 1873, Thomas organized a weeklong "grand music festival" at Steinway Hall in New York, featuring among other things, Rubinstein, William Mason, and the pianist Sebastian Bach Mills playing the Bach triple concerto in D-minor. The next month he was in Cincinnati, conducting a three-week music festival.

But his other endeavors did not go as smoothly. In 1876, Thomas took charge of music at the Philadelphia Centennial Exhibition, a mistake that nearly forced him into personal bankruptcy, as his costs were not guaranteed by the sponsors. To add to his woes, he was partially responsible for commissioning a new piece by Richard Wagner. The composer, who was raising funds to complete his theater in Bayreuth, charged the considerable fee of $5,000 and then delivered a work that was embarrassingly bad.[12]

In 1877, Thomas was elected conductor of the New York Philharmonic, displacing Leopold Damrosch. The Philharmonic was still a cooperative and about to encounter some competition from the New York Symphony

Damrosch was to organize. Thomas also retained his position with the Brooklyn Philharmonic and kept up his touring with his own orchestra, but his interests were now fragmented. In 1878, he returned to Cincinnati briefly to head the newly formed conservatory, but he returned the next year to New York and the Philharmonic.

In 1880, Thomas traveled to Europe to hear orchestras and opera. He was unimpressed and turned down an offer from the London Philharmonic to assume its direction and that of the opera at Covent Garden, returning instead to his New York activities. In 1888, he finally disbanded the Theodore Thomas Orchestra and focused his efforts on the Philharmonic; its cooperative structure, however, proved a frustration. When in 1890 he was approached by C. Norman Fay of Chicago to build and conduct another permanent, professional orchestra in that city, its expenses and deficits guaranteed by a group of wealthy Chicago families with names like Field, McCormick, Swift, Armour, and Pullman, Thomas jumped at the opportunity.[13]

His model would be the recently formed Boston Symphony Orchestra, established in 1881 and maintained through the efforts and watchful eye of Henry Lee Higginson, although Thomas was not the sort of man who would cede authority to a patron, as conductors of the Boston Symphony did. He moved to Chicago in 1891, established the new orchestra and trained it to his customary high standard. Ever the perfectionist, he programmed an uncompromising repertoire of symphonic music, defying what he termed the "indifference of the mass of people to the higher forms of music." His Chicago Symphony played not only the German masters like Beethoven and Wagner, but also the music of French composer Hector Berlioz and the Americans John Knowles Paine and George Whitefield Chadwick.[14]

Perhaps Thomas's most difficult moment in Chicago came at the World's Fair in April 1893. The pianist Ignacy Jan Paderewski, who had been engaged to play with Thomas's orchestra, insisted on using a Steinway piano, rather than one of the exhibiting manufacturers' instruments as the sponsors' policy mandated. Thomas sided with Paderewski, precipitating a committee investigation and uproar in the local press. The May 11, 1893 *Herald* attacked him as a "small despot by nature [with] an unscrupulous resistance to reasonable appeals."[15]

At this juncture, Thomas received an offer from Henry Lee Higginson inviting him to take the podium of the Boston Symphony, succeeding Arthur Nikisch who had returned to Europe. Thomas was tempted, for Boston was a musical center, with an active circle of composers, including Paine, MacDowell, and Chadwick. Moreover, Thomas had many friends and admirers there, as well as a summer home in nearby Fairhaven. But in the end he declined the offer, and shortly thereafter embarked on a campaign to build a proper concert hall for Chicago. Thomas, by now deaf in one ear and partially blind, conducted the opening concert at Orchestra Hall December 4, 1904; but he lived only long enough to conduct three more concerts there, dying there on January 4, 1905.[16]

Theodore Thomas's *New York Times* obituary described him as a prophet who had led American music "out of the wilderness." W. L. Hubbard, writing shortly after his death, called Thomas "one name which stands above all others." Perhaps the most astute summary of Thomas's career was made in 1917 by the New York music critic James Gibbons Huneker. Theodore Thomas, he wrote, established "the enchanted world of symphonic music" in America.[17]

NEW YORK AND THE DAMROSCHES

Thomas's contemporary and competitor on the New York musical scene was Leopold Damrosch (1832–1885), a conductor, composer, and violinist, and friend both of Wagner and Liszt. Though Damrosch had trained as a physician in Berlin, he decided his vocation was music, and by 1857, only three years after taking his medical degree, he was concertmaster of Franz Liszt's orchestra at the ducal court in Weimar. From 1858 to 1871, Damrosch conducted the Breslau Philharmonic. Little wonder that Thomas, who recognized real talent when he saw it and was always keen to sniff out any potential rivals, eyed him warily.[18]

Damrosch came to New York with his family to take charge of the Arion, one the finest of New York's many German singing societies. Even though such societies were amateur groups, their membership was strictly limited, and many if not most of the singers were of professional quality. More important, the organizations played a social and cultural role in the German community, wielding significant political and economic influence apart from their musical activities. Although Damrosch's talents would not be overly taxed by the Arion, he would have a good musical organization at his command, as well as powerful contacts in New York's German community, which included most of the city's prominent musical figures, among them the Steinways.

The next year Steinway sponsored a tour by the Russian piano virtuoso, conductor, and composer, Anton Rubinstein. Rubinstein made his New York debut with the Theodore Thomas orchestra on September 10, 1872. Privately, Rubinstein advised Damrosch, whom he had known in Europe, to form an oratorio society rather than compete with Thomas as an orchestral conductor. Damrosch followed his advice and in 1873 founded the New York Oratorio Society. For a while the two men collaborated, sharing conducting duties at combined concerts of the Oratorio Society's 40 singers and the Theodore

Thomas orchestra. Damrosch led the performances of Mendelssohn's *St. Paul* and Handel's *Messiah*. Thomas directed a performance of Beethoven's *Symphony No. 9*. Nevertheless, the two men did not get on well. Damrosch was courtly, courteous, and educated; Thomas was curt and imperious, and at some level envious of Damrosch's European polish, manners, and degree. Nor did Thomas care for Damrosch's conducting style, which was more emotional and intense than his own.[19]

The turning point came in 1875, when Steinway's piano-making competitor, Chickering, built its own hall and invited the German piano virtuoso, Hans von Bülow, to perform at its opening and then tour under Chickering auspices. Bülow, who had been Liszt's son-in-law and knew Damrosch from his Weimar days, asked Damrosch to organize and conduct the orchestra for the opening concert. Damrosch's performance at the concert established his presence as an orchestral conductor in the city, rivaling Thomas.

In 1876, Damrosch was elected conductor of the New York Philharmonic, on the retirement of its longtime conductor, Carl Bergmann. That same year he returned to Germany to attend Wagner's performance of *The Ring* at Bayreuth as correspondent for Charles A. Dana's *New York Sun*. Back on the podium of the Philharmonic, Damrosch presented the first act of *Die Walküre* and the third act of *Siegfried* in concert that season. The Philharmonic's playing improved markedly under Damrosch's direction. In Boston, *Dwight's* took notice, describing Damrosch in its issue of January 20, 1877, as "A very particular director, but who inspires his orchestra with something of his own musical fire and taste."[20]

Unfortunately, Damrosch's inspiration and musical fire did not attract large audiences, and the Philharmonic players had smaller profits to divide among them. Damrosch was blamed and at the next election, he was dismissed and Theodore Thomas designated the new conductor. Thomas was also allowed to retain his post with the Brooklyn Philharmonic and to tour with his own orchestra. Damrosch responded by forming another orchestra and scheduling performances to compete with Thomas's Philharmonic concerts. He managed to secure the score of Brahms' *Symphony No. 1* and to give its first American performance on December 15, 1877, although Thomas had been promised exclusive use of the score and parts so that he could conduct the American premiere. As it turned out, Thomas had to content himself with a second performance, which he conducted with the Brooklyn Philharmonic a week later.[21]

Thomas's departure for Cincinnati in 1878 left the New York scene open for Damrosch; however, the Philharmonic passed him over for a far less capable conductor. Damrosch immediately reorganized his orchestra as the New York Symphony and took steps to cut into both the Philharmonic's audience and the absent Theodore Thomas's following. He recruited some of the players left behind when Thomas took only 50 of his players with him. Damrosch also took over some of the Theodore Thomas Orchestra's scheduled dates at Steinway Hall, with the approval and assistance of William Steinway himself.[22]

The new orchestra gave the first of its many successful concerts on November 9, 1878. Thomas returned shortly from Cincinnati, however, and resumed his place as conductor of the Philharmonic. New York now had two orchestras—in addition to Theodore Thomas's own touring orchestra—and two talented conductors. In 1880, a group of New Yorkers formed the New York Music Festival Association. During May 1881, Damrosch staged the organization's first festival at the Seventh Regiment Armory in New York. An audience of 10,000 attended as Damrosch conducted a chorus of 1,200 and orchestra of nearly 300 in a program that included music by Berlioz, Handel, and Beethoven.[23]

Leopold Damrosch died early in 1885 in the midst of a season conducting at the Metropolitan Opera. His son and assistant conductor, Walter (1862–1950), finished the Metropolitan season, then surrendered the podium to a new conductor, Anton Seidl, and resumed his place as assistant. But Leopold's place as conductor both of the New York Oratorio Society and New York Symphony Orchestra was taken by Walter Damrosch. Thomas disbanded his touring orchestra in 1888 and three years later quit New York for Chicago.

Walter Damrosch's main concern was the lack of a good concert hall in New York. Chickering Hall and Steinway Hall, where both Thomas and Damrosch's father had conducted, were too small and better suited to solo recitals. In any event, Steinway had closed his hall in 1890, even before Thomas had departed the scene. But by good fortune, during the summer of 1887, Walter Damrosch met steel magnate Andrew Carnegie on board a ship to Europe. Carnegie was not especially knowledgeable about music, but he considered his fortune a trust and himself its guardian for the public good. He gave organs to numerous churches as a pious duty, just as he endowed many towns with public libraries as a civic duty. Musically, his personal tastes ran to sentimental songs, and he had little faith in the business acumen of musicians in general. In Carnegie's view, they lacked the kind of hard-headedness they needed to make a success of their talents. But he had liked Walter's father, and he liked Walter. The two men struck up a friendship. Indeed, once they had disembarked, Walter was invited to Carnegie's castle in Scotland and there met his future wife, the daughter of Maine senator and presidential candidate James G. Blaine.[24]

In March 1889, Carnegie formed a corporation with a view to building New York a proper concert hall as a business venture. As it turned out, the backers misjudged the profit potential and ended up underwriting losses. The hall opened May 5, 1891, with a six-day series of concerts. Peter Ilyich Tchaikovsky had been recruited by Damrosch to conduct some of his music, at a fee of

$2,500. Unfortunately, Tchaikovsky was not much of a conductor anyway and in addition was in a state of depression. Nevertheless, the concerts went well. The New York Oratorio Society sang not only Mendelssohn's *Elijah* and Handel's *Israel in Egypt,* but also a rather daring piece of programming by Damrosch, the first American performance of *The Seven Last Words* by Heinrich Schütz (1585–1672), a masterpiece from a virtually unknown musical era even to the most musically sophisticated in both Europe and America.[25]

Having lost Thomas in 1891, the New York Philharmonic meanwhile elected Seidl as conductor. Damrosch concentrated on honing his New York Symphony into the city's premiere orchestra. He reorganized it from a cooperative into a professional, salaried organization, like the Boston Symphony and Thomas's Chicago Symphony. He also formed the Damrosch Opera Company in 1894 to promote and perform German repertoire. In 1898, Seidl died suddenly at the relatively young age of 47. The Philharmonic passed over Damrosch to elect Emil Paur who had been conductor of the Boston Symphony Orchestra. That year, Damrosch closed out his opera company (at a profit), resigned as director of the New York Oratorio Society, and withdrew from the Symphony to rest and compose. Meanwhile, Paur was having problems with the Philharmonic. By 1902, the call came at last to Damrosch. Now he was conductor of the New York Philharmonic. But there were problems: the organization was in poor condition, membership had dropped, and players felt free to send substitutes to rehearsals and concerts when more lucrative opportunities presented themselves. Damrosch now focused on trying to do with the Philharmonic what he had with his Symphony Orchestra. But the resistance was too great. In 1903, he withdrew his name from consideration for reelection as conductor.[26]

He returned to the New York Symphony, taking with him the support of a former Philharmonic patron, Henry Harkness Flagler, a major stockholder in Standard Oil and the son of railroad magnate Henry M. Flagler. Among other supporters were the Seligmans, a prominent New York banking family, and even Carnegie, who, though he remained as president of the Philharmonic, gave generously to Damrosch and the Symphony. The professionalized New York Symphony was now the city's premiere orchestra. In 1906, the *Chicago Examiner* ranked it alongside the Boston and Chicago Symphony Orchestras and ahead of both the Cincinnati and Pittsburgh orchestras. Finally in 1909, the Philharmonic was at last reorganized into a professional salaried orchestra, subsidized by private philanthropy. A full 46 concert season and tour were booked, and the great composer and conductor Gustav Mahler, lured from Vienna by the Metropolitan Opera in 1907, took the podium of the Philharmonic. But Mahler was seriously weakened by the heart disease that would kill him within three years. The Philharmonic was on the mend, but still not a match for Damrosch's New York Symphony.[27]

Damrosch remained at the helm of the New York Symphony, and in many ways, its great years lay ahead. Under Damrosch's direction it premiered much of the new music composed in America after World War I, among other pieces, George Gershwin's *An American in Paris* and his *Concerto in F.* In 1928, it was finally merged with the Philharmonic to give New York its single great orchestra, the modern New York Philharmonic.

HENRY LEE HIGGINSON AND THE BOSTON SYMPHONY ORCHESTRA

Theodore Thomas's orchestra set the standards for musical quality in America, but it was Henry Lee Higginson's (1834–1919) Boston Symphony that set the pattern for organization and support. Thomas himself, busily organizing the Chicago Symphony in 1891, looked to the Boston Symphony as his model. Higginson had nowhere near the wealth of a Carnegie. His net worth probably never exceeded $750,000, a mere pittance compared to the fortunes of New York's robber barons.

Then again, a visitor to Boston in the Gilded Age would have found the city's stratified aristocracy neither self-consciously rich nor purposely ostentatious, and more cultured and intellectual than New York or Chicago's financial and industrial plutocracy. An intricate network of Harvard connections and intermarriage linked Boston's first families together. The great mercantile fortunes—great by pre-Civil War standards, that is—accumulated by their forbears in the sea trade of the Federal-era and textile mills of the industrial revolution were by century's end at rest in dividend-yielding trusts, drawn up by relatives who were lawyers and managed by relatives who were bankers, for the benefit of relatives as yet unborn. Long accustomed to having money, old Boston lived quietly and comfortably, interested itself in literature and certain social causes, and supported certain institutions, primarily Harvard, where its sons were educated and acculturated.

Although Higginson was connected to Boston's Brahmin caste, he was in fact a native of New York. He entered Harvard, but left before getting a degree to study piano and composition in Vienna. By 1857, he recognized that he lacked the talent to become a great musician, however hard he might work and practice. He returned to the United States, fought in the Civil War, and ended his service in the Army of the Potomac with the rank of major, a title he bore proudly for the rest of his life, along with a facial scar from a saber wound he sustained. He returned to Boston and entered the banking business as a partner in Lee, Higginson & Co. By the early 1870s, he had accumulated a modest fortune.[28]

Meanwhile, Boston and its cultural resources were growing. Back Bay had been filled in; indeed, Gilmore's 1869 Peace Jubilee was held on reclaimed land. Gilmore's choice of Boston had much to do with the fact that the city was already a musical center. It had the Boston Music Hall and was home to the foremost music periodical, *Dwight's Journal.* The touring Germania Society orchestra had made Boston its home base, and two of the city's entrenched musical institutions, the Handel and Haydn Society and the Harvard Musical Association, were under the direction of the former Germania musician, Carl Zerrahn. Boston had been especially welcoming of the Theodore Thomas orchestra since its first tour in 1869.

As early as 1873, Higginson conceived the idea of a municipal orchestra as a public institution, fully funded by private philanthropy; however, the financial panic of that year placed his plans on hold. By 1881, things had improved, and Higginson publicly announced his plan for a permanent "Boston Symphony Orchestra" consisting of "sixty selected musicians" and offering Saturday evening concerts. Unlike Carnegie a decade later, Higginson had no illusions about the Symphony as a profit-making venture. On the contrary, he was determined to keep ticket prices affordable. To that end, he budgeted a total annual budget of $100,000, half of which would be met by ticket sales and the other half from his own ample, but nevertheless limited, resources.[29]

With Higginson's generosity came a firm control of all the orchestra's affairs. John Sullivan Dwight, Higginson's friend and supporter, argued against any musical compromises, although he advocated the idea of a "Pops" series, inaugurated in 1885, as a way to satisfy the public taste for lighter music apart from serious concert programs. Higginson retained full authority over the Symphony's personnel and programming. His contracts guaranteed the Symphony's musicians employment for the season, but at the same time obligated them not to accept side engagements in dance ensembles or, for that matter, in any other performing organization except for the Handel and Haydn Society. He took special care that Symphony programs contain no "unworthy" music.

Higginson chose as the Boston Symphony's first conductor George Henschel (1850–1934) who directed its first concert on October 2, 1881, performing music by Beethoven, Schubert, Gluck, and Haydn. Henschel was a singer, pianist, and composer, rather than a conductor. By 1884, he had been replaced by Karl Gericke (1845–1925), a stern disciplinarian who transformed the orchestra into a superb ensemble. Its first New York concert at Steinway Hall in 1887 established it as the peer of the Theodore Thomas Orchestra, which disbanded the next year. By 1906, the Boston Symphony was generally acknowledged to be America's leading orchestra. Mahler described it in 1909 as "first class," in contrast with his own New York Philharmonic, which he characterized as "without talent."[30]

Having built his orchestra, Higginson now turned to the matter of a suitable concert hall. The leading architectural firm of McKim, Mead, and White were engaged, but Higginson was unsure of the acoustical properties of the amphitheatre design McKim submitted. In his usual forthright manner, he hired Harvard physics professor Wallace Sabine as acoustical consultant. Sabine, backed by Higginson, called for a different design altogether. Symphony Hall, redesigned in a rectangular shape and built at a cost of $750,000, opened October 15, 1900. Its acoustics vindicated the judgment of Higginson and Sabine, and it continues to be the one of finest concert halls in the world.

Higginson's controlling nature was such that he was unable to retain a conductor for very long. Gericke returned to Europe in 1889 and was succeeded by Arthur Nikisch (1855–1922), who left in 1893 before his contract had expired. Higginson tried unsuccessfully to entice Gericke back, offered the post to Thomas in Chicago, and then settled for Emil Paur, who also left in 1898 to take a clearly inferior position as conductor of the New York Philharmonic. This time Higginson was able to secure Gericke's services, but the relationship over next few years was stormy, and by 1906, Gericke departed once and for all to be succeeded by Karl Muck (1859–1940). Muck held the position until 1908, and then again from 1912 to 1918, when he was arrested and subsequently deported after a year's internment occasioned by the anti-German hysteria following America's entry into World War I. That very year, 1918, an aging and tired Higginson finally surrendered control of the Boston Symphony to a board of trustees.[31]

OTHER ORCHESTRAS AND THE END OF AN ERA

By 1918, several cities besides Boston had resident professional orchestras underwritten by private fortunes and controlled by trustees, among them Cincinnati (1895), Philadelphia (1900), San Diego (1902), Minneapolis (1903), Dallas (1911), Pittsburgh (1914), and Cleveland (1918). Leopold Stokowski (1882–1977), perhaps the most famous American conductor in the years after Thomas, had been at the helm of the Philadelphia Orchestra since 1912, and was introducing French and Russian music on his programs. In 1916, he and the Philadelphia gave the American premiere of Mahler's immense *Eighth Symphony*, the so-called "Symphony of a Thousand."[32]

The year 1918 marked a watershed in orchestral music. The United States had entered World War I in April 1917, and the nation's anti-German feeling quickly found a target in America's orchestras with their largely German membership and their programming of German music. Prominent figures like former President Theodore Roosevelt and Elihu Root, who had served as his Secretary of State, fanned the flames of hysteria. German musicians were boycotted, and public pressure was exerted to have German and Austrian music, at least the music of living German composers, dropped from concert programs. Orchestra rehearsals had customarily been carried on in German because of the large number of German musicians; during World War I, however, orchestras shifted to the use of English.

As a friend of the Kaiser, the Boston Symphony's conductor Karl Muck felt the full force of public and official displeasure. Even Walter Damrosch, fearing he too might come under such disapproval because of his German name, joined in the chorus of condemnation against Muck. The press and public demanded that Muck program patriotic airs. Never a tactful person, Muck refused, replying that the Symphony was not "a military band or ballroom orchestra." Bowing to public demand, he did open Symphony concerts with the "Star-Spangled Banner," but to no avail. Not even a firm and dignified public stand in defense of his conductor by Henry Lee Higginson could stem the tide of abuse. In March 1918, Muck was arrested and interred. A discouraged Higginson retired the next month. One year later Muck was deported. The uproar died down by the 1920s, although as late as 1923, Damrosch felt the need to open his autobiography with the statement "I am an American musician." The musical result was that French and Russian musicians and conductors, the latter refugees from the Russian Revolution, began to displace Germans in American orchestras; and programs included less German repertoire and more music from France, Eastern Europe, and Russia.[33]

2

Grand Opera

Perhaps the musical genre that most typifies the Gilded Age, at least from our viewpoint, is European "grand" opera, particularly the Metropolitan Opera's lavish turn-of-the-century productions in New York. The image arises of musical dramas by Donizetti and Bellini, and Verdi and Wagner sung by legendary artists, from Adelina Patti in the late nineteenth century to Enrico Caruso and Geraldine Farrar in the early twentieth; conducted by titans of the podium like Mahler and Toscanini; and patronized by the cream of New York's wealth. Astors, Vanderbilts, and Morgans attended, —the men in formal dress, the ladies opulently gowned and expensively bejeweled—and were seated in their row of private first-tier boxes, the so-called Diamond Horseshoe, watching and being watched by their peers and by the common folk in the orchestra and balcony seats. Henry James declared a box at the opera "the only approach to the implication of the tiara known in American law," the "great vessel of social salvation."[1]

And in fact, the picture is largely accurate. On any evening of the week, but especially Mondays when Mrs. Caroline Astor and her entourage customarily appeared at the Metropolitan, a glitter of diamonds in the first tier boxes faced a glitter of talent on stage. Mrs. Astor and others of her class invariably arrived late, left early, visited each others' boxes during intermissions, and conversed freely during performances. The Metropolitan was considered a suitable venue for society matchmaking, and young men of appropriate means customarily cruised the boxes seeking introductions and invitations to call on young ladies of similar breeding.

Occasionally the boxholders turned their attention to the stage, especially if a popular singer like a Jean de Reszke or Emma Calvé, and a generation later a Caruso or Farrar, was about to sing a favorite aria. But most of the time they were too preoccupied with their social rituals and conversations, whatever opera played before them. The purpose of those rituals was first and foremost to display the boxholders' resplendent finery, relegating the singers' opulent voices to secondary interest, and the actual operatic drama and music to a distant third. Dimly lit scenes in operas like Beethoven's *Fidelio* were staged with full lighting, lest they interfere with the boxholders seeing and being seen by one another and by the ticket holders in the gallery and orchestra seats.

To be sure, the Metropolitan had at least one serious competitor who aspired to a higher degree of musical and artistic integrity. Oscar Hammerstein's Manhattan Opera featured comparable talent and celebrity in such singers as Nellie Melba and Mary Garden. Hammerstein's productions appealed to those who came to see and hear opera, rather than to be seen and heard themselves. His boxholders imposed a far more rigid standard of behavior on themselves than the Metropolitan's boxholders would have tolerated.

Like the robber barons who owned the boxes in its Diamond Horseshoe and constituted its governing body, the Metropolitan dealt with the competition of a formidable and single-minded Hammerstein by the simple expedient of buying him out. In the end, the Metropolitan's victory was a mixed blessing for opera in America. Its operatic domination of New York and virtual national monopoly through its tours would not only retard the establishment of professional companies in other cities—an expensive proposition in any case—but also establish as the standard its own image of opera, and the idea of an elite audience for that opera. The Metropolitan's opulence was beyond the resources and capabilities of resident companies in other cities. Even the best of the local and regional opera companies looked a bit shabby after a visit from the Metropolitan's touring production.

Operatic melodies remained a popular and familiar part of the American musical scene; opera itself, however expensively staged, elegantly costumed, and performed by Europeans in what was perceived to be the European fashion and sung in European (though not necessarily original) languages, was steadily transformed into a cultural icon for America's new aristocracy of wealth. By century's end, the cream of New York's Society made a point of arriving in time for the second act of whatever was being presented and leaving before the conclusion of the performance to attend sumptuous dinner parties and evening balls at one or another of the palatial Italian villas and Renaissance châteaux rising along Fifth Avenue.[2]

OPERA AS MASS CULTURE

In Europe the public supported municipal opera houses, while court opera enjoyed aristocratic patronage. In America, however, no possibility of government support existed, and no aristocracy existed—at least not until the self-conscious newly rich of the 1870s. Moreover, America's primarily British tastes were not especially responsive to the continental operatic style, with its stylized drama, heightened musical emotion, and vocal fireworks. Nevertheless, the touring companies of the nineteenth century came close to gaining a firm and popular place for opera in American mass culture.

English lyric opera arrived in North America in the years before the Revolution and thrived after it. It was not opera in the sense we would understand it, but rather a play with spoken dialogue, interspersed with brief airs, usually in a popular style. An immensely successful eighteenth-century English operatic genre was "ballad opera," the best known of which was John Gay's *Beggar's Opera*. Ballad opera borrowed well-known tunes from folk songs to popular melodies, and fitted them with new texts. For citizens of American cities in the Federal period—except for New Orleans, in any case a French city and continental in its cultural outlook—opera then was simply a drama, usually comic, with interpolated music. Because theaters maintained small bands of musicians who entertained before and after plays and during intermissions, the line between an opera and a play could be somewhat blurred.

By the middle of the century, Italian opera became "the most significant force to hit the American performing world."[3] Traveling English, French, and Italian opera companies, with their large casts and high-quality soloists, brought Italian opera to much of the population. Opera gave voice to the passionate, emotional, and volatile American character. In an era that censured the expression of personal feelings, the opera singers vicariously provided a much-needed emotional release for their listeners. "Their skill at capturing, distilling, protracting, and communicating the human passions with utter conviction was surely the ingredient that enabled opera to cut across social and class lines, attracting a wide range of nineteenth-century American listeners in performance."[4]

Unlike today, Americans experienced opera as a part of their everyday lives and embraced it enthusiastically. By the 1850s, opera had become the reigning musical singing style throughout the land. Walt Whitman, after an evening at New York's Bowery Theater, thought the opera audiences represented democracy at its best "packed from ceiling to pit with full-blooded young and middle-aged men, the best average of American-born mechanics ... bursting forth in one of those long-kept-up tempests of hand-clapping ... no dainty kid-glove business, but electric force and muscle from perhaps two thousand full-sinewed men."[5]

George Templeton Strong, a recent and reluctant convert to operatic pleasures saw Bellini's *La sonnambula* at New York's Castle Garden in the summer of 1851. "Immense crowd. The Opera has created quite a furor. Everybody goes, nob and snob, Fifth Avenue and Chatham Street, sit side by side fraternally on the hard benches," he noted in his journal. His upper-class sensibilities shuddered at the audience's *outré* reaction to the soprano in Bellini's *Norma*. "The house was crowded and enthusiastic," he pooh-poohed; "the louder this lady screamed, the more uproariously they applauded, and her solitary windpipe was a fair match for the vociferous bravos of her 5,000 admirers ... Norma hollered so ... and so made the fur fly, that the exaltation of the audience knew no bounds."[6] Opera, and the musical style of the genre, soon permeated everyday life in America. Not only did it shape much popular music, but popular songs adapted from these operas soon found their way into almost every heart and home. These songs formed a major part of the song repertory in America: operatic songs were sung in the parlor, parlor songs were inserted into operas, any and all could appear on a concert. Arrangements of operatic music seemed to be limitless, such as the *Deux Quadrilles De contredanses pour le Piano Forte* from *La sonnambula*.

Opera's popularity crossed all musical boundaries. The touring European pianists after mid-century filled their concerts with glittering operatic transcriptions and fantasies on favorites such as *Lucia di Lammermoor, Norma, I Puritani, Lucrezia Borgia,* and others. That mainstay of American popular entertainment during the nineteenth century, the village band concert, rarely failed to include a number of operatic arrangements. In 1861, music from *Rigoletto* formed part of the band music accompanying President Lincoln's inauguration. Simplified arrangements fitted with texts in English were widely available for home music-making alongside the sentimental parlor songs of the era. Civil War era bands played music from operas, and soldiers on both sides marched and even fought to an accompaniment of operatic airs interspersed with patriotic songs and popular tunes. A number of touring companies introduced Americans to abridged and altered versions of Italian opera in English translation and often with the interpolation of popular songs and airs. Indeed, opera in translation became a significant presence on the American musical stage, alongside other kinds of lyrical and musical theater. Many towns had their own "opera houses," even if in many cases these were little more than modest assembly halls with small, bare stages and room for scarcely more than a piano in the orchestra pit. Gilmore's rendition of Verdi's "Anvil Chorus" from *Il Trovatore* was clearly the high point of his 1869 Peace Jubilee in Boston, although, in all fairness, the spectacle of the firemen playing their anvils caught the audience's fancy rather more than Verdi's music. Still, the memorable, singable tunes that are so much a part of opera's appeal, engaged the ears and affections of a large number of Americans. As a result, numerous Americans in cities and towns of any size were familiar with operatic melodies by Rossini, Mozart, Donizetti, Bellini, and Verdi.

Between the Civil War and World War I, however, Gilded Age fashion saw grand opera—as exemplified in the lavish productions of the Metropolitan in New York and on tour—as a reflection of its own opulence. In the eyes of most Americans at the end of World War I, opera had become an amusement for upper classes, an inchoate mix of temperamental prima donnas and displays of wealth. Meanwhile, a post-War generation faced the Great Depression. Local opera houses, those that had not already been given over to vaudeville, were converted into movie theaters. The Metropolitan maintained its prominence through recordings by its star singers and, beginning in 1931, its Saturday afternoon radio broadcasts; however, opera as a musical genre never regained the kind of following it had enjoyed before the Civil War.

OPERA AS HIGH ART

The major critical voices of the late nineteenth century divided over the matter of opera as High Art. In antebellum New York, the *Tribune* critic William Henry Fry, himself a composer of Italian-style opera, had advocated for the genre "as drama with good situations, exciting the genius of the composer," and for "the value of the music."[7] On the other hand, opera as Art music occupied a gray area in the view of John Sullivan Dwight in Boston, by far the more influential, first because of his biweekly *Journal of Music,* and second simply because he outlived Fry by precisely the 30 years in which the musical culture of the Gilded Age was formed. Nor was Dwight alone among his Boston colleagues. In an 1879 *Atlantic* article entitled "New York Theatres," Arthur Sedgwick characterized opera as an "imported luxury." As late as 1896, another *Atlantic* piece by William Biddle dismissed opera as an "artistic blunder."[8]

Not even Dwight would have gone *that* far. In fact, he was fond of Bellini's operas, although not Donizetti's; of Rossini's operas and even Verd's early work, although he was less enthusiastic about Wagner. But as Dwight viewed true musical Art with his critical eye and romantic bias, opera was like programmatic music that purported to tell a story or depict an object, and like most vocal music, drew attention to the performers' technical virtuosity. All were intrinsically inferior to the purely objective and abstract instrumental music of German and Austrian composers, in particular the symphonic works of Haydn, Mozart, Mendelssohn, and most of all Beethoven.

NEW YORK

No other American city approached New York as a center for opera before and during the Gilded Age. The city had long been extraordinarily fertile ground for the art form because of its concentration of Germans and Italians, with their cultural traditions embracing musical drama. Moreover, New York was America's financial center, and the growth of enormous fortunes during and after the Civil War resulted in an extraordinary concentration of newly rich who could patronize opera in what they perceived to be the style of an old-world aristocracy.

The city's earliest recorded operatic venture dates from 1794, when a French opera company fleeing the slave uprising in Santo Domingo staged English-language performances of Italian comic operas in Baltimore, New York, and Philadelphia. Two years later, the John Street Theater in New York presented a season including French opera in the original language.[9]

Between 1817 and 1824, the Park Theater in New York performed Mozart's *Don Giovanni*, Rossini's *Barber of Seville*, and other operas in English translation. For all practical purposes, however, serious Italian opera arrived in 1825 with Manuel Garcia, his company, and in particular his highly talented teenage daughter and pupil, better known by her later married name, Maria Malibran (1808–1836). Maria, an attractive young woman, as well as a fine singer and actress, was an instant success with the New York audiences. The company opened on November 2, 1825 at New York's Park Street Theater with a complete performance of Rossini's *Barber of Seville*, with ticket prices such that only the relatively wealthy could afford them. In a sense then, foreign-language opera in America was an entertainment for the relatively affluent from its beginnings.

Over the next year, Garcia's company staged other operas in Italian at the Park and Bowery theaters, including a performance of Mozart's *Don Giovanni* on May 23, 1826. Lorenzo da Ponte, who had composed the original libretto some 40 years before, had since relocated to New York and was teaching Italian at Columbia University. He prepared an English translation for sale to the audience.

The management of the Park Theater failed to renew the Garcia company's engagement for lack of sufficient public interest, and at the end of September, the troupe left New York to tour Mexico, minus Maria, its main attraction, who had married in 1826 to escape her tyrannical father. Maria remained in New York with her husband, who went bankrupt a short time later. She gave concerts, appeared in English lyric operas, and sang in the choir of Grace Church. In the fall of 1827, she returned to Europe and enjoyed great success singing in its major cities. But once again, bad luck dogged her steps. In 1836, she suffered a riding accident and later that year died from her injuries.[10]

Back in New York, the Park Theater presented both French and Italian opera from 1827 to 1833. Meanwhile, the 84-year-old da Ponte organized an Italian Opera association in 1832. He had support from several wealthy families, 16 of whom committed $6,000 each. By the spring of 1833, he was building his own opera house, a matter not altogether to the liking of one prominent knickerbocker. On April 9, John Pintard, warden of the Huguenot Church next door, St. Espirit wrote his daughter, "We are to be annoyed by the erection of an opera house on vacant ground in the rear, a very bad neighbor." He seemed slightly resigned a month later, on May 31, when he wrote, "A Fine Opera House is erecting in the rear of our French Church wh[ich] I do not much relish."[11]

Da Ponte's Italian Opera House opened on November 18, and a day later one of its affluent boxholders, New York's former mayor Philip Hone, remarked in his diary on the blue hangings, gilt trim, armchairs, and sofa in his private box. Still, he wondered, "Will this splendid and refined amusement be supported in New York? I am doubtful." His reservations were prophetic; by 1835, Da Ponte's venture had accumulated a deficit of $30,000. Hone blamed the venture's failure on the incomprehensibility of foreign language to most New Yorkers and public resentment of luxurious boxes for the wealthy few. The building was sold the next year and in 1839 it was destroyed by fire.[12]

Over the next few years, a number of New York theaters attempted operatic productions, albeit with mixed results. Niblo's Garden sponsored Italian opera from 1843 to 1848, including a successful seven-night series in 1848 by a touring company from Havana. Palma's Opera House opened February 3, 1844, with Bellini's *I Puritani*. Palma's theater had no boxes; rather, it seated its whole audience of some 800 on benches, as did most other theaters. On the other hand, its raked floor, unique for the time, allowed the audience a better view of the stage.[13]

For a few years at mid-century, New York's leading operatic theater was the Astor Place Opera House. It was owned by its stockholders, who leased the house to an impresario or manager whose job it was to book singers, plan a season, and endeavor to turn a profit. The Astor Place opened November 22, 1847 with a performance of Verdi's *Ernani*. Between 1848 and 1852, Max Maretzek (1821–1897), a native of what is now the Czech Republic and former chorus master at London's Covent Garden, staged several Italian operas there, including Donizetti's *Lucia di Lammamoor* and *Anna Bolena*, and Mozart's *Don Giovanni*. The paying audience of single-ticket buyers tended to be sparse, partially because of high prices but largely because the area of Astor Place was unsafe. Anti-English riots of May 7 and 10, 1849, which had nothing to do with the theater's operatic productions, depressed attendance even further. Meanwhile, Maretzek's other productions in Castle Garden at the southern tip of Manhattan did rather well. Bellini's *La Sonambula*, on July 29, 1851, drew an "immense crowd," according to diarist George Templeton Strong as mentioned previously.

German opera also drew crowds in New York during the 1850s. On a number of occasions it had been performed in English for mixed audiences; however, the city's large German population ensured a demand for it in its original language. The Stadt-Theater opened in September 1854 for staging both drama and opera in German. A month later, Weber's *Die Freischütz* was presented. But the Astor Place Opera House's location in a neighborhood plagued by street gangs spelled failure. By 1852, its brief period of operatic splendor was fast drawing to a close.[14]

THE NEW YORK ACADEMY OF MUSIC

In 1852, with the Astor Place Opera in its death throes, a new house, to be called the New York Academy of Music, was being planned further uptown, in the fashionable area around 14th Street. Although the Academy received a charter from the New York State legislature as an educational institution, the promised school never materialized. Instead, it was owned by its 200 stockholders, each of whom paid $1,000 and received in return a seat to use or dispose of at will, as well as share of the income, including rent. As with the Astor Place Opera, the Academy's stockholders, acting through a board of directors, planned to lease the theater to a manager who would assume all risks and overhead, produce operas for their pleasure, and pay his expenses, including their rental charges, out of the box office proceeds from single ticket sales.

Once again, the scheme fell short of their hopes. Negotiations with Maretzek broke down, and in March of 1854, an actor named James H. Hackett was engaged as manager; the Academy opened October 2, 1854, with his production of Bellini's *Norma*. The title role was sung by the celebrated soprano, Giulia Grisi (1811–1869); however, scarcely half of the 4,600 seats were occupied for the event, and subsequent productions played to even smaller audiences, sometimes as few as 250. The problem was that although the Academy's acoustics were excellent, more than half the seats had a poor view of the stage. Moreover, many of the best seats were held by the stockholders and could not be sold, even on evenings their owners did not occupy them. Nor did it help that the Academy was poorly lighted and inadequately ventilated, and most of all that the single ticket prices were simply too high. By the end of December 1854, Hackett gave up. He was followed in quick succession by four other managers over the next three years, the best known of whom, the renowned violinist Ole Bull (1810–1880), lasted but two weeks.[15]

Dring the next 24 years audiences at the Academy endured a constant turnover in companies and impresarios. Max Maretzek staged a number of operas himself and conducted performances for other managers. Bernard Ullmann and the Strakosches, Maurice and Max, uncle and nephew, who had enjoyed success as impresarios, took their turns at the Academy and emerged from the experience poorer but wiser. To complicate matters further, the hall suffered a major fire in 1866 and was rebuilt with fewer seats and therefore even less box office revenue. Yet in spite of these vicissitudes, the Academy steadily gained attention and prestige for excellent productions featuring such stars of the era as Giulia Grisi (1811–1869), Adelina Patti (1843–1919), and Christine Nilsson (1843–1921). By the 1870s, the cream of New York's society customarily attended its performances, and old families held the small number of boxes at the Academy against efforts by any among the newly rich who might try to acquire one.

Opera in English translation was still widespread in America in the Civil War era, and even European impresarios like Maretzek and Maurice Strakosch occasionally mounted such productions in New York. Theaters with somewhat less lofty pretensions, like Jim Fiske's Opera House, offered Italian and French grand and light opera in English translation; however, at the elite Academy, opera was performed in French and Italian, although not necessarily in the appropriate language. For instance, Maretzek conducted Gounod's *Faust* at the Academy November 25, 1863, with Clara Louise Kellogg (1842–1916) in the role of Marguerite, sung in Italian, rather than the opera's original French. *Faust* quickly became a favorite, even though it lacked the flowing, frothy melodies of Italian opera, so loved by singers and audiences alike.[16]

In 1873, the Academy presented Verdi's *Aida* in its American premiere, with Christine Nilsson in the title role, before it was heard either at London's Covent Garden or the Paris Opéra. But at the same time, the expense of paying stars like Nilsson, Grisi, and Kellogg and the tightened resources occasioned by fewer salable seats after the fire, necessitated economizing in other areas. Costumes became threadbare, scenery was shabby, and the lower salaries paid to supporting cast, chorus, and orchestra often resulted in pedestrian performances.

But the Academy's focus and specialty was Italian opera, which relied for its effect on enchanting arias superbly sung. Neither a prima donna like Adelina Patti, for instance, nor her audience, paid much attention to scenery or even her acting. When it was time for an aria, she came downstage and sang to them, regardless of the dramatic context. And they loved her for it. She would respond to their applause with an encore like "The Last Rose of Summer," or "Comin' thro' the Rye," in total disregard for the dramatic situation. The *New York Post* critic, Henry Fink (who coined the term *nightingale* for singers like Patti), wrote that she was "more interested in showing off her lovely voice than in the music she sang ... [but] she was so glorious, so incomparable."[17] Frances Alda, a celebrated Metropolitan Opera soprano of the early twentieth century, never forgot the first and only time she heard Patti, age 65 and well past her prime, at a concert in Paris. "I went home in a daze, unable to sleep all that night," Alda wrote. The next day she told her teacher, the renowned Matilde Marchesi, that there was no point in her continuing. "I know I'll never sing like Patti."[18]

The watershed moment in the Academy's fortunes occurred in 1878, with the arrival of Colonel James Henry Mapleson (1830–1901). Mapleson had studied violin and voice at the Royal Academy of Music in London, had served in the artillery, and had begun producing opera in London theatres in 1861. His early success was such that August Belmont, chairman of the Academy's board of directors, sought him out in 1868. Nothing came of the overture, and in 1876, Mapleson visited cities in the United States to arrange a tour for his troupe from Her Majesty's Theatre in London.

In the fall of 1878, Mapleson's company opened its tour with a series of Italian and French operas at the Academy in New York. The superb performances brought an immediate response. In October, Bizet's *Carmen* was introduced to Academy audiences, with Minnie Hauk (1851–1929) in the title role. Its gritty realism repelled some, but its marvelous melody and drama ensured its success. Meanwhile, Mapleson was also overseeing the London season at Her Majesty's Theatre, shuttling scenery and singers back and forth across the Atlantic. From December to February, Mapleson took his American company on tour, appearing with great success in seven cities. In February he was back in New York to finish the season, and by spring the Academy's stockholders and their directors must have been impressed with the manner in which he had balanced some 300 operatic performances on two continents an ocean apart. Once again, they invited him to take over the Academy's productions.

In addition to Mapleson's management skills and flair for publicity, the directors doubtless took the measure of the man, his British accent, and his personal demeanor. Mapleson was energetic, handsome, impeccably dressed and groomed, tactful, and skilled in disarming his temperamental singing stars and focusing their artistry on the production at hand—in short, the sort of person who becomes the natural leader in any group he is a part of and turns heads anytime he enters a crowded room. Nor was Mapleson unaware of his own worth. Too many before him had failed, and the Academy had all but exhausted the pool of possible candidates for the post. Accordingly, Mapleson bargained for concessions his predecessor stood no chance of securing. The directors gave him the lease rent-free; moreover, they agreed to an almost unheard of provision, whereby Mapleson would receive compensation for the 200 frozen stockholders' seats. Under those conditions, Mapleson, along with his Royal Italian Opera Company, embarked on an eight-year term as the New York Academy's longest-lived—and last—impresario.

THE GILDED AGE AND THE METROPOLITAN OPERA

Sometime in Mapleson's second year, 1879 or early 1880, a confrontation took place between Mrs. William K. Vanderbilt and the Academy's chairman, August Belmont, over her desire to purchase a box. Although the affair had nothing to do with Mapleson or his company, it began the chain of events that would spell the end both of his American career and opera at the Academy of Music. The few boxes were coveted, closely held, and jealously watched over by the old knickerbocker families who owned and guarded them as a sort of social bulwark against the rising tide of newly rich.

Mrs. Vanderbilt did not get her box at the Academy, but neither was she inclined to withdraw gracefully from such battles. By late winter, plans were afoot by a group of subscribers that included Goulds, Whitneys, Morgans, Astors, Vanderbilts, and even some members of so-called old New York families like the Roosevelts and Goelets, to build a new opera house. The Academy's directors took due notice and met with the group on March 31, 1880. Belmont offered to renovate the old Academy, adding another 30 or so boxes, but his concession was too little and too late. By April 11, "fifty-five gentlemen of wealth and influence" had purchased 60 boxes at $10,000 each, and incorporated the Metropolitan Opera-house Co., Ltd.[19]

Designs were drawn, land acquired on Broadway at 39th Street, and the new Metropolitan Opera House rose to a final cost of $1.7 million. Its auditorium seated 3,045, but there were enough exits to empty the theater in three minutes in an emergency. Construction was of brick, masonry, and iron; the curtain was asbestos; and the stage, prone to fire because of painted scenery and effects, was protected by a rudimentary sprinkler system.[20]

The new Metropolitan has been called "a semi-circle of boxes with an opera house built around them, a private club to which the general public was somewhat grudgingly admitted."[21] Priority had been given to providing a generous number of boxes—122 in all—together with salons and other rooms for the comfort and convenience of the owners and proprietors of the house, who held the first-level, or *parterre*, boxes in what became known as the Diamond Horseshoe. Boxes outside the Diamond Horseshoe were leased for the season or rented. The exterior of the building was relatively plain. Downtown at the Academy, Colonel Mapleson loftily dismissed the new house as the "yellow brick brewery." Little did he suspect that he would shortly find himself in the professional struggle of his career. If the new Metropolitan was severe outside, inside was quite another matter.

Sumptuous though the boxholders' area might be, working space for the performers was at a premium, and rehearsal space was inadequate. Chorus and dancers had no place of their own to practice, and even the stars' dressing rooms were spartan in their furnishings. The ones on the women's side had plumbing fixtures in the open; those on the men's side had no plumbing facilities at all. Perhaps worst of all, there was little storage space, most of it beneath the stage. Sets had to be carried to and from warehouses for performances, and as the Metropolitan was a repertory company, staging a different opera every night and two on Saturdays, scenery was often left in an alley outside the stage doors between productions and scene changes, regardless of the weather.

Like the Academy of Music and the Astor Place Opera House, the Metropolitan's owners set up a board of directors and contracted with an impresario to manage and produce the season of opera. On December 31, 1882, the board announced that it had contracted with Henry Abbey (1846–1896). Abbey's strength lay in the theater, rather than opera, so he hired Maurice Grau (1849–1897) as his assistant. Born in what is now the Czech Republic, Grau had grown up in New York, studied law at Columbia University, and managed the tours of pianist Anton Rubinstein and composer Jacques Offenbach. In 1873, he had organized an English-language opera company with the renowned soprano Clara Louise Kellogg. In short, he was an ideal choice for Abbey; in fact, as it turned out, the Metropolitan would enjoy some of its most successful years under Grau's management in the next decade.

At the Academy, Mapleson assured the *Times* that the uptown upstart did not worry him. The Metropolitan might have an elegant new house, scenery, and costumes, he reminded the *Times* readers, but his Royal Italian Opera Company at the Academy had the great singers. Shortly thereafter, Mapleson left for Europe; during his absence, Abbey managed to steal some of the Academy's best voices, including Christine Nilsson. Mapleson returned to find himself in a bidding war for artists, who were playing off one impresario against the other. Mapleson even had to go to court to prevent further defections from the Academy to the Metropolitan. He did manage to hang on to his brightest star, Adelina Patti, but at a steep increase in her performance fees that he could ill afford.

The Metropolitan Opera opened October 22, 1883, with the hugely popular *Faust,* sung in Italian with Nilsson in the lead role. Her rendition of the "Jewel

Song" brought the house to its feet. Mrs. Caroline Astor deigned to attend, decked in diamonds and pearl moonbursts; someone said she looked like a walking chandelier. Like every Monday, she appeared at precisely 9 o'clock, greeted her guests from her box, promenaded during intermissions, and exited grandly before the last act of whatever opera happened to be on the boards. The same night, Mapleson staged the equally popular *La Sonambula* at the Academy, featuring the celebrated soprano, Etelka Gerster (1855–1920). Prominent New Yorkers had to make a choice between two equally attractive offerings; Mrs. Paran Stevens, one of the few grandes dames of New York society who truly loved music and opera, managed to attend portions of both. On October 23, the *New York Times* reported on the rival boxholders of the two theaters, "Something more than hundred of our best families are ... irretrievably committed to a social war of extermination." By December, both Abbey and Mapleson were feeling the economic effects of their competition. Their respective tours took the two companies to the same cities, and at least in their Chicago engagements, the two companies found themselves in the same hotel at the same time.

In the end, Mapleson won out against Abbey, but his victory turned out to be a hollow one. Abbey had spent too much and lost some $300,000, and the Metropolitan's directors refused to renew his contract for the next season. The directors briefly considered offering Mapleson the position, but decided against it. What saved the Metropolitan was German opera. Compared to French or Italian singers, Germans were inexpensive; any two cost less than Nilsson alone. New York's large German population, estimated at 250,000, could be counted on as well. The directors then turned to Leopold Damrosch, who offered to present a season of German opera, recruiting less expensive singers from Germany and using his own New York Symphony as the orchestra and his New York Oratorio Society as the chorus. Abbey's six-dollar top ticket would be scaled down to three dollars for the 562 downstairs "parquet" seats.

The first full season in 1884–1885 of 21 weeks presented 101 performances, of which 44 were of Wagner's *Tannhäuser, Lohengrin,* and only the second performance of *Die Walküre* in New York. Demand for tickets ran high. Even though the German operas lacked the aria and choral showpieces of the Italian repertory, the audience listened with rapt attention. The combination of German opera, and French and Italian opera sung in German, drew large numbers of German-speaking ticket buyers, and the Metropolitan had a good autumn. But Damrosch was overextended. In February he fell ill during a rehearsal and died shortly after. His son, 23-year-old Walter, finished the season, and the directors voted to continue with German opera and engaged Anton Seidl (1850–1898) for the next season.[22]

Seidl had been Wagner's assistant at Bayreuth in 1876, and had played a part in the premiere of the *Ring* cycle. He was the most eminent European musician to come to this country yet and would impact opera in America more profoundly than any conductor before or since. Wagner died in 1883, just as his popularity was rising sharply in America. Seidl broke with Bayreuth to escape the stifling politics, became an American citizen, and bought a summer home in the Catskills. Over the next six seasons, he would transform the fledgling institution into the world's leading German opera house. Seidl was a fine conductor, highly regarded not only by his orchestral players but by his singers, as well. Walter Damrosch was assigned to conduct French and Italian operas, which were sung in German. Among the productions were *Carmen,* and even *Faust,* the French libretto of which was rendered in German, except for the leads who sang their roles in Italian.[23]

Seidl presented the first American *Tristan und Isolde* in 1866 and the first American *Ring* cycle three years later, culminating the assimilation of German opera in the United States. Carl Bergmann had presented the first Wagner opera production in America of *Tannhäuser* at the Stadttheater in 1859, followed in 1871 by the first *Lohengrin* under Adolf Neuendorff, who also led the first American *Die Walküre* at the Academy of Music. Wagner was gaining respectability and more luxurious theaters. At the Met, Seidl held sway three and four times a week, presenting the operas of the *Ring* tetralogy 16, 10, 13, and 11 times, respectively, in 1888–1889. In the seven seasons under Seidl, the Met had given 599 staged performances (in New York and on tour), of which 320 were works by Wagner. No administration since has even approached this record.[24]

The audiences were caught up in rapt attention. "One could hardly listen to 'Götterdämmerung' among throngs of intensely young enthusiasts, without paroxysms of nervous excitement," Henry Adams declared. The composer Sidney Homer went even further, swooning "A new world burst forth! Life would never be the same again, the commonplace was banished from our ... lives forever!"[25] Wagnerites shushed the boxes, darkened the house (something new), chided the boxholders for arriving late, and generally annoyed the monied set—exceedingly—who were paying most of the bills.

Downtown at the Academy, Mapleson resolutely continued presenting Italian opera. It was clear that New York could not support two full-scale opera houses, and discussions began on some means of combining resources. Outright merger was suggested, as was the sharing of a single company between the two houses and performances on alternate evenings. In the end, no arrangement came about. By 1886, Mapleson, deeply in debt and being pursued by creditors, threw in the towel in 1886. "I cannot fight Wall Street," he announced, and then departed for England.[26]

Although German opera continued to be popular with ticket holders at the Metropolitan, many of whom were German themselves and all of whom were music lovers, the boxholders who owned the House were increasingly restive. They viewed their boxes as extensions of their drawing rooms and felt free to carry on conversations during the acts, visit back and forth, encourage matches between young men and women of proper families, and in short carry on as if the single ticket holders were either not there or had come to behold their finery and to watch the goings-on of their social betters in the boxes, rather than the performance onstage. To be sure, an aria sung by a favorite star would elicit the boxholders' attention; however, for their purposes the Metropolitan was primarily a venue for socializing. The brief acts, engaging arias, and multiple intermissions of Italian opera were ideally suited to such rituals; Wagner's lengthy acts were not.

And, the wealthy masters of the Met were not about to be lectured and scolded. The directors met secretly in 1889 and terminated German opera. In January 1891, they announced that during the next season, 1891–1892, the Met would give performances in Italian and French only. This decision brought outpourings of support from the German listeners. The final performance of *Die Meistersinger* had a half hour of applauding, cheering, and stamping. Emil Fischer, who had played as Hans Sachs, made a brief statement in English. Every member of the chorus presented Seidl with flowers, after which he thanked them. Only the entrance of workmen to tear down the set dispersed the crowd.

Ignoring protests from ticket holders, the directors called back Abbey and Grau in 1891, and the Metropolitan once again became an Italian opera house, now without competition from the defunct Academy. Italian and French operas were given in their original languages. German operas were sung in Italian. Abbey and Grau reinstituted a star system with a stable of highly paid singers like Emma Eames (1865–1952) and the brothers Jean (1850–1925) and Edouard de Reszke (1855–1917), the former a tenor and the latter a basso.

In spite of the precautions taken by its builders, the Metropolitan suffered damage on August 27, 1892, from a fire that started in the painted scenery stored under the stage. The season was canceled while the theater was rebuilt, and 51 of the 70 boxholders took the opportunity to withdraw from the corporation. The remaining 19 along with 16 new subscribers paid $30,000 each for which they received 100 shares of stock in the new Metropolitan Opera and Real Estate Company and one of the 35 *parterre* boxes in the renovated Diamond Horseshoe. They agreed to an annual assessment of $100 a share, $10,000 a box for maintenance. Newly painted and furnished with electric lighting, the Metropolitan opened for the 1893 season under the management of Abbey and Grau. Mrs. Astor occupied Box 7; Mrs. William K. Vanderbilt Box 4; and J. Pierrepont Morgan, chairman of the new board of directors, occupied the center box, number 35. An additional 19 boxes in the so-called Grand Tier, above the Diamond Horseshoe, could be leased for the season.[27]

More than a whiff of arrogance tainted the new arrangements. The circle of boxholders had tightened, so that Morgan's family and partners held 12 of the boxes, and Vanderbilt family members another 11. Each box bore a brass plate with the owner's name, and no box could be sold or transferred without the approval of the board of directors. No Jews or Roman Catholics were eligible to own boxes. The Astor Place and Academy aristocracy had been somewhat more subtle about their prejudices, possibly because they socialized and in some cases intermarried with members of the city's old Sephardic Jewish families whose New York roots went at least as far back as theirs, to the days of colonial New Amsterdam. Men like Morgan, on the other hand, were simply beyond caring whom they offended. The directors met in Morgan's library. Women in all their finery were on prominent display in the boxes and probably had a good deal of influence on Metropolitan affairs through their husbands and fathers; however, (as was customary at the time) only men could sit on the board.

The Metropolitan continued to operate at a loss, and in 1896 a group headed by piano manufacturer William Steinway attempted to reorganize its finances, but not until Maurice Grau took over complete management after Abbey's death in October of that year, did the company become fiscally solvent. Grau reorganized the musical forces and strengthened further the star system, hiring and firing singers in accordance with their box office appeal, and maintaining a galaxy of greats, like Lilli Lehman (1848–1929), Ernestine Schumann-Heink (1861–1936), Lillian Nordica (1859–1914), and Nellie Melba (1859–1931), along with Eames and the de Reszke brothers. Under Grau's management, the Metropolitan introduced Puccini's *Tosca* to America, presented Mozart's major operas, and instituted profitable tours, traveling from city to city on the Metropolitan's own special train. The policy became original language for productions. French operas were done in French and Italian operas in Italian. German opera returned to the repertoire, sung in German. But Grau also found it necessary to cut back on the chorus, orchestra, and ballet corps. Scenes were omitted to economize, and the costs of star-studded productions were offset with hastily rehearsed, second-rate performances by third-rate singers at reduced prices on off-nights.[28]

Grau retired in 1903, and his successor, Heinrich Conried (1855–1909), took up the lease. He reorganized the performing arm yet again, establishing it as the Conried Metropolitan Opera Company (CMOC), the first resident troupe with its own board of directors separate from that of the Metropolitan Opera and Real Estate Company (MOREC). The CMOC had use of the Hall and box office, rent-free, and in return staged an opera each evening during the week, and two on Saturday. Conried continued Grau's policy of spending lavishly on stars and stinting on staging and ensembles. Gatti-Casazza (1869–1940), who took over management of the Metropolitan in 1908, found it necessary to restore discipline among the singers, restrain their independence, and curb their influence on the company's operations. Conried disdained modern French opera and passed up performing rights to Massenet's *Thaïs* and Debussy's *Pelléas et Mélissande*. Yet he was capable of daring strokes. On Christmas Eve 1903, he staged the American premiere of Wagner's *Parsifal*, over the Wagner family's objections and in spite of its international copyright, to which the United States was not a party.

Again on January 22, 1907, Conried mounted the first American performance of Richard Strauss's *Salome*, with the great Wagnerian soprano Olive Fremstad (1846–1951), precipitating a crisis with the boxholders and directors of MOREC. J. P. Morgan's daughter was particularly scandalized, not so much by the notorious Dance of the Seven Veils (Fremstad was not a dancer and a body double was substituted for the dancing), but rather by Fremstad's closing scene in which she caressed the head of the Baptist. Ever the actress, she had visited the city morgue to learn for herself how it felt to handle a severed head. Heeding his daughter's indignation, Morgan, as chairman of the MOREC board of directors, ordered that subsequent performances be canceled. Kahn and the CMOC board gave way and the production was withdrawn.[29]

Metropolitan politics only added to the headaches that nature and a new competitor were giving Conried. The San Francisco earthquake of April 18, 1906, struck during the Metropolitan tour appearance there. Although none of the performers were injured, properties and musical instruments were destroyed, causing his company a significant financial loss. But Conried's most serious challenge came from outside the precincts of the Metropolitan. On December 3, 1906, Oscar Hammerstein opened his Manhattan Opera House in direct competition with the Metropolitan. We will turn to Hammerstein presently; for the moment, however, by way of countering the combination of the San Francisco earthquake, the *Salome* debacle and Hammerstein's competition, Conried enagaged Gustav Mahler (1860–1911), renowned at the time more as conductor of the Vienna Imperial Opera than as a symphonic composer. Mahler, already weakened by the heart disease that would take his life three years later, agreed to a three-month season at the Metropolitan each year and made his debut on January 1, 1908, conducting Wagner's *Tristan und Isolde*. A month later Conried resigned as manager of the Metropolitan.

Kahn now took over day-to-day management, personally underwriting deficits of about $100,000 each year.[30]

Mahler conducted superb performances of Beethoven's *Fidelio,* Mozart's *Don Giovanni,* and Wagner's *Siegfried* at the Metropolitan. He was a demanding person and offended some boxholders by insisting on silence from the audience. Kahn considered engaging him to replace Conried. Morgan and the MOREC directors preferred a manager they knew and trusted, specifically Andreas Dippel, an adequate tenor whose chief attribute was his ability to step into any number of roles on short notice. As for Mahler, he was under no illusions either about his own stamina or the challenges at the Metropolitan. He liked Americans, but considered the Metropolitan inferior to European houses. In the end, Kahn turned instead to the seasoned impresario of Milan's La Scala, Giulio Gatti-Casazza (1869–1940); and Gatti immediately enlisted La Scala's brilliant conductor, Arturo Toscanini (1867–1957) to accompany him to New York. To placate Morgan's group, Dippel was appointed administrative director, and played a sometimes discordant role in Metropolitan affairs until his departure to run the Metropolitan's subsidiary Philadelphia and Chicago Grand Opera companies in 1910.[31]

Toscanini's temper and musical brilliance were already legendary, and he immediately impressed the Metropolitan's musicians by conducting rehearsals without a score. He was equally at home with Italian, French, and German opera. Although he and Mahler respected each other, it was only a matter of time before the two men tangled over Toscanini's insistence on conducting a performance of Wagner's *Tristan,* an opera Mahler considered his territory. Although a compromise of sorts was worked out whereby the two would alternate, Mahler's health and enthusiasm were flagging. He withdrew from the Metropolitan in the fall of 1909 to conduct the New York Philharmonic, then returned to Vienna early in 1911, dying there that spring.

The era of Gatti-Casazza and Toscanini was the high point for the Metropolitan, largely because of Kahn's support. The star system continued unabated with the addition of such singers as Enrico Caruso (1873–1921) and Geraldine Farrar (1882–1967). In an operatic tradition that idolized sopranos, Caruso, a tenor, may well have been the most popular operatic star of all time, and Gatti-Cassaza's most potent weapon in his war against Hammerstein's Manhattan Opera. Caruso was born in Naples, the 18th of 20 children and the first to survive beyond early childhood. He did not burst upon the opera scene in Italy; rather, he served an apprenticeship in provincial and metropolitan Italian houses and made his Metropolitan debut November 23, 1903. Critics were lukewarm. It was Caruso's good fortune that his career coincided with the early days of recording. Earlier greats like the de Rezke brothers left no recordings; and even Patti was well past her prime when she made her discs. Caruso began recording in 1904, quickly making his name a household word, even among those who never set foot inside the Metropolitan. Through it all, he remained a simple, jovial man whose modesty was such that he turned down offers of extravagant fees beyond his customary stipend.

Farrar grew up outside Boston, studied in Europe, and made her debut in Berlin. A media darling from her first appearance onstage and linked romantically with the German crown prince, she sang the lead in the Metropolitan's 1906 premiere of Puccini's *Madame Butterfly*; carried on—and broke off—a torrid affair with Toscanini; and retired from the Metropolitan in her forties at the height of her powers. Farrar's great soprano voice is attested to by her many recordings. She was also a superb dancer and a strikingly attractive woman who appeared in silent movies. The audience response to her final curtain call on April 22, 1922, bordered on hysteria.

Both Kahn and Gatti-Casazza were dissatisfied with the Metropolitan's building. Gatti was frustrated with the lack of storage and rehearsal space, and Kahn wanted more low-priced seating. The two men tried to launch a campaign for a new opera house, but to no avail. Kahn tried to include a new Metropolitan Opera House in the plans for Rockefeller Center, but efforts were thwarted by the stock market crash of 1929. Not until 1966, when the Metropolitan moved to Lincoln center, did it have an adequate opera theater.[32]

On the other hand, the era of Gatti's management and Kahn's support resulted in new artistic triumphs for the Metropolitan. Puccini's operas with their lyrical melodies and real-life plots became a staple of the repertoire, as did the earthy, so-called *"verismo"* operas such as Leoncavallo's *I Pagliacci* and Mascagni's *Cavalleria Rusticana*. The staging of these newer operas affected the way older repertoire was done. Audiences now expected more than the sort of unsophisticated blocking, generic scenery—hastily-built interior and exterior sets usable in a variety of operas—and careless acting. If the American premiere of Richard Strauss's *Salome* in 1907 had scandalized some in the audience, the first American performance of his *Elektra* in 1910 was greeted with a 15-minute ovation. That year, the Metropolitan presented a two-month season of opera performances in Paris, financed by Kahn and other wealthy board members.[33]

Kahn was also sensitive to matters of budget, and in this he had at least the acquiescence of Gatti, who, in the words of Frances Alda (who was Gatti's first wife and therefore knew him particularly well), "never lost sight of the box-office receipts in the cause of ART."[34] Toscanini, on the other hand, resented any economizing that compromised his own artistic standards. Out of patience (of which he was always in short supply) with Gatti and Kahn, and unhappy because Geraldine Farrar had ended their affair, Toscanini walked out of the Metropolitan in 1915 and left for Italy. He subsequently returned in 1926 and became America's leading conductor, but he never again mounted the podium at the Metropolitan Opera.[35]

HAMMERSTEIN AND THE MANHATTAN OPERA

Having overcome its operatic competitor, the Academy of Music, in 1906, the Metropolitan found itself in yet another rivalry, this time with an immigrant cigar maker and opera enthusiast named Oscar Hammerstein I (1846–1919), who, in 1908, would declare to the Philadelphia *North American,* that opera was the "most elevating influence upon modern society after religion." No wonder the music critic Henry Krehbiel later characterized the irrepressible Hammerstein as "quixotic." In 1863, Hammerstein immigrated alone from Germany as a youth. Although he had talent and training in music, and even composed, Hammerstein chose instead to go into the cigar-making business and made money from a cigar molding machine he invented. Meanwhile, he maintained an avid interest in music and, in 1871, joined in sponsoring a season of German opera at the Stadt Theatre.[36]

By 1889, he had made even more money in real estate and was financially able to indulge his impresario ambition. On September 30, he opened the Harlem Opera House, far enough uptown from the Metropolitan that he felt he could work out some sort of cooperative arrangement. In March 1890, he approached the Metropolitan's management, but his proposal was dismissed out of hand. Hammerstein thereupon began aggressively recruiting Metropolitan singers like Lilli Lehmann and engaged Walter Damrosch as conductor. Although he enjoyed some successes at first, the venture subsequently failed, largely because of Hammerstein's tendency to overextend himself financially. Over the next few years, he built one theater after another, trying in turn opera in English, popular musical theater, and vaudeville, all with varying degrees of failure and success. Deciding that he had garnered sufficient experience, the 60-year-old Hammerstein returned to his main love, grand opera, intent on competing with the Metropolitan by focusing on artistic integrity rather than social opulence. On December 3, 1906, Hammerstein's Manhattan Opera House opened with Bellini's *I Puritani.*

Hammerstein was using his own money and was thus able to maintain full control. He recruited singers from Europe and hired Mapleson's former stage director. He insisted on realistic sets, careful staging, and historically accurate costumes. His chorus was made up of young, enthusiastic singers, a mix of students and professionals who were an integral part of the dramatic action.

More important, he eschewed the star system and encouraged teamwork in his company. He prohibited encores, which interrupted the dramatic flow, and conversation in the boxes. With little interest in cultivating wealthy patrons, he sought to attract a diverse audience and build a following for opera as art rather than display. In this he saw eye-to-eye with Kahn, and indeed Kahn could sometimes be found sitting with Hammerstein in the latter's box at the Manhattan Opera.[37]

In spite of his aversion to the star system, Hammerstein managed to recruit several leading singers from the Metropolitan and from Europe, among them Nellie Melba (1861–1931), Lillian Nordica (1859–1914), and Luisa Tetrazzini (1871–1940). He took advantage of Conried's disdain for modern French opera to secure American performing rights to Massenet's *Thaïs,* Charpentier's *Louise,* and perhaps his greatest triumph, Debussy's *Pelléas et Mélisande,* which received its American premiere at the Manhattan Opera on February 19, 1908. Melisande was sung by Mary Garden (1874–1967), a superb actress and Debussy's own choice for the part in the Paris premiere. With such stellar offerings, Hammerstein began attracting fashionable people who customarily attended the Metropolitan, even though he disdained such patronage. His 1907–1908 opening night audience included such old New York names as Stuyvesant and Rensselaer, Consuelo, Duchess of Marlborough, and her brother, William K. Vanderbilt. By the next year, the Manhattan's opening night drew not only August Belmont, one-time chairman of the old New York Academy's directors, but also Andreas Dippel and Otto Kahn from the Metropolitan, the latter of whom joined Hammerstein in his box.[38]

Metropolitan stars Farrar and Caruso faced off against the Manhattan's Garden, Melba and Tetrazinini. Disregarding the reaction to the Metropolitan's performance of Strauss's *Salome* in January 1907, Hammerstein mounted his own production in January 1909, with Mary Garden in the title role, this time with great success. He was planning another house in Chicago to compete with the newly established Chicago Grand Opera, which the Metropolitan supported. But once again, Hammerstein had overreached himself. *Salome* was greeted with outrage by the clergy in a Philadelphia performance, and a planned Boston performance was canceled. Moreover, he had miscalculated the number of fashionable opera lovers who could be drawn away from the Metropolitan by his productions.

By that time it had again become clear, as it had been 20 years earlier, that New York could not support two opera houses. Among other things, star singers were playing the two houses against each other for higher fees. In January 1910, the *Times* reported that the Metropolitan was seeking to engage Hammerstein as director of its French operas. Although the Metropolitan promptly denied the story, the truth was even more striking. In spite of their seemingly productive and warm partnership, Kahn had wearied of the feuding between Gatti-Casazza and Dippel, and considered releasing Gatti-Cassaza and replacing him with Hammerstein. But nothing happened, and any prospects of a talked-about merger evaporated.

The ending was far less dramatic. The Metropolitan simply had more resources than its competition. In April 1910, the once again overextended Hammerstein was paid only $1.2 million for the sets and property from his opera house. In return he surrendered his Philadelphia opera house, scenery, and performing rights and agreed not to produce opera for 10 years. Dippel took over the Philadelphia and Chicago operations for the Metropolitan, and Hammerstein sailed away to Europe. He was dead within 10 years.

OPERA IN OTHER AMERICAN CITIES

After the Civil War, many smaller cities and towns built their own "opera houses" for concerts and touring productions, from minstrel shows to actual operas. Such theaters and halls varied in size, facilities, and seating. In some towns, a few folding chairs accommodated the audience, and the orchestra "pit" provided scarcely room for a piano. Elsewhere, as in the mining boom town of Virginia City, Nevada, for instance, opera houses might replicate the opulence of New York, albeit on a smaller scale, including boxes for those who could afford them.

As the nation's largest city and the financial center for its emerging industrial might, New York could support an expensive grand opera establishment. Most other American cities could not follow suit in the years before World War I. Even as they established their own resident orchestras, approaching and even surpassing New York's, those cities were unable to maintain resident opera companies at anything like the quality of the Metropolitan. In fact, the various touring companies, especially those of the Metropolitan Opera, Mapleson's company from the Academy of Music, and Hammerstein's Manhattan Opera, had the effect of undermining attempts to establish local resident companies, even in large cities.

NEW ORLEANS

Continental origins and traditions gave New Orleans a reliable base and head start in the establishment of opera. By 1791, the city had a French opera company and a year later an opera house. Even after it became a part of the United States in 1803, New Orleans remained European in its outlook. A dozen or more operatic performances were presented in 1805–1806, and in 1810, the Theatre d'Orleans formed its own permanent company. In a little more than four years between 1820 and 1824, the Orleans Theater saw 464 performances of 140 operas by 50 composers, an average of two operas a week. Between 1827 and 1833, a touring company from New Orleans presented opera in northern cities, including New York, Boston, and Philadelphia, as well as French-speaking Quebec. In December 1859, the French Opera House opened. Its productions enjoyed the patronage of New Orleans's Creole aristocracy. Unfortunately, Louisiana's secession in April 1861 and subsequent occupation by Union forces kept the house closed until 1866, when opera resumed. By the 1870s, the resident company at the French Opera House was again touring.

The house was something of a Creole tradition. It had been built in an upper-class neighborhood, within walking distance of the homes of the old families, and boxes were passed down from generation to generation. But as the French Quarter declined in the 1890s and the notorious Storyville became an officially recognized red-light district, with bars and bordellos, the opera and the Opera House fell out of fashion. Soon Dixieland was drawing more listeners than divas. In 1915, the House was severely damaged by a storm, and four years later it was destroyed by fire. This was not completely bad news. It was in this same Storyville and during this same period that America's greatest contribution to popular music—jazz—fermented and developed.

BOSTON

Nineteenth-century Boston did not prove especially hospitable city for opera. The city's Puritan-rooted social establishment had inherited an instinctive mistrust of operatic emotion and passion. Moreover, the city's old-monied upper classes shunned the opulent display of New York's newly rich. Finally, Boston's musical elite and its musical establishment were largely influenced by John Sullivan Dwight and his *Journal,* and Dwight considered German instrumental music the highest form of musical art. Nevertheless, a group of prosperous Bostonians planned an opera house in 1852, purely as a commercial enterprise and tourist attraction. The house had no resident company of its own, but presented performances by touring opera companies during the 1850s and 1860s.

In 1908, Eben Jordan, an amateur singer and heir to a department store fortune, established a house with a resident company. Jordan agreed to underwrite deficits for three years and hired as manager Henry Russell, Jr., whose touring San Carlo Opera Company had presented Italian opera in Boston during its tour the previous year. Like Hammerstein's house, no encores were allowed to interrupt the productions, and no latecomers were seated after the curtain had gone up. The company produced some modern operas, including *The Pipe of Desire* (1905) and *the Sacrifice* (1910), works by the Boston composer Frederick Converse (1871–1940). Nevertheless, support for opera was insufficient. Not even the highly popular Felix Weingartner (1863–1942), who conducted between 1911 and 1913, could improve the company's fortunes enough to make up for mounting deficits. By 1914, the house was bankrupt and it closed the next year.

PHILADELPHIA

The Philadelphia Academy of Music, founded in 1855 as a commercial venture, opened on February 25, 1857, with a performance of Verdi's *Il Trovatore*. The Academy was to include a school whose students would also function as chorus singers and orchestra players to the star leads; however, neither the school nor resident company of stars materialized. Instead, throughout the Gilded Age, the Academy presented opera by touring companies. Nevertheless, some events of note occurred. The future King Edward VII of England heard Patti sing there during his 1860 visit, and Gounod's immensely popular *Faust* received its American premiere at the Academy on November 18, 1863.

CHICAGO

In the years before and after the Civil War, touring opera companies made the city a regular stop. Crosby's Opera House, built in 1865, was destroyed in the fire of 1871 and rebuilt in 1873. The sumptuous Auditorium Theater, designed by the eminent Chicago architect, Louis Sullivan, opened in 1889. But Chicago did not have its own company until 1910, when the Chicago Grand Opera Company was established. Initially, the company relied heavily on singers from New York and the Metropolitan. In any case, its history and that of opera in Chicago properly belong to the years after World War I.

SAN FRANCISCO

San Francisco had an active musical life, including touring opera performances, during the gold rush years of the 1850s, beginning with a performance of Bellini's *La Sonambula* January 24, 1851. The completion of the transcontinental railroad in 1869 raised the level of artistic and cultural activity to the city. Mapleson's New York Academy company and the Metropolitan tours regularly brought San Francisco audiences stars such as Patti and Caruso. Indeed, the Metropolitan was in San Francisco in 1906, when the earthquake struck. Other touring groups included Clara Louise Kellogg's English opera company in 1877 and Theodore Thomas's American Opera Company, whose costs were underwritten by his New York patroness, Jeanette Meyer Thurber. The American Company toured for two seasons with its own ballet corps, chorus, scenery, and costumes, presenting American singers performing grand opera in English translation.[39]

San Francisco had several operatic theaters before the earthquake, of which the best known during much of the Gilded Age was the Tivoli, which operated at three successive locations between 1875 and 1906. Beginning as a beer garden, the Tivoli built a 1,000-seat theatre in 1879, in which a resident company of singers, and a small but balanced orchestra presented a variety of operas and operettas. The performances were good, albeit on a modest scale, at least by New York standards, and the audience could buy printed translations of foreign-language productions to follow along with the action on stage.

By the turn of the twentieth century, opera in the United States had become completely sacralized. Wagner—along with Beethoven—illuminated the American experience more than any other European masters transplanted here. Music Historian Joseph Horowitz argues that "Wagner not only dominated America's musical high culture for a generation; his world of music and ideas—Wagnerism—inflected general intellectual discourse as no musician's had before."[40] When Theodore Thomas, a noted Wagner advocate, premiered the American premiere of *The Ride of the Valkyries* in 1872, the public responded by leaping onto chairs and shouting. In St. Louis, where Seidl presented the *Ring* on tour, 4,000 crammed the 3,500-seat Music Hall. Whereas Wagnerism in Europe had become associated with decadence, socialism, and sometimes even nihilism, in America it served to counterbalance the materialism and rapaciousness of modern industrial capitalism; it served as therapy.

Wagner presented to American audiences, especially to the women, opportunities to experience emotional and aesthetic depths left unexplored in proper Victorian society. One 1890 New York review called the *Tannhäuser* Bacchanale, with its sexually explicit eroticism, "beyond comparison the most intoxicating piece ... ever composed.... If an abstainer wants to realize the voluptuous dreams of an oriental opium-smoker, he may have the experience without bad after-effects by simply listening to this ballet music."[41] For many, Wagnerism epitomized bourgeois genteel conventions while illuminating some of the deep emotions unrealized in earlier artistic experiences.

In so doing, it brought opera full circle, back to Dwight's earlier position on absolute instrumental music as an idealized experience, offering spiritual uplifts and moral catharsis. In concluding the story of opera in nineteenth-century America, Wagnerism went beyond Verdi and reconnected High Art to the canonized German concert composers.[42]

Critics, Composers, and Conservatories

In the decade before the Civil War, two of America's leading music journalists opened a debate about the nation's musical destiny. They asked whether American composers should seek a distinctive style for America's cultivated or concert music or embrace the German symphonic style of such composers as Haydn, Beethoven, and Mendelssohn as a universal standard of musical excellence. Young composers of the period in Eastern Europe and Russia were debating the same issue as they began to abandon inherited German Romantic forms and forge nationalistic styles inspired by their indigenous music. In America, the controversy found opposing adherents in William Henry Fry (1813–1864) in New York and John Sullivan Dwight (1813–1893) in Boston.

Born to a relatively well-to-do Philadelphia newspaper publisher, Fry began composing music in his school days at a Catholic boys' academy, Mount St. Mary's, in Emmitsburg, Maryland. By age 20 he had produced four orchestral overtures, all of them heavily influenced by his favorite Italian operatic composers, Donizetti, and Bellini. He also began his first opera and his career as a music critic, writing for his father's *National Gazette*. His opera *Aurelia the Vestal* (1841) had an English-language libretto patterned on that of Bellini's *Norma*, but was never performed.

In 1841, Fry moved to New York and began writing for Horace Greeley's *Tribune* and continued composing. In June 1845, his opera *Lenora*, also in English and modeled on Bellini, received the first of several performances in Philadelphia, followed by a New York production. Fry spent the years between

1846 and 1852 in Paris as correspondent for the *Tribune*. On his return Greeley appointed him music editor, and in that capacity Fry gave a highly publicized series of lectures on music at Metropolitan Hall in November 1852. It was a prominent and visible vantage point in New York's musical establishment that Fry engaged Dwight by advocating for an artistic "Declaration of Independence" from Europe. Fry envisioned a distinctively American musical movement corresponding to the painters of the Hudson River School, with their depictions of American landscapes and subjects, or the city's Young America literary movement of the 1840s. By no means did Fry reject European styles; indeed, he firmly believed that Italian opera was the highest of musical genres and urged Americans to accomplish what the British had not in the development of English-language opera. In the decade that followed, Fry also wrote his most successful programmatic symphonies, *Niagara* and *Santa Claus*.

Fry encountered both allies and opponents in New York. On one hand, he was supported by the equally prominent composer, performer, and teacher, George Frederick Bristow (1825–1898), who resigned his seat in the string section of the New York Philharmonic as a protest against its departure from the explicit provision in its original charter requiring it to program at least one work by an American composer each year. Bristow's opera *Rip Van Winkle* had several performances in New York in 1855, and, 20 years later, his American-themed *Arcadian* Symphony was played by the Philharmonic during its 1874 season.

Whereas Fry was a professional composer and musician, John Sullivan Dwight was a musical amateur who advocated an idealized, transcendent type of music. To be sure, he played the flute and had helped launch the Harvard Musical Association, but Dwight was first and foremost a romantic with a pronounced sympathy for German idealism. Fry was scion of a wealthy Catholic family; Dwight came from old Puritan stock of modest financial circumstances and was chronically short of money. Dwight graduated from Harvard in 1832 and completed his studies for the Unitarian ministry there four years later, although he had little success in the churches he served, at least in part because of a certain carelessness and even laziness on the one hand and a scholar's detachment from the practical duties of his calling on the other.

Dwight was one of a group of young ministers who met at the Boston parsonage of George Ripley beginning in 1836 to discuss religion and philosophy in the context of German philosophical idealism and romanticism. As such, he moved in the rarified intellectual atmosphere of Boston's transcendentalist movement from its beginnings. Dwight became an intimate of such luminaries as Ralph Waldo Emerson and Margaret Fuller and finally left his pulpit in Northampton (much to his congregation's relief) and the active ministry to join George Ripley's idealistic community at Brook Farm in 1840, remaining there until it closed in 1847. During his years at Brook Farm, Dwight contributed numerous articles on music to the transcendentalist periodicals, the *Dial* and the *Harbinger*. In a real sense, he was the musical spokesman for New England transcendentalism.[1]

Dwight married late, in 1852. Neither practical nor wealthy, neither punctual nor industrious, he had heretofore supported himself by writing essays and articles and by translating Goethe and Schiller. Now he sought a more reliable means of gaining a living and with that in mind borrowed money from friends and established *Dwight's Journal of Music*. In 1858, he delegated the business side of advertising, publishing, and circulation to the Boston publishing firm of Oliver Ditson, although Dwight retained editorial control. *Dwight's Journal* probably never had a paid circulation of more than 750; however, Ditson provided numerous complimentary copies, and during its 30-year run, it became the most influential musical periodical in America.

Dwight's correspondents from cities and hinterlands across the country reported on a variety of American musical activity, from minstrel shows to music teaching, from amateur events to touring virtuosos, from Gilmore's Peace Jubilee to church music news from various cities. *Dwight's Journal* was also a prominent platform for its editor's musical philosophy. Ever the transcendental idealist, Dwight defined music as a universal expression of emotion and spirituality, much as words were expressions of intellect and ideas. The truest music needed neither the words of songs nor opera to give it meaning, nor underlying programs or stories to render it comprehensible. Indeed, such literary encumbrances only served to block music's innate essence. Music was completely self-referential, and thus it required neither literary nor pictorial associations to find meaning. Accordingly, the truest and best music was instrumental, cast in the strict contours of classic sonata and symphonic form, transcending, as it were, both sung words and story line.

Dwight's Journal argued that such music, exemplified in the work of the German and Austrian symphonists and especially Beethoven ("unspeakable inspiration," Dwight said), was by definition universal and rose above any particular national or indigenous significance. Put simply, Dwight embraced the German symphonists and their nonrepresentational instrumental forms as the universal ideal of music, transcending any nonmusical elements, literary or geographic. As he put it, "Art soars above all narrow nationalities."[2]

Dwight had little patience or respect for showy performers and their virtuosity. He viewed the popular pianist Louis Moreau Gottschalk (1829–1864) with misgivings. Gottschalk loved performing in Boston, but he never received the kind of press notices from Dwight that other music journalists bestowed on him as a matter of course. Dwight expressed similar reservations about operatic arias, beloved both by prima donna singers and their doting fans. In

Fry's scheme of Italian opera and musical Americanism, words were what imparted meaning to music; in Dwight's vision of musical universalism, music itself was the language, for it alone communicated emotion, whereas words were signifiers for thought.

Dwight respected the operas of Bellini, Rossini, and Verdi, although he disliked most Donizetti and reserved judgment on Wagner. For Dwight, unlike Fry, the melodies of Italian opera served first and foremost as an effective means of attracting audiences, whose tastes could then be guided to a mature appreciation of German instrumental music, which Dwight characterized in the *Journal's* first issue, "the True, the *ever* beautiful, the Divine." On the other hand, Dwight was generous about Fry's last opera, *Notre Dame of Paris,* performed in Philadelphia in April 1864 under Theodore Thomas's direction. In the May 16, 1864 issue of the *Journal,* he wrote "Mr. Fry's reputation will be greatly augmented by this work. Many of its attributes are of an order which the most famous composers are glad to be credited with."[3]

Dwight's wife died in 1860 while he was away on his only visit to Europe. On his return he moved into rooms at the Harvard Musical Association, took up duties as its librarian, and outlived his *Journal* by more than a decade, dying in 1893. After a run of 30 years, Ditson and Dwight had disagreed over editorial aspects of the *Journal* and parted ways. Dwight was unable to keep the periodical afloat without Ditson or to find another agent. *Dwight's Journal of Music* finally ceased publication with the September 3, 1881 issue, but his musical ideas had found other advocates. By the 1870s, other critics like Henry Krehbiel were following Dwight's lead and intellectualizing music in the context of German idealism, in books as well as leading periodicals such as *Atlantic, Harper's,* and *Century.*

Fry and Dwight defined two opposing intellectual positions in American music. Dwight's view prevailed at least until the end of the century, in part because of the articulate Fry's premature death from tuberculosis in 1864, but primarily because of the prestige and influence that accrued to *Dwight's Journal* in the years that followed. By the time the journal ceased publication, the Boston Symphony had been formed by Henry Lee Higginson—the first of several resident professional orchestras that would be established in American cities in subsequent years.

CRITICISM'S GOLDEN AGE

The years from 1890 to World War I bloomed into a golden age of music criticism. Major city newspapers and magazines alike maintained one or more critics on their staff. As a whole they were cultured and widely educated in the arts and literature; they were capable writers and shrewd commentators on music and the arts. The artistically gifted William Foster Apthorp (1848–1913), for instance, studied with Paine at Harvard and alongside John Singer Sargent in Florence. He wrote for *Dwight's Journal* in its last years and *The Atlantic* between 1872 and 1877. In 1881, he became principal critic for the *Boston Transcript,* among whose subscribers were Boston's oldest families, and the first writer of program notes for the Boston Symphony orchestra's concerts.

Among other critics in Boston was Louis Elson (1848–1920), who taught at New England Conservatory, wrote, and lectured. But Apthorp's real successor was the aristocratic Philip Hale (1854–1934), who graduated from Yale in 1876 and studied the organ abroad before returning to Boston, eventually becoming critic for the *Herald* from 1903 to 1933, and succeeded Apthorp as program annotator for the Boston Symphony Orchestra. Witty, cutting, and opinionated, Hale was clearly a snob. But he was also systematic and erudite and could defend his snobbery. He especially enjoyed taking jabs at the New York musical scene, Krehbiel, and Dvořák's following. Hale was an early advocate for both Debussy and Stravinsky, respected Richard Strauss, and was unafraid to challenge the cult of Beethoven with pithy observations about weaknesses in this or that piece.[4]

Hale's polar opposite in Boston was his Harvard classmate and fellow Paine student, the kindly Henry T. Finck (1854–1926), who wrote for the *Boston Evening Post.* Finck and Hale agreed in their distaste for the *New York Tribune*'s chief critic, Henry E. Krehbiel (1854–1923). Krehbiel taught himself music before moving to New York from Cincinnati in 1880 as editor of the *Musical Review.* A year later he began at the *Tribune,* New York's most influential paper. Krehbiel also taught at Juilliard's predecessor, the Institute of Musical Arts, lectured, studied multicultural music, and wrote several books. Part of the Bostonians' antipathy was professional. Krehbiel advocated the Americanism of Thurber and Dvořák, as opposed to the aristocratic European orientation of Hale, Finck, and the Boston composers. But Krehbiel's large and forceful demeanor managed to anger even the patient Finck, who called him "dominating and arrogant."

Personifying Gilded Age music criticism was James Gibbons Huneker (1857–1921), a Philadelphia native who began his career writing for the *Evening Bulletin.* Huneker went to Paris in 1878 hoping to become a concert pianist, failed, and salvaged the trip by writing travel articles and talking with Edouard Manet, Edgar Degas, Victor Hugo, Émile Zola, and Gustave Flaubert, among others. All totaled, he made 20 trips to Europe, meeting virtually every art and music dignitary, including Johann Strauss, Claude Debussy, Matthew Arnold, and others. He settled in New York, taught at the National Conservatory for a few years, and in 1900 became music critic for *The Sun.* In 1917, he moved to *The Times*. In his prime, Huneker was America's highest paid critic, although he always seemed short of money and forced to moonlight as a freelancer; by 1904, he was turning out 5,000 words a day. Writing easily and quickly on all the arts, he referred to himself as a "steeplejack of the arts." Huneker was a man about town in New York, who at one time or another knew such major writers as Whitman and Shaw, composers like Strauss and Debussy, and the painter Henri Matisse. The first of his 20 books, *Mezzotints in Modern Music* (1899), is penned in his elegant prose as are the books that followed, including his biography of *Chopin* (1900), whom Huneker idealized; at the same time, he decried the modern trends encroaching on concert music at the turn of the century even as he tried to understand them, dismissing them as "decomposition."

Huneker was the last American critic who knew enough about art, music, literature, and drama to write about them all with depth and insight. He knew his world was passing and he passed with it. Along the way he disliked nearly all the modern devices, especially the movies, phonograph, the telephone, and the automobile. His health began to decline as the Gilded Age waned with the war years. He died as the last great critical voice of a genteel, civilized way of living.

COMPOSERS IN AMERICA

It must have been gratifying to Dwight's Eurocentric musical universalism that two strong signals of America's musical maturity had appeared during his lifetime and that of the *Journal*. First, collegiate music departments and conservatories were thriving, especially in Boston; second, and probably even more gratifying to his sense of accomplishment, 1870s Boston had been attracting an extraordinarily talented school of composers, almost all of whom had studied in Germany. The group clustered around John Knowles Paine (1839–1906), Harvard's first professor of music. Indeed, by 1885, the *Musical Herald* referred to the city, in somewhat of an exaggerated but a nevertheless understandable tone, as America's "musical centre."[5]

After being raised in a musical family in Portland, Maine, John Knowles Paine studied in Berlin from 1858 to 1861. On his return to Boston he became organist of Old West Church; a year later he became chapel organist at Harvard and began giving lectures on music. In 1872, he was appointed instructor and, in 1875, Harvard's first professor of music. He quickly became a prominent figure on the American musical and cultural scene. At the poet Celia Thaxter's summer colony on Appledore in the Isles of Shoals, off the New Hampshire coast, Paine summered with artists and writers such as Childe Hassam and

for church, which display his best efforts. His Symphony of 1885 is seldom if ever heard, and his *Regulus* overture, although well received both in London and Munich, soon disappeared from the orchestral repertoire. His stage works likewise failed to gain much of a foothold, even though his opera *Mona* (1910) won a $10,000 prize from the Metropolitan, which staged the work in 1912. Critics such as Rupert Hughes greeted it with more respect than enthusiasm, commenting in 1915 that it was "scholarly, musicianly and masterful," but lacked melody and dramatic flow.[7]

Parker's greatest influence on American music came through his composition students at Yale, some of whom, like Quincy Porter (1897–1966) and Roger Sessions (1896–1985) remained prominent well into the twentieth century. The greatest of his Yale students, of course, was Charles Ives (1874–1954). Although he was frustrated at Parker's stern personal and musical formality, Ives acknowledged that Parker taught him structure, discipline, and technique. It is notable that, once on their own, Parker's students—Sessions and Ives especially—often adopted compositional idioms sharply opposed to Parker's innate conservativeness.[8]

ARTHUR FOOTE

Arthur Foote was born in Salem as the youngest child of a newspaper publisher. He entered Harvard intending to become a lawyer, studied with Paine, and led the Harvard Glee Club for two years. After graduation in 1874, he changed his plans and, in 1875, earned Harvard's first M.A. in music. Although he visited Germany the next year and attended the opening of Wagner's theater in Bayreuth, Foote took no formal European training. Returning to this country, he taught piano and music theory privately, played the organ for many years at First Church in Boston, and gave recitals and chamber music concerts. Late in life he was offered the music chairmanship at the University of California, but was reluctant to move to Berkeley or to take on such a responsibility at that stage in his career. Instead, he remained in Boston and joined the piano faculty of New England Conservatory.

Modest and unassuming, Foote's music reflects that aspect of his character. His writing shows care and formality, characterized by lyrical melodies, simple but elegant harmonies, and clear structure. Most of his music consists of smaller works: piano and organ pieces, choral music, and songs. He is probably at his best in his chamber music, notably the Violin Sonata (1889) and the Piano Quintet (1897). Among the larger compositions are three cantatas for chorus and orchestra: *The Farewell of Hiawatha* (1885) for male voices, *The Wreck of the Hesperus* (1888), and *The Skeleton in Armor* (1897) for mixed voices, all on Longfellow texts. Other important works are the Cello Concerto, three suites for strings, an orchestral suite, and a "Symphonic Prologue," *Francesca da Rimini* (1890). The third Suite for Strings (1908) was probably the most successful of Foote's orchestral pieces.[9]

EDWARD MACDOWELL

Born in New York, Edward MacDowell spent much of his life after 1876 in Europe, where he studied first at the Paris Conservatory (Debussy was a classmate) and after two years moved to Stuttgart and then Frankfurt. By 1880, he had a reputation as a pianist, although he hated to practice, was nervous before concerts, and preferred composing. In 1882, he visited Franz Liszt in Weimar, and Liszt later arranged for some of MacDowell's piano music to be published by the prestigious German house of Breitkopf & Härtel. MacDowell's work was also gaining attention in America, largely thanks to Teresa Carreño (1853–1917), a renowned Venezuelan-born concert pianist who had taught him as a youth.

In 1884, MacDowell married an American student of his, Marian Nevins, and four years later the young couple returned to America, living in Boston between 1888 and 1896, his most productive years. Carreño had introduced Americans to his First Piano Concerto in 1888, a few months before MacDowell's return from Europe, and he gave the first American performance of his Second Piano Concerto himself with the New York Philharmonic in March 1889, repeating it a month later with the Boston Symphony. Two of his most popular orchestral works, the *Suite for Orchestra* (1891–1895) and the *Indian Suite* (1896), were completed during his Boston years.

Although not yet 40, in the late 1890s, MacDowell was the best known of America's serious composers; however, his most creative years were behind him. His friends and family persuaded him to accept a professorship at Columbia University, and he moved to New York in 1896. That year he bought a farm in Peterborough, New Hampshire, as a summer refuge for rest and composing. MacDowell found himself charged with developing and teaching virtually a complete music curriculum and took his duties seriously. Always frail and nervous, the pressures drained him. In 1902, he went on sabbatical and, when he returned the next year, he found his program had been reorganized by Columbia's new president, Nicholas Murray Butler, which prompted his very public resignation in June 1904, provoking recriminations on both sides in New York's newspapers. He and Marian continued to spend their winters in New York and their summers in Peterborough; however, the Columbia affair, as well as injuries he sustained in a traffic accident, weakened MacDowell's already fragile constitution. His mental and physical health deteriorated steadily and he died in 1908.

MacDowell took as his models late European romantics such as Liszt and his teacher, Joachim Raff, rather than the earlier, more classically influenced romantic masters such as Beethoven, Mendelssohn, and Schumann. Like Liszt, MacDowell sought a more narrative musical style, inspired by his love for literature on one hand and nature on the other. For this he relied on such subjective elements as engaging melody, colorful harmony, and dramatic dynamic contrasts.

Not surprisingly then, MacDowell wrote no symphonies or operas. His large works include two brilliant piano concertos, a handful of symphonic poems, and the orchestral suites. He also wrote more than 40 songs: melodic, lyrical, and expressive. Even his four piano sonatas have evocative subtitles: "Tragica," "Eroica," "Norse," and "Keltic." MacDowell was at his best as a miniaturist, and most of his music consists of brief, descriptive, and atmospheric piano pieces grouped in sets with evocative titles such as *Woodland Sketches, New England Idylls,* and *Fireside Tales,* which continue to be performed in the twenty-first century.

MacDowell drew on Native American motifs, but only as devices. He was distinctly in accord with the view of the other Boston composers in regard to European musical styles and forms. His closest stylistic identification was with his friend and contemporary, the Norwegian composer Edvard Grieg (1843–1907), whose music MacDowell admired. One can hear the older man's influence in both MacDowell's piano miniatures and his concertos.[10]

AMY MARCY CHENEY BEACH

Amy Beach was probably the most gifted of the Boston group. An only child, born in Henniker, New Hampshire, she showed such talent that at age four her parents moved with her to Boston, where her musical genius drew the attention of such prominent men like the pianist William Mason and Dr. Henry Harris Aubrey Beach, an eminent physician her father's age and scion of a prominent Boston family. She had begun composing when she was four years old and published her first pieces in 1880 when she was 13 years old. She also possessed a superb piano technique and musical maturity beyond her years, making her debut at age 16 in the autumn of 1883 and two years later performing Chopin's F-minor Piano Concerto with the Boston Symphony Orchestra.

In 1885, when she was 18, she married Dr. Beach, and he insisted that she give up public performance and devote her efforts instead to composing.

Whatever may be said of her husband's overbearing Victorian attitude, he deserves some thanks for her development as a composer. Even though her music was signed "Mrs. H.H.A. Beach" he at least supported her efforts. After Dr. Beach's death in 1910, she resumed her public performing in Europe and America. After the start of World War I, she divided her time among her New York apartment and homes in Vermont, Cape Cod, Massachusetts, and the MacDowell Colony in Peterborough, New Hampshire. And she continued to produce fine music.

Beach wrote her larger works during the late 1890s, including a choral *Mass in E-flat* (1892) with accompaniment for small orchestra and organ, her *Gaelic Symphony in E minor* (1894) and a Piano Concerto in C-sharp minor (1899). Most of her work is in smaller forms, including songs, character pieces for the piano, and choral music for church use. Her piano music is excellent, but her best writing is probably her chamber music. Her Sonata in A minor for violin and piano (1896), and the Piano Quintet in F-sharp minor (1907) are masterpieces. Beach's music is strong, energetic, and characterized by exquisite melodies, colorful harmony, shifting tonalities, and a complete command of classical form and romantic style.[11]

COMPOSERS AND AMERICANISM

Antonin Dvorák exerted a profound influence on American music. A major musical nationalist in his own country, he was sympathetic with the aspirations of Thurber, Seidl, and Krehbiel, and much taken by the black spirituals his student and assistant, Henry Thacker Burleigh (1866–1949) sang for him. A May 21, 1893 *New York Herald* article headed, "Real Value of Negro Melodies," quoted Dvorák: "I am now satisfied ... that the future music of this country must be founded on what are called the negro melodies."[12]

The statement provoked the Boston musical establishment. In his *Boston Journal*, the aristocratic and waspish critic Philip Hale wrote sarcastically of Dvorák the "negrophile" seeking musical inspiration in the "jungles of the Bowery and the deserts of Central Park." In the *Boston Herald* for May 28, 1893, which printed reactions from the city's leading composers, Paine took a somewhat lofty tone, "It is incomprehensible to me how any thoroughly cultivated musician or music critic can have such limited and erroneous views of the true functions of American composers." Chadwick likewise pleaded unfamiliarity with "the real negro melodies," but opined, "Such negro melodies as I have heard, however, I should be sorry to see become the basis of an American school of musical composition." Beach was the most thoughtful. She did not question the beauty of "negro melodies" but rather wondered if they were any more typically American than songs of "Italians, Swedes or Russians." She also pointed out what Dvorák evidently missed: that the minstrel songs he admired were actually written by white composers like Stephen Foster. Beach looked out at the prevailing Anglo-American culture and suggested that vernacular influences were more properly to be drawn from Celtic and British sources, "inherited with our literature from our ancestors."[13]

Dvorák's music was generally respected by his American colleagues; however, his views on a distinctive American music continued to provoke controversy. Two months before he returned to Europe, he reminded the readers of *Harper's* in February 1895, that "germs for the best of music lie among all the races that are commingled in this great country."[14]

In Boston, Edward MacDowell snapped back, "National music has no place in art." Nevertheless, he and the other Boston composers had come to terms with vernacular materials. MacDowell's *Indian Suite* (1894) used Native American melodic elements, but the piece earned him a sharp rebuke from the waspish Hale. "I go to a concert to hear music," wrote Hale in the *Musical Courier* for February 5, 1896, "not to study or discuss folklore." For MacDowell, however, those Native American folk materials were just that— folk materials to be adapted and recast into a "universal" art music structure, in a similar manner to Haydn's use of folk melodies within a classic structure. "[N]ationalism, so-called, is merely an extraneous thing that has no part in pure art." In a similar manner, composers such as Chadwick and Beach who responded to Dvorák in the May 28, 1893 issue of the *Boston Herald,* increasingly borrowed from vernacular music to create a distinctly American flavor in many of their works.[15]

THE YOUNG AMERICANISTS

A number of composers of the younger generation were more receptive to Dvorák's ideas than their elders. Minnesota native Arthur Farwell (1872–1951) earned an engineering degree from Massachusetts Institute of Technology in 1893 while studying composition with Chadwick; he then went abroad for further work in Germany and France. After a year as lecturer at Cornell he returned to Boston where in 1901, he founded the Wa-Wan Press in suburban Newton Center. Farwell proposed to publish the music of composers like himself whose work was inspired or based on folk, Native American, and African American music and who were unable to interest mainline music publishers like Schmidt and Ditson. Between 1901 and 1912, when the Wa-Wan Press was discontinued and its catalogue sold to G. Schirmer, it provided its subscribers with an issue each of vocal and instrumental music every quarter.

In all, 37 composers were published by Wa-Wan Press, including Farwell's own work adapting materials from American Indian music; pieces by Harry B. Gilbert (1868–1928), a pupil of MacDowell who drew on African American themes; and music by Rubin Goldmark (1872–1936), a Dvořák pupil who also drew on Native American music, who went on to teach George Gershwin and Aaron Copland. Farwell also served as music critic of *Musical America* from 1909 to 1914.

The music of Farwell's generation represents the populist, egalitarian spirit of the early twentieth-century Progressive Era, rather than the Eurocentric artistic elitism of the late nineteenth-century Gilded Age. One can scarcely imagine a Paine or Chadwick in Farwell's role as supervisor of New York's public concerts, writing and producing music for civic events, considering music "a simple and available pleasure for all," as he later wrote, and directing community groups, as he did in New York after 1910.[16]

CHARLES IVES

Charles Ives (1874–1951) was born in Danbury, Connecticut, the son of a Civil War bandmaster who passed on to his son his fascination with unorthodox musical effects.[17] By the time he entered Yale, young Charles was already a superb performer and composer. He studied with Horatio Parker, who gave him a sure technical facility, but was totally unsympathetic with his musical ideas. Rightly convinced that he could not support himself adequately with music, Ives moved to New York after graduation, joined the Mutual Life Insurance Company, and later became a partner in the firm of Ives and Myrick, retiring quite well off on New Year's Day, 1930. In 1902, he gave up his last paid engagement in music as organist at New York's Central Presbyterian Church. Unfortunately, he left much of his choral and organ music behind, and it was discarded and lost when the church moved to a new building in 1915.

As Ives embarked on his musical career in the 1890s, the performance of his cantata *The Celestial Country* (1892) met with an indifferent reception. He also attempted to interest professional musicians in his music, which met with disdain, if not downright hostility. Deeply hurt by these rejections, he retreated, composing prolifically in isolation until about 1917, when poor health forced him to abandon most of his creative work for the rest of his life. It appears that this isolation, however, brought a certain liberation to Ives, for it was at the same time that he began to move beyond the romantic language of the Boston classicists and experiment with an increasing array of avant-garde compositional styles. From roughly 1905 to 1921, when he effectively ceased composition, he produced one of the most original and astonishing bodies of American music.

Ives's music falls into three broad categories: choral, instrumental, and vocal.

Choral Music

Most of the large amount of choral music is early, written before 1902, during his years as a church organist. The choral works reveal Ives's clear indebtedness to his Victorian artistic heritage, something he later attempted to obscure. Most pieces were for the church: some 40 sacred choruses. Best known are the settings of *Psalm 67* (1898), composed on a bitonal structure of G minor and C major, and an extended setting of *Psalm 90* (1898–190) for choir, organ, and bells, supported by a low C throughout on the organ. Of the secular choral works, the most well known are *Three Harvest Home Chorales* (1898, 1902) for chorus, brass ensemble, and organ, set in a complex counterpoint and three sonic portions.

Instrumental

Ives's major works include four numbered symphonies, the *Holidays Symphony*, two three-movement sets, two piano sonatas, four sonatas for violin and piano, two string quartets, and one piano trio. He also composed many smaller piano and organ pieces, including the popular *Variations on America*.

Ives drew his intellectual and aesthetic inspiration from the idealism of the New England transcendentalists, which found one of its richest expressions in his monumental and distinctly original *Piano Sonata No. 2 (Concord)* and *Essays Before a Sonata*. Even though he had written the work between 1909 and 1915, Ives did not announce the piece to the musical community until 1920, when he printed and distributed his *Concord Sonata* to critics and musicians, most of whom considered it the work of a crank. Only a few musicians, like critic and composer MacDowell, biographer Lawrence Gilman, and the composers Lou Harrison and Henry Cowell, recognized Ives as a genius. In his notebook, later published as his *Memos* in 1972 by Ralph Kirkpatrick, he reacted angrily to the incomprehension of his music. Typically, "And when the Nice Old Ladies (i.e., critics and academics) say "no design—formless—all music should have design and form"–Yes, Sarah, but not your designs and forms—No, Sirree! In this Sonata they're spitting about, there is design—somewhat more than there should be, it seemed to me–and the form is obvious, but it isn't drabbed on every milestone on the way *up* or *to* or *on*."[18]

The sonata, as Ives explains in the *Essays,* "is an attempt to present (one person's) impression of the spirit of transcendentalism that is associated in the minds of many with Concord, Mass., of over a half century ago. This is undertaken in impressionistic pictures of Emerson and Thoreau, a sketch of the Alcotts, and a *scherzo* supposed to reflect a lighter quality which is often found in the fantastic side of Hawthorne." He saw Emerson as "America's deepest explorer of the spiritual immensities," found a deep affinity with Thoreau, and in Hawthorne he noted "a sensitiveness to supernatural sound waves" and a substance charged with "the phantasmal, the mystical."[19] As Crawford observes, the four-movement sonata expresses the ultimate Ivesian synthesis. By casting the New England Transcendentalists in a respected European form, Ives demonstrates their universality as well as their Americaness. He accomplished this by synthesizing a traditional form with disparate vocal elements and combining sonata-style thematic development with quotation and layers, masterfully demonstrating his own command of the composer's craft.

Vocal

His *114 Songs* followed in 1924, again printed at his own expense and distributed to an uncomprehending establishment with a wry postface that did little to endear them to critics: "I have not written a book at all—I have merely cleaned house."[20] The housecleaning is not so much a *magnum opus* as an *opus compendium.* The collection includes songs written throughout Ives's compositional life—an enormous variety of styles, from parlor-song harmony to cowboy songs to tone clusters. Perhaps the two most well known are "The Circus Band March" (1894), which captures a slice of small-town life with its vocal line supported by a festive march in the piano, and the lengthy "General William Booth Enters Heaven" (1914), in which Ives combines astringent dissonance with phrases from the revival hymn "There is a Fountain Filled with Blood."

Even with all of its aggressive modern aspects, Charles Ives's music incorporates the past not as history, but as an ongoing tradition—the past enduring in the present. He weaves all of this together with original material and in original ways, in thick textures of complex harmony and counterpoint, involving quotation and layering, often with multiple simultaneous tonalities and rhythms. In this manner, Ives anticipated mid- and late twentieth-century musical idioms, although he worked in isolation, and his music was largely beyond the composers and performers of his own era. With his strong classical training, eccentric early musical influences, and his emphatic rejection of conventional musical standards, Ives was uniquely qualified among American composers to synthesize the indigenous and lasting elements of our folk, sacred, and popular music. As Gilbert Chase so aptly puts it, "We can take almost the whole body of American folk and popular music, as we have traced it from the early psalmody and hymnody of New England, through the camp-meeting songs and revival spirituals, the blackface minstrel tunes, the melodies of Stephen Foster, the fiddle tunes and barn dances, the village church choirs, the patriotic songs and ragtime—and we can feel that all this has been made into the substance of Ives's music, not imitated but assimilated, used as a musical heritage belonging to him by birthright."[21]

Not surprisingly, Ives found no place in the American concert world of his own time. As far as musicians of the Gilded Age were concerned, even those who studied alongside him under Parker at Yale and knew he wrote strangely eccentric music, they had little, if any, inkling of his artistic existence. Sadly, his name does not appear in Rupert Hughes and Arthur Elson's *American Composers,* published in 1915. Even the appearance of his *Concord Sonata* in 1920 failed to evoke much reaction beyond derision and bewilderment.

Other than private readings, Ives did not hear his music played before World War I. In 1910, Walter Damrosch attempted the second movement of Ives's relatively conservative *First Symphony,* written under Parker's tutelage. Ives was wealthy enough to pay theater musicians (who were used to playing anything put before them without comment) to read through his work; his *Washington's Birthday* was played at the Globe Theatre after hours in 1914; and violinist David Talmadge gave a private performance of a violin sonata by Ives in Carnegie Hall in 1917. But public recognition would have to wait until Ives was in his last years and long after he had stopped composing. The *Second Symphony of 1901* was not performed until Leonard Bernstein conducted it 50 years later. His *Third Symphony,* completed in 1904, received its premiere in 1946, with Lou Harrison conducting, and was awarded the Pulitzer Prize a year later. His *Fourth Symphony,* completed around 1914, received its first full presentation by Leopold Stokowski and the Philadelphia orchestra in 1965. Its four movements not only capture the musical world of nineteenth-century America but summarize Ives's life work; more than a dozen of his earlier pieces are quoted in this work. After a short Prelude, movement two (*Allegretto*) depicts a Pilgrim journey and quotes dozens of tunes, including "Marching Through Georgia," "In the Sweet Bye and Bye," "Turkey in the Straw," and many others. The third movement (*Andante moderato*) consists of a double fugue on the hymn tunes "From Greenland's Icy Mountains" and "All Hail the Power of Jesus' Name." The fourth movement (*Largo maestoso*) is a recomposition of Ives's "Memorial Slow March" based on the hymn "Nearer, My God, to Thee." By the time of the symphony's delayed premier, Ives had begun achieving international recognition as an uncommonly broad artist and greatly original composer.

CONSERVATORIES IN AMERICA

As touring artists gained increasing popularity in America during the 1850s and 1860s, expedited by the expanding railroads crisscrossing the country, American musicians began to emulate these artists as performers and composers. To accomplish this, they sought high-level professional training themselves. They understood that success in the concert hall and opera house followed a long educational study with excellent teachers. For much of the nineteenth century, Americans understood that such professional training could be had only in Europe. After all, weren't virtually all of the performing artists either Europeans such as soprano Jenny Lind, pianists Anton Rubinstein, violinists Henryk Wieniawski and Ole Bull, or Americans who had studied there, such as pianist Louis Moreau Gottschalk? Nearly all the respected composers from Dudley Buck to Horatio Parker likewise had made the long European circuit to gain their education. Also accelerating this press for professional level music training was the growing call for more widely accessible general education.

Americans had always sought some instruction in singing and playing, which had been addressed since the 1700s in the New England singing schools. Lowell Mason's work in Boston and the founding of the Boston Academy, as well as the spread of music education, added to the call for better music teaching. Moreover, as the American performers and composers returned from abroad, they continued doing what musicians had done ever since colonial days—they taught to enable them to pursue their careers in music. Gradually, colleges, universities, and conservatories started adding music to their curricula or devoting themselves entirely to professional music instruction. Gilded Age Boston led the way, and it must certainly have been in this light that Horatio Parker, who knew well the musical scene in both cities, complained to Henry Krehbiel of New York's *Musical Courier,* that New York, unlike Boston, disdained musicians as nothing more than "entertainers," and their work as inferior to the other arts and sciences.[22]

In Baltimore, George Peabody founded an arts institute in 1860, although his plans were not fully realized until 1868 because of the Civil War. Oberlin's conservatory was established in Ohio in 1865, and two years later Florenz Ziegfeld, father of the notorious early twentieth century showman of the same name, set up the Chicago Musical College. Earlier that same year, two institutions opened in Boston. German-born Julius Eichberg (1824–1893), violinist, church musician, and superintendent of Boston's public school music, led the way in establishing the Boston Conservatory especially for the training of singers and string instruments. Not far away, Eben Tourjée (1834–1891), a Rhode Island music teacher who edited the *Massachusetts Music Journal,* founded the New England Conservatory on the European model. In 1872, Tourjée helped establish a college of music at Boston University to grant degrees in music. Paine spoke at its inauguration and became its first professor of music, in addition to his Harvard appointment. Otherwise, the faculty of the college was essentially identical with that at New England Conservatory. Harvard's formal establishment of a music professorship for Paine in 1875 and a music department of its own thus ratified Boston's status as the nation's center for serious musical training.

One by one, other cities followed Boston's lead. Cincinnati created its own conservatory in 1867, and the Philadelphia Music Academy established one in 1869. Cincinnati had its second institution, the Cincinnati College of Music, in 1878; the Detroit Musical Academy was founded in 1880; and the Chicago Conservatory and American Conservatory in Chicago were established in 1885 and 1886, respectively.

JEANETTE MEYER THURBER, ANTONIN DVORÁK, AND THE NATIONAL CONSERVATORY

New York did not have its own conservatory until 1885. Jeanette Meyer Thurber (1851–1946), a native New Yorker, had studied at the Paris Conservatory before her marriage to a wealthy New York merchant. She began energetically to support musical endeavors, among them Theodore Thomas's American Opera Company. In connection with that project, she and a number of other wealthy patrons—Andrew Carnegie, August Belmont, and William K. Vanderbilt, among others—underwrote an American School of Opera as a training school for the company. A year later, the opera venture had failed, and the school's name was changed to the National Conservatory. Thurber's dream of government support for the arts in general and her school in particular never came to pass, although the National Conservatory did receive a congressional charter in 1891.

Students of any race, national origin, or gender were admitted, solely on the basis of their talent, and Thurber herself underwrote scholarships for African American students. Tuition was nominal, and expenses were to be met by patrons' gifts (Thurber herself gave $100,000), as well as the regular donations expected of successful graduates. The star-studded faculty included pianist James Gibbons Huneker (1857–1921), later to gain fame as a critic not only of music, but of all the arts; cellist Victor Herbert (1859–1924), who would go on to eminence as a stage composer; Horatio Parker; Anton Seidl (1850–1897), a Wagner disciple and perhaps America's leading conductor along with Theodore Thomas; and some years later composer Rubin Goldmark (1872–1936), who later taught George Gershwin and Aaron Copland, among others.

When the National Conservatory's first director returned to Paris in 1889, Thurber determined to replace him with a major composer. She turned to the celebrated Czech composer Antonin Dvorák (1841–1904), who was regarded as Europe's most important composer after Brahms. Dvořák disliked travel and unfamiliar surroundings; however, his celebrity on one hand and his affinity for vernacular, or "nationalist" elements in his own music, on the other made him too attractive a prospect for Thurber to give up on. In the end, her salary offer of $15,000 proved irresistible. Dvořák accepted the Conservatory directorship and arrived in late September 1892.

Dvorak completed his *Symphony in E minor*, subtitled "From the New World," during his first year in America. Acclaimed in advance by Krehbiel, it was introduced by the New York Philharmonic under Seidl's direction in a public rehearsal in Carnegie Hall, December 15, 1893, and formally premiered in a concert the next evening, achieving instant and lasting popularity. During the next few years the symphony provided a model for American composers. Both Beach's *Gaelic Smphony* of 1894 and Charles Ives's *First Symphony*—a student work—follow Dvořák's symphony. The actual "new world" elements are not literal. The themes of the first two movements resemble African American spiritual melodies and minstrel songs, and Dvořák maintained that the last two movements were inspired by Longfellow's *Song of Hiawatha*. Some critics, then and since, have been more inclined to hear elements of Dvořák's own native Bohemian folk music in the symphony.[23]

Thurber's National Conservatory began to decline even before Dvořák's departure in April 1895 as the 1893 economic depression began taking its toll on the school's benefactors, including Thurber's husband. Moreover, the public mood was shifting from fascination with Gilded Age wealth, opulence, and High Art, and toward Progressive Era populism. Not even the indefatigable Thurber could keep the institution afloat, although it lived on, at least on paper. After the turn of the century, Frank Damrosch's Institute of Musical Arts—later the Juilliard School—siphoned off the best music students further. Although the National Conservatory held out as a legal entity until 1952, no recorded activities appear after 1930.

The musical leaders of the Gilded Age transformed the American musical landscape. First, they developed the serious, professional musical criticism that elevated the discourse about music to a level where it had intelligence, insight, and substance. In this way, it could compete with other disciplines, including the visual and literary. Second, the musicians and musical advocates established outstanding, world-class musical training institutions that became one of the Gilded Age's most priceless legacies to the United States. Now, American students could remain in this country to study, gaining a musical education every bit as thorough and artistic as anywhere in Europe. And finally, the passion and energy of late nineteenth-century musicians in this country demonstrated that elite, sophisticated European music and its American practitioners could evoke the same compelling excitement from everyday Americans as any other music.

Church Music

4

Gilded Age church music prospered and expanded enormously, becoming one of the major cultural forces in Victorian America. As congregations multiplied across the land, so did the music programs and instruments they installed to fill their often resplendent sanctuaries. After the Revolution, the United States had been a largely unchurched society. A generation later, however, the height-ened passions of the Second Great Awakening generated a religious fervor that has never abated. In 1835, the noted French visitor Alexis de Tocqueville compared religious life in America and France. "In France I had seen the spirits of religion and of freedom almost always marching in opposite direc-tions." But in America, he explained, religion "never intervenes directly in the government of American society," but should nonetheless "be considered as the first of their political institutions."[1] The new religious enthusiasm soon unleashed a wave of reform movements—abolitionism, temperance, female suffrage, and worker's rights—which joined Christian Romantic thought with the first strains of Darwinian evolutionary arguments, energized by the exhilaration of the newly emerging millenarianism. It all came together: God and history merged into a linear progression of the fittest, which meant the triumph of Protestant, Anglo-Saxon culture over the barbarism of heathen, uncivilized cultures and lands.

By the onset of the Civil War, a new formality found its way into the wor-ship of all denominations. This increased reverence accompanied a revival of historicism in many congregations, probably affecting Episcopal churches the most, given their traditionally structured liturgy. The British Oxford Movement of the 1830s had prompted the so-called Ecclesiology movement, with its focus on renewing the connection to the medieval church along with the restoration of ancient rituals and traditionalism. These developments accelerated the press for more refined choral singing, larger organs, more dignified hymns, and professionally trained directors and organists. In a real sense, the movement was undergirded by the tendency of the newly rich upper class to see itself as an aristocracy in the medieval sense.

In addition to the dominant cultural authority the Victorian church assumed in national life was its move toward High Culture, especially in the Northeast. The support of High Culture in church music enabled the growing middle and upper classes not only to affirm their cultural taste but also to discreetly stratify themselves socially, intellectually, and aesthetically. Spiritually, one can see how the passion for choral and organ music functioned as an antimodern musical statement for a bourgeois society that found itself adrift in an unreal culture of blurred moral distinctions, infected with a platitudinous optimism that undermined the firm ground of Protestant theology. As society grew increasingly secular during the Gilded Age, the organized church saw its influence on American moral and social life recede. Puritanism had offered a solid metaphysic through which people constructed a framework of meaning out of the chaos of everyday experience. As Victorian theology supplanted Calvinism and accommodated itself to bourgeois culture, however, it lost its supernatural framework, which undermined the sense of an ordered universe; reality itself seemed uncertain. Cultural historian T. Jackson Lears aptly sums it up, "A weightless culture of material comfort and spiritual blandness was breeding weightless persons who longed for intense experience to give some definition, some distinct outline for substance to their vaporous lives."[2]

To fill the vacuum left by the explanatory collapse of sturdy Calvinistic theology, many turned to High Culture in search of meaning, value, and authority. These prospering Protestant bourgeoisie sought genteel literature, art, drama, and music as an antidote to the disruptive, rowdy manners, foreign tongues, and papist religion of the new immigrants. This newly affluent class also included the men who had made large fortunes in the rapidly industrializing economy of the postbellum era. In an unfocused, half-conscious effort to align themselves with some external symbol infused with historical meaning, they underwrote the construction of large neomedieval and Romanesque edifices, capped with towering spires, enshrining large organs and beautiful chancels. Such neomedievalism affected urban and suburban churches of all denominations from the 1870s on. But many, if not most, of the latter day barons and prosperous bourgeoisie favored the Episcopal Church owing to its historical connection and its aesthetic component. It also helped distance them from the working class, which was largely drawn to the more evangelical styles of worship. Fashion, wealth, and religion came together to create a religious aesthetic of formality and opulence. Charles Willeby, writing in *The Etude* of 1891, articulated the widespread belief about music's ameliorative power in and out of the service:

> Music is not mere pastime. Its effects are both powerful and beneficial, not only upon the cultured few, but upon the uncultured many.... If the lower orders could have as much of music as of the low literature with which they beguile their spare hours, there would be a large decrease in crime. Music imparts only good influences, while this low class of literature incites its coteries to commit the crimes and practice the vices of which they read.[3]

The immensely wealthy families who underwrote museums, orchestras, and opera houses in the second half of the nineteenth century viewed themselves as an American aristocracy and enthusiastically supported much of this growth in the church and its music. In the years after the Civil War, they built themselves great homes patterned on European manors and chateaux, which they filled with paintings and decorative art from Europe. Many had already replaced their earlier and more modest houses of worship with great gothic and Romanesque churches, ornamented with striking stained glass, elegant decorative arts, large organs, and luxurious furnishings.

Larger churches and their antiquarian furnishings inevitably lent themselves to increased formality and ceremonial. Even though the Episcopal Church in this country was generally "Broad" or "Low Church" in nature, the growing influence of the Oxford movement from England exercised a continual influence in the gradual move toward more elaborate ritual and richer liturgy. In an attempt to recapture the mystery of medieval worship, Episcopal churches began replacing the old word-centered, meeting-house style of churches with Georgian and classical revival churches; the preferred style was the gothic. Gradually, the focus of the now recessed chancel was shifted from the dominating pulpit to the altar table; stained glass replaced plain windows, and choirs and organs moved from the gallery to the front. Public worship became more mystical and aesthetic with the appearance of candles, colors, incense, and Eucharistic vestments for the clergy. Majestic processions and recessions of clergy opened and closed the services, accompanied by crucifers, candlebearers, and—gradually—surpliced choirs with paid singers. Now, the clergyman was obliged to move several feet from pulpit to lectern to altar during worship, and music provided a decorous cover for these movements. The increasingly choreographed and aesthetic quality of worship began to

influence churches of other denominations, which sought to emulate the choral services in the larger churches and few cathedrals.

Music in the Victorian church involved three overlapping practices: the
choir and choral music, centered on the anthem; the organ with its voluntar-
ies and accompanying support; and a vibrant congregational hymnody.

THE SOLO QUARTET AND CHOIR

In the Puritan worship of the seventeenth and eighteenth centuries, singing in the worship service had largely been limited to metrical psalms and a
rare short anthem. Interest in choral music in the service began growing in
the days of William Billings (1746–1800) and other New England composers.
During the first decades of the nineteenth century, choirs spread most rapidly
in the mainline Protestant denominations of Methodist, Presbyterian/Con-
gregational, Episcopal, and Baptist congregations—churches whose worship
service comfortably found a place for the anthem. Many Catholic and Jewish
congregations followed suit as well. When congregations began to separate
the choir out as an ensemble that prepared special music for the service, it
opened up a number of new possibilities—and challenges. For the first three
decades of the century, voluntary singers mainly composed the choirs. But
with little formal training on the part of the choristers, the organists, or the
leaders, few groups reached a level where they could sing anything but the
simplest music. Churches that became dissatisfied with the volunteer chorus
choirs, and who grew affluent enough, sought a higher standard of music by
employing professional singers. This also helped them display their cultivated
tastes by "improving" the service music on an operatic model. To that end,
they engaged four professional singers—a soprano, alto, tenor, and bass—
who sang every Sunday, both as soloists and together as a quartet.

By the 1840s, the number of urban congregations using professional singers had increased rapidly, influenced by the rising popularity of Italian opera.
In the years just before the Civil War, the practice become fairly widespread.
Many churches installed a quartet as soon as the budget permitted. Indeed,
some had systematically replaced their "chorus" choirs with quartets. The
music of such groups, pronouncedly operatic in style, was deemed to be finer
than the efforts of amateur volunteers and a sign, especially to visitors and
potential new members, of the congregation's enhanced affluence, sophistication, and taste.

At the same time larger churches started acquiring bigger organs. Whereas
the older, more modest instruments were usually situated in a gallery along
with the volunteer choir, Protestant churches tended to display the new organs,

beautifully cased, at the front of the church, behind or alongside the pulpit, in clear view of the congregation and admiring visitors. As the pulpit area usually offered much less space than a gallery, there was often sufficient room for only a quartet and organist. Even churches that kept their volunteer chorus choirs often hired a quartet to lead the amateurs and furnish concert quality solos for the enjoyment of the congregation.[4]

An 1861 survey of more than 130 New York churches showed that 72 of them had solo quartets, including 14 of 17 Roman Catholic churches and 24 of 31 Episcopal churches. Other Protestant churches varied depending on denomination. Eight of eleven Dutch Reformed congregations employed quartets. On the other hand, only 7 of 24 Presbyterian churches had quartets, whereas 12 had chorus choirs and 5 relied on congregational singing. Baptists and Methodist churches maintained their revival-era tradition of lusty congregational singing and volunteer choirs. Only four Baptist churches (the most fashionable ones in the city) had adopted solo quartets, as opposed to nine who maintained their chorus choirs. Similarly, only four Methodist churches (again, the most fashionable) used quartets as opposed to 16 churches with large and flourishing volunteer choirs.[5]

Clergymen of all denominations complained about theatrical music in church, and many prominent church musicians publicly endorsed volunteer "chorus" choirs as more appropriate for worship. But church trustees with an eye on parish finances understood that professional singers and operatic-style music attracted affluent new members of the proper sort; it also elevated the pew rents. Accordingly, church music committees contracted with quartets and organists for a year at a time, often through agents, and had no hesitation about making a change for better or more renowned musicians or to save money.[6]

By the same token, singers generally regarded their church work as simply another engagement, and all four singers in a quartet might move together, often with the organist, if another church made them a better offer. Contracts often included an extra benefit allowing singers the use of the church for presenting one or more recitals during the year. Young singers, aspiring to concert and operatic careers, could make more than enough money to pay for their lessons and gain performing experience and visibility. Moreover, the pressure of singing Sunday after Sunday on relatively little rehearsal helped them sharpen their musical skills and sight reading. Singers in urban churches averaged about $250 a year, generous for part-time work in the 1860s and 1870s. Leading Boston churches paid as much as $750, a modest but adequate living wage at the time; and at least one New York church offered more than $3,000 to lure an especially illustrious soloist. By the 1870s, it was possible for a singer to live comfortably (although by no means as extravagantly as an operatic prima donna, of course) by combining church solo work and private teaching.[7]

The rise of the solo quartet accelerated the growing demand for higher quality, more professional choral music in the service. At the same time, choral music rapidly came to be viewed as a central pillar in High Culture, ensuring that ensemble singing remained the most widespread type of organized music performance through the end of the century. Gradually, the better continental composers became popular in the United States, and around mid-century native composers began imitating these European musicians. Even though few native composers attained the musical quality of Felix Mendelssohn (1809–1847), John Stainer (1840–1901), or Charles Gounod (1818–1893), the European model brought out the finest abilities in the more talented Americans.

American composers and publishers provided large amounts of music for church soloists and quartets, including solo songs and anthems for the full quartet. Some pieces were adapted from operas by composers such as Gioacchino Rossini and Charles-François Gounod; others were written in the fashionable European operatic style or in the style of the popular, sentimental parlor songs with which middle-class families of the era entertained themselves and each other. Some rather good quartet anthems were written by prominent composers such as George Whitefield Chadwick (1854–1931) and Arthur Foote (1853–1937), although such pieces do not represent their best work.

In other words, the overall quality varied. A fairly low but not atypical level is represented in the works of George William Warren (1828–1902). A native of Albany and largely self-taught in music, he served churches in Albany and Brooklyn and in 1870 became organist and music director of St. Thomas Church in New York. Warren is remembered today only for his hymn, "God of Our Fathers"; however, he was highly regarded in the last decades of the nineteenth century for such works as his *First Easter Cantata* (1875) for solo quartet, subtitled "The Singing of Birds." The piece had a lilting 6/8 rhythm and an accompaniment garnished with pictorial trills in imitation of bird twitters. His *Second Easter Cantata* (1878) was a setting of the text "Fill the font with roses," by the popular sentimental poet Mrs. Lydia Sigourney.

On the other hand, the anthems and service music of Dudley Buck (1839–1909) represent some of the best work in the genre.[8] As an American who was trained in the European tradition, he was received with enthusiasm when he appeared on the scene as a composer of religious music. Although Buck was not a threat to the superiority of European composition; he was the best that America could then bring to the field of church music. A native of Hartford, Connecticut, Buck dropped out of Trinity College after two years, at age 18, to study in Leipzig, Dresden, and Paris. He returned to Hartford, in 1862, as organist of the North Congregational Church and quickly acquired a reputation as a concert organist, composer, and conductor. In 1869, Buck was appointed organist of St. James's

Church in Chicago; two years later his church, home, and studio were destroyed in the great Chicago fire. He moved to Boston, where he taught at New England Conservatory and served as organist of St. Paul's Church and the nearby Music Hall. In 1875, he moved to New York, as assistant conductor of the renowned Theodore Thomas Orchestra.

From 1877 on, Buck concentrated on church music, becoming director of music at Holy Trinity Church in Brooklyn. Too good a musician not to recognize the musical shortcomings of the quartet and too much of a pragmatist to think he could do anything about them, Buck wrote in 1877, "We have simply to deal with the fact [that quartets] exist, and whatever the signs of the future may be, they unfortunately form at present the majority."[9]

Buck's two volumes of anthems became the most popular collections in the last third of the century. His first *Motette Collection* (1864) found immediate success, and the *Second Motette Collection* (1871) firmly established his reputation. The *National Cyclopaedia* reported in 1897 that both collections enjoyed a "popularity which is still unabated."[10] Buck's volume not only offered professional quality anthems, but appeared just as this interest in sacred music began accelerating. In the first place, the compilation offered longer pieces that breathed the air of the Mendelssohnian oratorio rather than the Protestant hymn or the Italian aria. Second, the work reflected a shift to American compositions: of its 33 compositions, 14 were by Americans, including 10 by Buck himself. And third, the music was written for both amateur and professional singers, with the latter providing musical support and performing the solos. With different levels of musical difficulty available, Buck could compose more challenging music than that composed solely for chorus choirs. In sum, the *Motette Collection* demonstrates his ability to challenge amateurs without overwhelming them, while at the same time giving professional singers music appropriate for their ability and training. These sacred works, anthems, helped inaugurate a new tradition of American choral music composed in a romantic musical idiom. Buck's quartet anthems made generous use of individual soloists; at the same time, however, they were also written to be effective with a chorus choir. His numerous anthems for mixed quartet enjoyed immense popularity with American quartets, choirs, and congregations. Although sometimes facile, Buck's music was rarely trite and never cheap. He was a superb melodist, highly gifted in both counterpoint and harmony, and a meticulous craftsman.

Seeking to emulate the beauty, mystery, and High Culture of Episcopal worship, churches of all denominations began purchasing and singing Buck's choral music, which set texts that worked well either in the liturgical Episcopal service or, taken out of context, succeeded admirably as an anthem for other Protestant worship. The "Festival Te Deum" (1873) is an extensive setting of the historic *Te Deum* text, one of nine Buck composed. The optimistic tone and melodic elegance held great appeal for the church-going public during the Gilded Age, and it went through a number of reprintings into the twentieth century. It was still being performed nearly a century after its composition. As recently as 1949, Buck's *Te Deum* remained among the top anthem favorites for worship, according to an informal survey of nearly 100 choir directors.[11] The anthem provides the soloists and choristers ample opportunity to reflect on, adore, and celebrate the majesty of God above a robust accompaniment and stirring choral passages. The vigorous organ writing also showcases a critical ingredient of the Victorian musical practice.

The New York Herald for July 5, 1890 proclaimed, "[F]ew would deny Dudley Buck's claim as foremost writer of Protestant Church Music."[12] The main reason for this evaluation surely lies in Buck's concentration on sacred music. Outside the popular sphere, the church was the primary place where Americans encountered American compositions, whether as choir singers, congregation members, or listeners to oratorios, cantatas, anthems, and organ works. To these genres Buck devoted much of his effort as a composer. And he did so in the spirit of blending elevation with accessibility. Buck's many years of working with choir members gave him a sure sense of their tastes and technical limitations. He learned to write for them anthems that offered challenge and substance, and the thrill of participating in a kind of expression that, while praising God, also touched their hearts.

Buck retired in 1903 and died only a few years later. His pupils, such as R. Huntington Woodman (1860–1943), William H. Neidlinger (1863–1924), and Harry Rowe Shelley (1858–1947), continued writing in his style, but in general they lacked his spark. Shelley, who also studied with Antonin Dvořák in Europe, was probably the most popular and successful of the three. His career was spent at churches in Manhattan and Brooklyn, and his quartet anthems enjoyed almost as much popularity as Buck's, especially his attractive 1887 setting of Frederick William Faber's 1854 text, "Hark, hark, my soul."

The success of Buck's anthems accelerated the reverence and authority Victorian America accorded the church choir and choral music, which, along with the band, became the most popular and ubiquitous performing organization in the nineteenth century. Social reformers believed in the democratizing potential of choral music and its ability to edify and uplift the congregation. For the first time, virtually everyone could join a respected organization and benefit from the artistic thrill of making fine music while discharging their proper Victorian duty, while also enriching their soul. For these reasons, the choir and its music remained central to American musical high culture well into the twentieth century.

HISTORICISM AND MALE CHOIRS

Although most churches of all denominations hung on to their professional quartets for decades, an opposing historicist movement was very much alive in a number of liturgically oriented parishes from the 1840s on. Lutherans and German Reformed churches in America revived musical and liturgical traditions that had been dormant since the evangelical revivals of the early nineteenth century, largely because of the wave of German immigrants who arrived during and after the 1840s. Stained glass and altar crosses were restored, as were kneeling and chanting.[13]

Episcopalians began to revive their historical worship traditions, including choirs of men and boys, in place of women or girls. As early as 1861, the *American Musical Directory* showed choirs of boys and men in a few New York churches.[14] To be sure, most male choirs simply led the congregational singing of simple hymns and service music, or sang much the same sort of music as the solo quartets did; however, a handful of churches had already begun experimenting with using male choirs specifically to chant psalms and canticles in the manner of English cathedral ritual. By the 1870s, some wealthy Episcopal churches had both a quartet and a choir of men and boys (sometimes with a group of women, hidden from view, to support the boys' singing).[15]

The Rev. William Croswell, rector of Church of the Advent in Boston, one of the earliest parishes of the so-called ritualist movement, had tried to replace the church's volunteer adult quartet with boys as early as 1849; however, it was not until Henry Stephen Cutler (1822–1902) was hired, in 1852, that the boy choir was established. Cutler, a native of Boston, had studied in Germany and England during the 1840s, just as the English boy choir tradition was beginning to recover from a lengthy period of institutional indifference and incompetent leadership. Two years later, *The New York Musical World* reported that Cutler had both the regular choir and a group of probationers, with rehearsal and services daily except for three weeks of vacation in August. The group's repertoire included at least five English anthems and five services, among them one each by Tallis and Byrd.[16]

Cutler was called to Trinity, New York, in 1858 to take over the duties of the incapacitated Edward Hodges. A year later he weeded out the women left over from the regime of his predecessor and shortly after he moved the choir out of the west gallery. Instead, the 16 boys and 6 men were divided on either side of the chancel in spite of the difficulties of coordinating and supporting the group with the gallery organ, some 150 feet away. The *American Musical Directory* described the service as:

the "Cathedral" or "Choral Service," that is, the clergy *intone* the prayers, and the *Amens* and all other responses are by the choir and people in full harmony. This is the only church in this country, where the English cathedral service is presented in its integrity [*sic*], although an approximation to it is attempted at the Church of the Holy Communion ... and at the Church of the Advent, Boston.[17]

Elsewhere, male choirs had been instituted in the late 1850s at both St. Mark's and St. James the Less in Philadelphia and at St. John's in Detroit. By the 1860s, Church of the Atonement, St. James, and several other Chicago churches dismissed their solo quartets for boys and men.[18] In 1873, the Rev. John Sebastian Bach Hodges (1830–1913) established a choir of men and boys at St. Paul's Church, Baltimore, along with a day school for the boys.[19] That year, St Mark's in Philadelphia managed to secure as its choirmaster J. Kendrick Pyne (1852–1938), organist and choirmaster of Chichester Cathedral. Pyne was the first experienced trainer of boys' voices to work in an American church; however, he remained in Philadelphia scarcely two years, then returned to England in 1875 as organist and choirmaster of Manchester Cathedral, where he spent the rest of his career.[20]

By the turn of the century, the boy choir movement had caught on to the extent that Episcopal churches with no particular bent toward ritualism had begun forming male choirs. Such congregations had little interest in chanting. Instead, they expected their boys and men to sing much the same body of anthems as other Protestant church choirs, along with elaborate anthem-like settings of service music by contemporary English composers, as well as Americans like Horatio Parker. Indeed, Parker was the only one of the major American composers at the turn of the century to focus significant creative effort on writing music for the church.

ROMAN CATHOLIC MUSIC

A similar attempt at historical restoration was somewhat less successful in Roman Catholic churches of the period, where the musical fashion consisted of masses in quasi-operatic style, sung by solo quartets with or without volunteers. In 1861, according to the *American Musical Directory* survey, almost all the Catholic churches in New York, including the new St. Patrick's Cathedral on Fifth Avenue, had professional quartets or double quartets. The exceptions were a few ethnic German parishes, whose congregations enjoyed singing as a part of their culture, and these churches became the nucleus for an attempted reform of Catholic church music.

After mid-century, a new musical culture began to influence some American Catholic services. The Cæcilian movement, founded in Germany, sought to restore the exclusive use of chant and polyphony in Catholic liturgy. In the Midwest, St. John's Abbey was established in the 1850s in Collegeville, Minnesota, as a monastery and a seminary. By the 1870s, the community was using Gregorian chant and polyphony, under sway of the Cæcilians.

Influenced by church musicians such as Karl Proske (1794–1867) and his pupil, Franz Xavier Witt (1834–88), German musicologists were editing and publishing masses, motets, and liturgical music by Renaissance masters such as Giovanni Pierluigi da Palestrina and Orlande de Lassus. At the same time, French scholars and particularly the Benedictine monks of Solesmes in France were editing and publishing an authoritative version of Gregorian chant for practical use.[21] In 1868, Witt and others founded the Cæcilia Society to restore the use of Gregorian chant and polyphony and to promote the composition of new liturgical music in the archaic style. Swiss-born John Baptist Singenberger (1848–1924) established an American branch of the Society in 1873, when he became professor at the Catholic Normal School in St. Francis, Wisconsin. Singenberger himself wrote Catholic liturgical music and instruction books on the singing of chant. By 1878, his American Cæcilian Society had some 3,000 members.[22]

All but a few Catholic churches ignored or rejected the Cæcilian reforms, and those churches that adopted them encountered resentment in the pews. A letter from "A Parishioner" of Chicago's Holy Name Cathedral in the November 17, 1878, issue of the *Chicago Tribune* complained of "this unholy, unheavenly substitute for the grand old Catholic music."[23] Most Catholic clergy simply ignored the Cæcilian movement, even though its principles were endorsed by Rome. New York's Catholic churches still had their quartets in the 1890s.[24] Indeed, even the *Motu Proprio* of Pope Pius X, issued on November 22, 1903, making the movement's principles the official position of the Vatican on church music, changed little if anything in America's Catholic church music.[25]

MUSIC IN SMALLER CHURCHES

Professional quartets were found mainly in affluent city churches who aspired to demonstrate their new-found economic status by employing the finest singers available. In smaller churches from city to village, the gospel hymn quickly took hold, leading amateur choirs and untrained directors to clamor for appealing music in a similar style that could be easily learned. Following mid-century, their demand was met by a regular flow of pieces with simple texts set syllabically to repetitive melodies with engaging rhythms and uncomplicated harmony in a generally sentimental style recalling the over-refined style of composers such as the extremely popular Isaac Woodbury (1810–1858).

Concurrent with this demand for new music was a technological revolution in music printing that lowered the price of individual anthems enormously. Individual copies of anthems had appeared in the 1840s in England when, in 1844, J. Alfred Novello bought a three-year-old magazine that included an anthem in each monthly issue, which Novello renamed *The Musical Times and Singing Class Circular.* This magazine made multiple copies of the octavo pieces available for church as an alternative to the costly hardbound collections used by cathedral choirs. The term *octavo* derived from the move to imprinting eight pages on one sheet at a time, which produced smaller, vertically aligned choral scores. Novello ushered in the modern era of choral music publishing in 1846, when it published Vincent Novello's vocal score reduction of Handel's *Messiah,* which was sold in 12 monthly numbers beginning in August 1846 and costing six pence per number. Another important innovation appeared in his resolute adoption of the treble clef for all the upper voices, a controversial decision at mid-century. In 1852, Oliver Ditson & Company in Boston became Novello's American representative and soon dominated choral-music publishing in this country.

The technological development that most immediately impacted the spread of choral music came from improvements in music printing after about 1860.[26] The critical development in printing technology came from the introduction of steam-driven offset lithography in this country. About 1860, Julius Freidländer devised a mechanical steam press for printing music, which made it possible to print music from the highest quality plates on sized paper at an amazing cost reduction of 800 percent. Within a few years this new technology appeared in this country when Oliver Ditson began publishing octavo choral works in 1876. This new format, printed on steam-driven, cylindrical presses, lowered the price of anthems and oratorio scores considerably, making it possible for an entire choir to have a copy of each anthem for every Sunday. It also gave American composers more immediate access to publication.

The most significant collections for smaller churches were the serial publications of choir music, a counterpart to the gospel song collections being issued periodically in series. The first such periodical appeared in 1874, entitled *The Parish Choir.* In 1892, John P. Vance (1867–1897) of Chicago offered by subscription his *Choir Herald,* each issue of which contained anthems, most of them by Vance himself. Edmund S. Lorenz (1854–1942) hit the jackpot when he founded what became the largest supplier of church music by subscription in 1894, when he issued the first number of *The Choir Leader.* The periodical was aimed at volunteer choirs and contained a column of advice, along with "music of a simple or only moderately difficult character." Vance died in 1897, and Lorenz bought *The Choir Herald* and began publishing it with music a grade easier than *The Choir Leader*. In 1913, Lorenz added a periodical with still easier music, *The Volunteer Choir*.

Lorenz specifically targeted small churches with unsophisticated congregations, untrained and unbalanced choirs, and volunteer directors with minimal background and neither the time nor the knowledge to select individual pieces of music for their choirs from the usual catalogues. The music in the periodicals offered such churches music for every Sunday of the year, with a consistent level of difficulty and a consistent style of composition. Most of the pieces were written by in-house composers to fairly transparent formulas or adapted from the classical repertoire, instrumental and vocal. In some cases, popular anthems, from the "Hallelujah Chorus" from Handel's *Messiah* to Shelley's "Hark, Hark My Soul" and "The King of Love My Shepherd Is," for instance, were simplified and shortened for use by more modest groups.

HYMNODY

Hymnody has been one of the central musical experiences of all Americans since the Puritans began colonizing the country in the seventeenth century. Not surprisingly, the first full-length book printed in the English-speaking colonies was a metrical psalter, *The Whole Booke of Psalmes* (Cambridge, MA, 1640; published thereafter as *The Psalms, Hymns, and Spiritual songs of the Old and New Testament*), known as the *Bay Psalm Book*. With the great camp meetings in the first decades of the nineteenth century, a much looser, spontaneously improvised type of revival and folk hymnody began emerging. After mid-century the growing interest in worship reforms alongside the press for High Culture in many Northeast churches accelerated the separation between folk and revival hymnody, and a more sophisticated, professionally composed congregational song. This divergence in both content and form took two distinct but related tracks: (1) denominational—Episcopalians, Methodists, Baptists, Presbyterians, and others, including those denominations with European backgrounds, such as German-speaking Lutherans and Mennonites; and (2) private/commercial, which reflected the contemporary secular markets of popular song, Civil War ballads and marches, and minstrel songs. These volumes responded to the need of numerous religious organizations, namely, Sunday schools, temperance groups, revivals, home singing, and educational. Its repertory included a diverse array of camp-meeting choruses, folk hymns, revival songs, and others.[27]

The reform movement for a higher quality hymn had emerged first in the late 1820s and 1830s when Lowell Mason (1792–1872) and Thomas Hastings (1784–1872) led the way. Mason moved to Boston in 1827 from Savannah, where he had been an obscure partner in a dry-goods store. In his work with his colleagues in Boston, he encouraged musical literacy by introducing music into the public schools, improving the quality of church choir performance, establishing choral societies, and holding musical conventions that offered needed musical instruction to American choral leaders, church choir directors, and music educators. Having begun his career in the field of sacred music, he gradually realized that techniques of singing-school instruction could be applied outside the sacred realm: ongoing classes could be maintained, correct use of the voice could be demonstrated, basic music skills could be taught, and new music could be composed according to more "scientific" European principles.

Mason and Hastings eschewed the emotional, spontaneous ecstasy of the revival song for a more rational hymnody, mildly evangelical in doctrine, and sentimental in tone. They insisted that hymns were for the edification of the believer and must be composed with scientifically correct harmonies on uplifting, appropriate texts, in a heartfelt simplicity and a dignified, devotional style. Mason composed or arranged 1,600 hymn tunes and compiled 80 music collections, which contained a number of hymns that became favorites during the last part of the century: "Joy to the World," "O For a Thousand Tongues to Sing," "Nearer My God to Thee," and "My Faith Looks Up to Thee."

Concurrent with these reform efforts of Mason and others was the appearance of officially sponsored denominational hymnals. These various groups gradually supplanted the use of metrical psalmody and the hymns of Isaac Watts and other hymns of English origin with hymns of their own writers. Mason, Hastings, and their followers energetically supplied tunes for these hymnals and actively encouraged better choral and congregational singing through their lectures, teaching, and musical conventions—short-term training courses for music teachers and church musicians. The Methodists had had an authorized hymnal since 1784; the Episcopalians issued their first hymnal in 1827; and the Presbyterians, in 1829, followed by other denominations during the next decade.[28] Most scholars on the subject agree that the Unitarians, assisted by liberal Congregationalists and what Theodore Cuyler called "godly women" writers, produced more popular hymns of high quality than any other denomination.[29]

During the 1850s, these two trends, the popular revival song and the more musically sophisticated, literary hymn, overlapped in many of the mainline hymnals. Perhaps the single most influential and widely used publication at mid-century was the book produced by Henry Ward Beecher (1813–1887), pastor of Brooklyn's fashionable Plymouth Church and one of the most notable figures in nineteenth-century America. Edited by his music director, Darius Jones, the *Plymouth Collection of Hymns and Tunes,* first published in 1855, contained 1,374 hymns selected by Beecher from a wide variety of sources. This work was significant not only for its literary and musical comprehensiveness but for the way it printed the texts and the tunes together, something new in American hymnody. Most hymnals published before the Civil War contained texts only, which meant that congregations sang just a small number of old familiar tunes. The first books that printed both texts and tunes were designed for revival meetings, not Sunday services. The *Plymouth Collection* changed all that with its new format, instigating a new era in hymn singing. Now a whole world of excellent tunes and words of all styles and origins opened up to the worshipper. At times the words might be under the tune on the same page or on facing pages. Most usable was the arrangement with one or more stanzas printed between the staves. Moreover, these volumes were in the upright form we know today, which made them easy to use and follow.[30]

In addition to a new format, the style of hymns following mid-century underwent a fundamental transformation, strongly influenced by the Oxford Movement and Victorian English hymnody. Felt first in the Episcopal Church, these influences expanded into other denominations: Presbyterian, Methodist, Congregational, Dutch Reformed, and Lutheran, and, by the end of the century, Roman Catholic. This new type of hymn tune gradually supplanted much of the earlier work of Mason and Hastings. Nicholas Temperly, in his excellent study of *The Music of the English Parish Church,* explains how the new style of hymns came about. As he observes, hymn singing and choral music had become *artistic* forms of expression, as the Victorian parish church tried to emulate the cathedral and the concert hall. The fundamental transformation occurred in the treatment of the melodic line. In the traditional metrical psalm and hymn, each syllable of the text was harmonized by a single chord, with the harmony changing virtually every beat. Temperley continues, "In the 'old way', each note of the tune had been an event in itself; when this style gradually collapsed, the series of events was still recognised in the succession of chords. It is difficult to find any significant exceptions to this in congregational psalm or hymn tunes before the Victorian period." Victorian composers moved away from this principle and made the melody and harmonic motion independent of the syllables in the text. Now, the melody became thoroughly interdependent with the harmony, where the tune could function as a passing note or even sustain a succession of changing chords underneath it. The musical line now moved on through each of the independent phrases of the metrical psalm with the continuous harmonic motion prevailing in romantic composition. The Victorian hymn "tune" now became only one element in the musical texture: "Singing hymns was now almost like singing in an oratorio chorus—the summit of many Victorians' musical ambitions. Thanks to the skill of a Dykes, Barnby or Stainer, they could sing a tune that was no more difficult than one of the traditional psalm tunes, but in doing so could feel the thrill of participation in something that sounded like great music."[31]

Another new aspect of these hymns was their literary quality, as well as their tendency to emphasize the more uplifting side of Protestant theology. As the emerging capitalist market economy of industrializing America grew more harsh, hymns offered some compensatory consolation. Hymn writers strove to articulate the confident Victorian alliance of society and heaven imbued with Christian assumptions of love and charity. As Ann Douglas puts it: "hymnology facilitated the process by ignoring hell and highlighting heaven." Hymns no longer sought to frighten the believer with their horrific scenes of hell and damnation. Nor did they address the intellect but imparted a comforting religion of the heart. Austin Phelps, who co-authored the most important hymnology treatise in nineteenth-century America, argued that hymns should be literary in quality, tasteful, and beautiful. He wrote that "sacred song instinctively looks heavenward." It should edify and uplift, acting as a kind of "tonic to the worshipper." Phelps explained that "actual and tangible horrors do not belong to poetry." He easily cited many lines from Isaac Watts as unfit for a "Christian Hymn": "Eternal plagues and heavy chains,/Tormenting racks and fiery coals."[32] Contrast these lines with deep comforting and relief of John Greenleaf Whittier's enduring "Dear Lord, and Father of Mankind" (1872):

> Drop they still dews of quietness,
> Till all our strivings cease;
> Take from our souls the strain and stress,
> And let our ordered lives confess
> The beauty of thy peace.

THE GOSPEL HYMN

To many Americans, both those who looked on and those who took part, the Civil War had a crusading spirit or revival, an aura of a religious struggle for the abolition of sinful slavery. In an era in which Americans were far more overtly and self-consciously religious than they had been since the age of the Puritans in the seventeenth century, many a foot soldier went into battle, and to his death, fresh from one of the frequent revival meetings held in the camps of both armies, with a Bible or hymnal (that is, a collection of religious poetry) in his pocket. Such Civil War songs as "We are Coming, Father Abraham" clearly evoked religious connotations; George F. Root's "Battle Cry of Freedom"

(1862), and especially the tune that was sung in the North to "John Brown's Body" and after 1861 to Julia Ward Howe's "Battle Hymn of the Republic" were direct outgrowths of camp meeting torchlight marches.

Rural congregations sang eighteenth- and early nineteenth-century folk hymns, or white spirituals. At the same time, a more sentimental type of hymn with simple melody and harmony and catchy rhythm, and patterned on popular parlor songs, marches, and quicksteps, appeared in the 1840s as part of the Sunday school movement. By the 1850s, collections of these so-called Sunday school hymns were being published quarterly and sold by subscriptions in series. In the postbellum period, such pieces would be christened "gospel songs," after the title of a popular collection put out by Philip Paul Bliss (1838–1876) in 1874. Such hymns readily found a place in the revivals that began in 1857 among adults, many of whom had fond memories lingering from their childhood Sunday schools. In the years after the Civil War, these new revivals were focused on the city, where they began to draw immense crowds.

The new urban revivals, which added the organizational structures developed by showmen such as P. T. Barnum to the old rural camp meeting, had as their format dynamic preaching, rousing singing, passionate prayers, and individual testimony. Whereas white spirituals focused on grace and salvation, gospel hymns involved texts that testified to intimate, personal, and highly emotional sentiments. Typical is the intensely personal testimony from the popular collection *Gospel Hymns:*

> O I love to talk with Jesus,
> for it smooths the rugged road;
> And it seems to help me onward,
> when I faint beneath my load;
> When my heart is crushed with sorrow,
> and my eyes with tears are dim,
> There's nought can yield me comfort
> like a little talk with him.[33]

Even the most unlearned could immediately sing the attractive, simple harmonies set with the regular, infectious march or waltz rhythms. The hymns were invariably in a strophic form, usually with a refrain that was easy to remember, and spoke with an emotional directness lacking in the earlier shape-note melodies. Increasing the accessibility of the gospel hymns was their similarity in style and form to the parlor songs that were growing in popularity with the urban middle class. Indeed, the gospel song became a parlor song with sacred words.

The gospel song found its first great flowering in the immensely popular meetings led by Dwight L. Moody, a Boston shoe salesman, who moved to Chicago and established both a thriving church and the pattern of carefully planned and executed traveling "crusades." His partner was Ira D. Sankey (1840–1908), son of a Pennsylvania legislator. He directly appealed to listeners' emotions, accompanying himself on a small reed organ. With the vigor of a field marshal brandishing his baton, he directed the singing with great bravura. So popular was Sankey's music that a 24-page pamphlet of them was combined with a collection published by Bliss and issued as the first of six *Gospel Hymns and Sacred Songs* (Cincinnati, 1875) that appeared from 1875 to 1891 and then combined into a single collection, *Gospel Hymns, 1 to 6 Complete* (Chicago, 1894). By 1900, the volume sold more than 50 million copies. As evangelical Protestant worship adopted many of the characteristics of the revivals, gospel hymns became the predominant musical medium in both rural and urban churches, especially in the South and West.

Seeing the large amounts of money to be made in writing and publishing gospel hymns, others followed Sankey's lead. Perhaps the most successful of these men was Homer Rodeheaver (1880–1955). He was the musical partner of the early twentieth-century evangelist Billy Sunday who prepared the crowds for the sermon with his informal, chatty, and enthusiastic platform style. He, like his colleagues, synthesized the older gospel style of the 1870s and 1880s with the secular music of the prewar generation to produce hymns and solo songs with lilting melodies, syncopated ragtime rhythms, and barbershop quartet harmonies. The deeply personal and sentimental texts followed the mold of those created by Fanny Crosby (1820–1915), the blind poet and author of nearly 9000 texts, and other nineteenth-century writers. These gospel hymns met and still meet the need for simple, direct, heartfelt music that is easily learned and sung by large numbers of people. Roheheaver co-founded a major gospel-music publishing house that became enormously successful and set a pattern of sacred-music publishing active today.[34]

AFRICAN AMERICAN SPIRITUALS

Before the Civil War, southern blacks worshipped as and where their owners decided; however, free blacks in the North had formed separate congregations before 1800, adopting the hymnody of their parent white churches and denominations, at least initially. In the South, the slaves' worship music consisted for the most part of spirituals, many of them in call-and-response form with a soloist answered by a group. These pieces resembled lined-out psalmody, which had persisted in southern churches long after it had died out in the North; although in point of fact, call-and-response structure was and is a major trait in African music and could be seen in the work songs slave gangs themselves used to coordinate the effort and exertion required for a particular job.[35]

Black spirituals were largely improvised, led by a singer to whose call the group responded with a set phrase. They were open-ended, continuous, and often quasi-improvisatory. But even in the group singing, extemporaneous ornamentation abounded, such as melodic turns, held notes, and quarter tones. Sections of different hymns and spirituals, black or white, might be interpolated, and choruses borrowed from other pieces. The effect could be chantlike and hypnotic. The texts of black spirituals reflected real, day-to-day earthly trials. Blacks identified with the Israelites, enslaved by the Egyptians, and Old Testament places and terms took on special meaning. Canaan, for instance, was the "promised land," meaning free soil. Even as freedmen following the Civil War, their lives were harsh and difficult, and they were subject daily to indignities if not persecution from whites.

The sense of individual sin and repentance that characterized white evangelical hymnody and doctrine figured far less in the black spiritual; nor did black texts reflect the Calvinist sense of personal unworthiness and Judgment dread. Salvation came at death, not after; the day of jubilee brought rest from the meanness of life and white man's oppression; Jesus often merged with Moses as a single symbol of deliverance who redeems man, not through his suffering but as the victorious head of an army:

> Ride on, King Jesus! Ride on Moses, Ride on King Emanuel
> No man can hinder me. I want to go home in the morning.[36]

With emancipation, such phrases lost their significance. Newly freed southern blacks, now able to establish their own evangelical churches, began adding to the spiritual the same gospel hymns used in neighboring white evangelical churches.

WHITE AUDIENCES AND THE BLACK SPIRITUAL

Ironically, just as newly freed southern blacks were suppressing their traditional spirituals, those pieces were about to gain a following among whites. The first printed collection of black spirituals, collected and edited by three whites, appeared shortly after the end of the Civil War, *Slave Songs of the United States* (New York, 1867). Most significantly, nine students from the all-black Fisk University in Nashville formed the Jubilee Singers, under the direction of a white faculty member. They toured the northern states and Britain singing concerts of spirituals to raise money for their institution. Another black college, Hampton Institute, followed suit two years later. The two choirs quickly gained a following for spirituals among white audiences in America and then in Europe.

On the other hand, white audiences were unaccustomed to the improvisatory style and rhythmic freedom of the original spirituals. The touring versions sung by both groups were recast into concert arrangements with European-style harmonies and rhythms. It is through such arrangements, adopted for concert by college choirs, white and black, that the body of black spirituals have come down to the present. Arrangements by trained and talented musicians like Dvořák's student Henry T. Burleigh (1866–1949) have a haunting beauty to them, but at the same time, they are far from the way slaves sang them as they worshipped in their antebellum plantation praise houses.[37]

Ironically, even as spirituals gained a hearing among whites in the years after the Civil War, their use in black churches declined. Newly emancipated blacks, anxious to leave behind them the cultural artifacts of their bondage, moved increasingly toward the adoption and adaptation of white gospel songs that had gained currency late in the century.

ORGANS AND ORGANISTS

The 1840s saw the first real development of the organ in the United States. Population increases resulted in larger, more sophisticated urban congregations, which soon began demanding louder organs for their larger churches, which led to a growing interest in the instrument to the general public. Americans had always been fascinated with complex mechanical devices, and partially because of the sheer size and cost of the new instruments, audiences flocked to see and hear them. On October 7 and 8, 1846, the new Henry Erben organ in Trinity Church, Wall Street was dedicated by 21 different organists.[38] The *New York Express* reported the next day that 17,939 people attended, causing utter chaos for the exhibition. Similarly, the arrival and inauguration of the Boston Music Hall Organ in 1863 had occasioned a good deal of press coverage and public interest.

Beginning in the 1850s, organs became more mechanically complicated and tonally varied. Equal temperament was quickly adopted after 1850 to play the orchestral transcriptions that were rapidly coming into vogue. Organ recitals also were becoming popular features of American musical life during the same decade, almost always played by European immigrants, performing variation sets, pedagogical works, orchestral transcriptions, as well as notorious storm scenes, where they held a number of pedals down at once and laid their arms on the keyboard to imitate the power of a thunderstorm. The growing popularity of the recitals in turn encouraged bigger, more standardized organs, with at least two complete manuals and a pedal board with 25 or more pedals, with greater tonal variety and force to imitate the varied orchestral colors. As the number of recitals increased, improvisations gave way to music written for the instrument and works transcribed from operatic and symphonic compositions. Even so, the immensely popular storm scenes continued. Henry Lahee humorously relates how they could be "so vivid that people involuntarily reached for their umbrellas. On one occasion an old woman rushed out of the church in great excitement, saying she had left the front door open, and she was afraid her best carpet would get wet."[39]

The largest church organ in America before the Civil War was the instrument in Trinity Church, New York, built by Henry Erben (1800–1884) in 1846. It had three manuals and about 35 stops.[40] During the decades after the Civil War, American organ builders were influenced by the 1863 organ in the Boston Music Hall, built by E. F. Walcker of Ludwigsburg, Germany. Over twice as large as the Trinity Church organ, it had a reedy sound and a variety of novel solo colors and quasi-orchestral effects. American organs began to take on a similarly colorful, orchestral sound. The opening of the Great Organ in Boston proved to be one of those major turning points in nineteenth-century American musical life. The high cost of the organ—a staggering $60,000—dramatically symbolizes the powerful authority Victorian society now ascribed to organ music and the setting provided for it. The evening drew all the ranking cognoscenti from the area, as well as reviewers from all over the Northeast, who inundated the event with articles; *Dwight's Journal* extended its coverage through three issues, in which Dwight used the opportunity to press for more professional organ literature and better playing (November 14, November 28, December 12, 1863). The instrument never functioned properly, and in 1881 was removed from the Music Hall stage for the newly formed Boston Symphony Orchestra. It was completely rebuilt and reerected in the Memorial Music Hall in Methuen, Massachusetts, where it is heard every summer in a series of recitals.

Erben (along with the Hook brothers in Boston) had been the most prominent organ builder in America up to the Civil War. But Erben was past his prime by the mid-1860s, although he stayed in business until his death in 1884. A number of younger builders vied for Erben's primacy, including Hook and Hastings in Boston; however, it was another New Yorker, Hilborne Roosevelt (1849–1886), inventor, engineer, and first cousin of future President Theodore Roosevelt, who took the lead in organ manufacturing. Roosevelt's family name and the extraordinary quality of his instruments, large and small, earned him a fashionable clientele. The social and artistic circles he moved in included the very men who designed and furnished the newer, larger, and more sumptuous churches of the Gilded Age: men such as artists Louis Comfort Tiffany and John LaFarge, the sculptor August Saint-Gaudens, and the architect Stanford White. At its height, his Roosevelt Organ Works had shops in New York, Baltimore, and Philadelphia and instruments all over America and in Rome, Italy.

Roosevelt's organs were among the first to use electrical key and stop action in place of earlier mechanical or tracker action. Electricity allowed larger organs to be built and divisions of pipes to be placed at a distance from one another and from the organist. Roosevelt's largest organ was built between 1879 and 1895 for the Episcopal Cathedral of the Incarnation in Garden City, Long Island, financed by the New York department store magnate, Alexander T. Stewart. Its 114 sets of pipes were placed in the chancel, the tower, and an adjoining chapel.[41] Electricity also allowed the introduction of fan blowers and higher wind pressures, resulting in fuller more colorful tone, culminating in the orchestral organs of the early twentieth century.

With an increasing number of American organists going abroad for study, especially men such as John Knowles Paine (1839–1906), Dudley Buck, and Eugene Thayer (1838–1889), who had worked in Berlin with the eminent Bach specialist, Karl August Haupt, programs in the 1860s began to assume their modern form, with pieces by Bach, Handel, Mendelssohn, and other European masters. Buck and others had studied in the conservatories of Leipzig, Berlin, and Munich under stern professors who assigned them to write large works in the traditional eighteenth-century European genres: preludes, fugues, canons and trios, and sonatas. Back home, their early works were often preludes and fugues, which proved too elitist for American audiences. They then wrote preludes, postludes, impromptus, and character pieces. The sparkling canons and trios often built on hymn tunes and displaying skillful counterpoint were generally teaching pieces for gaining independence in the hands and feet. They also produced splashy works such as "Grand Sonatas" or "Grand Concert Fantasias" to demonstrate their technical expertise and to appeal to the musical elites. These generally fit the Mendelssohnian model with multiple movements in traditional forms, the outer movements often displaying flamboyant virtuosity while the inner ones could possess a naively touching charm; one movement generally involved an extended passage in the fugal "learned style." All of these served to fit the Victorian program to improve music and connect it with the revered past, albeit an imported German past.

The most popular genre in American organ literature in the decades between 1860 and 1890 was the variation form, which had virtually vanished in classical European organ composition by this time. Variation technique, however, proved exactly the right genre for organ music in the United States.

Improvisations on a favorite hymn tune to demonstrate the different tonal qualities of the instrument had long been a feature of American organ dedications. Concert variations were simply a formalized, written-out extension of this practice. They also held immediate appeal to the relatively unsophisticated American audiences. Even the simplest workman delighted in the clearly followable elaborations on "Annie Laurie," "Home, Sweet Home," "Old Hundredth," "Vesper Hymn," "Hail! Columbia," "The Star-Spangled Banner," "The Last Rose of Summer," or the national anthems of Austria and Russia.

Buck's variation cycles comprise some of the most sophisticated music found in nineteenth-century American organ literature. Perhaps nowhere did he so completely synthesize the sacralized, esoteric, abstract instrumental literature of the high cultural tradition with its aesthetic opposite—common popular song—as in the variation works. Buck convincingly assimilated the various contrapuntal structures and made them an intrinsic, unforced part of his own musical voice. He composed his first set of variations on "The Star Spangled Banner" for his Hartford concert series, premiering it on October 3, 1866, then repeating it on October 20 by popular request. The set is framed by two contrasting but complementary variations, presenting the theme first in the immediately accessible hymn style with which his audiences would have been familiar and concluding with a nearly 100-measure fugue on a four-measure motive derived from the opening of the tune.

Beginning in the mid-1870s, foreign artists like the Parisian master Alexandre Guilmant (1837–1911) toured the United States. A prolific composer as well as a performer and researcher, Guilmant introduced American organists and audiences to large amounts of historical organ literature by heretofore unknown composers, as well as his own works, which gained immediate popularity. The foremost American concert organist at the turn of the century was Clarence Eddy (1851–1937), a native of Greenfield, Massachusetts, and pupil of Dudley Buck. He studied in Europe with Haupt, and quickly gained a reputation for his virtuosity before returning to Chicago, where he made his home. Eddy toured the country, performing serious organ literature from various periods. In 1877, he began presenting his 100 recitals in a two-year series, each concert anchored by a Bach work. But he also introduced transcriptions of orchestral literature into his programs, thereby initiating a fashion; such transcriptions became a major part of many if not most organists' repertoire in the years after World War I.[42]

By the first decades of the twentieth century, church music in America had come of age. Churches of all denominations and economic strata enthusiastically embraced the new musical styles, increasing their budgets and volunteer participation. The more affluent urban congregations continued their support for the solo quartet (with or without a chorus choir), refined European choral

and operatic music, and noble hymnody, accompanied by a professional organist on a good-sized instrument, often newly acquired. Middle-class congregations sought to emulate the excellent taste and genteel elegance of the socially
elite churches and, if they could afford it, enjoyed similar music in their services. The smaller churches with unsophisticated congregations, untrained
choirs, and volunteer directors turned to the anthem periodicals that offered
such churches music for every Sunday of the year, with a consistent level of
difficulty and a consistent style of composition. They joyfully sang the gospel
hymns and songs that had immediately accessible texts and formulaic music.
Church music had come a long way since the days of the plain meeting house
for services of unaccompanied metrical psalms, a rare anthem, and the most
rudimentary organ music.

New York's Academy of Music on 14th Street, completed in 1854, sits between 3rd Avenue and Irving Place, and was one of the city's top performing spaces for theater and opera. Picture Collection, The Branch Libraries, The New York Public Library, Astor, Lenox and Tilden Foundations.

The Rialto Theater at 42nd Street and 7th Avenue in Manhattan. One of the first major Movie Palaces. Billy Rose Theatre Division, The New York Public Library for the Performing Arts, Astor, Lenox and Tilden Foundations.

Lowell Mason (1792–1872) led the way in establishing music education in the United States; he was the first musician to become rich practicing his art. Music Division, The New York Public Library for the Performing Arts, Astor, Lenox and Tilden Foundations.

A crowd waits to enter the Great Hall of the 1876 Philadelphia Centennial Exhibition on May 10, 1876, as the Gilded Age moves into high gear.

Dudley Buck (1839–1909) was the central figure in transmitting Romantic choral and organ music to this country from Europe following the Civil War.

Charles Ives (1874–1954) was one of the most important and iconoclastic figures in American classical music.

George Chadwick (left; 1854–1931) clowns with composer Victor Herbert (1859–1924) in this 1890 photograph by exchanging hats.

John Sullivan Dwight (1813–1893), the leading spokesman for High Musical Art through his journal *Dwight's Journal of Music*, which he edited from Boston from 1852 until 1881.

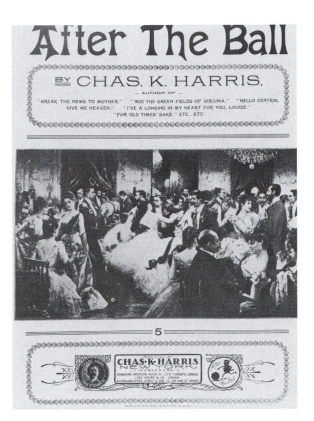

"After the Ball," by Charles K. Harris was one of the most enduring and touching songs to emerge from the Gilded Age.

The French Opera House in New Orleans stood at the corner of Bourbon and Toulouse Streets from 1859 until 1919, when it burned. It was the most fashionable establishment in the city in the years between the Civil War and World War I.

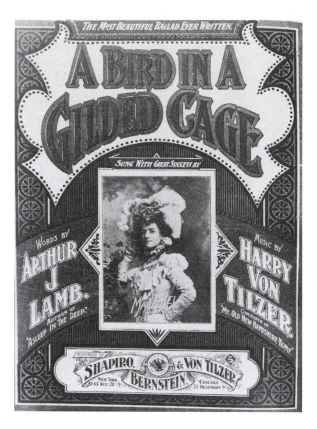

"A Bird in A Gilded Cage," by Arthur Lamb and Harry von Tilzer was one of the most popular and moralizing popular songs of the period.

The Black Crook, which opened on September 12, 1866, is considered the first musical with a unifying plot and music. Library of Congress.

Scott Joplin (1868–1917), the most well-known composer of ragtime.

Mrs. Caroline Astor (1830–1908), in a portrait by John Singer Sargent, the reigning monarch of New York society during the Gilded Age.

Adelina Patti (1843–1919) age sixteen, pictured here as Amina in *La Sonamula* which ran in 1859, the year of her American operatic debut.

Matilda Sissieretta Jones (1869–1933), known more widely as Black Patti. She was the leading soprano of Black Patti's Troubadours. Her voice was admired for its richness and power.

Theodore Thomas (1835–1905) in his middle years. The most famous conductor in the country at that time and one of the primary forces behind the spread of European symphonic music.

James Reese Europe (1881–1919) leading an ensemble of New York City's Clef Club members in 1914.

Oscar Hammerstein's Manhattan Opera House was a modern, democratic theater built to highlight musical productions, rather than the Metropolitan's design, which emphasized social structure. Library of Congress.

The Metropolitan Opera House in New York, about 1890. The architect gave the rich shareholders their demand for "a semi-circle of boxes with an opera house built around them." Library of Congress.

Gustav Mahler (1860–1911), the demanding, energetic, and brilliant conductor of the Metropolitan Opera in the first years of the twentieth century. Library of Congress.

Irish immigrant Patrick Sarsfield Gilmore (1829–1892) became America's most prominent band director in the years following the Civil War, and championed the notorious Monster Concerts. Library of Congress.

Edward A. MacDowell (1860–1908) departed from the classicism of the Boston group and identified with the modernist "New German School" of Franz Liszt and Richard Wagner. Library of Congress.

Amy Marcy Cheney Beach (1867–1944), known then as "Mrs. H. H. A. Beach," was one of the Boston Classicists and referred to by Chadwick as "one of the boys." Library of Congress.

Irish-born musician Victor Herbert (1859–1924) became America's greatest composer of operettas, composing more than 40 between 1894 and 1924. Library of Congress.

George M. Cohan (1878–1942) Americanized the musical stage with his direct, energetic, and brashly patriotic works, which featured many of his more than 500 songs. Library of Congress.

Louis Moreau Cottschalk (1829–1869) was the most famous and accomplished American pianist at mid-century. He achieved a unique artistic synthesis by blending the folk rhythms of the New World with the elegant melodies and styles of French pianism. Library of Congress.

John Philip Sousa (1854–1932) became America's band leader by the turn of the century. With his 136 marches, he remains perhaps our most famous native composer. Library of Congress.

Amateurs and Entrepreneurs
on and off the Stage

The Gilded Age experienced an explosion of professional and amateur ensemble music making across the country. Works for the American stage grew prodigiously. Most of the popular antebellum styles—burlesque, minstrelsy, opera, melodrama, dance, and plays with songs—continued, but they transmuted, metastasized, and cross-pollinated. Added to this tradition were the emerging new styles: spectacle/extravaganza, operetta (including imported works from France, Germany, Austria, and Britain, and "light operas" by American composers), musical comedy, and expanded variety/revue shows. After about 1870, all of these forms coalesced and evolved along two roads: drama and variety, although those roads often intersected.[1] Dramatic works based on some minimally coherent plot emerged from the British ballad opera, melodrama, pantomime, and elaborately costumed extravaganza, all of which involved music, story, and action, and led to operetta and musical comedy. Variety shows, including vaudeville and later burlesque, originated in similar European productions and American minstrel shows, which continued their popularity to the end of the century and beyond.

Spectacle and opera likewise enjoyed growing audiences. Spectacle would merge with burlesque to become the revue-extravaganzas of the early twentieth century. One branch of opera grew pious, rid itself of its interpolated songs and skits, assumed a more reverential demeanor (in the original languages), became socially stratified, and developed such a sacralized atmosphere that it disappeared from the popular houses, retreating mostly to the few theaters exclusively devoted to its production, such as the Metropolitan Opera in New York and the Chicago Lyric Opera. The other side of opera took a more popular path, sought a more inclusive appeal, abandoned recitative for dialogue, reined in the more excessive vocal displays, and insisted on romantically happy endings. This became comic opera and operetta. Fueling this rich stew of new musical theater activity was the dynamic economic engine of Gilded Age America, driven by relentless industrial expansion, spreading transportation networks (which encouraged traveling shows), rich immigrant talent, and the growth of cities, which created vast new eager, affluent audiences.

By the time of the Civil War, the theatrical experience was ripe for renewal, given the endless parade of heavy-handed comedies, dreary melodramas, and wooden classics that had been the main fare for decades. Music and musical performance had been intrinsic to almost every nineteenth-century playhouse. Even those theaters that never mounted musical offerings kept large orchestras in their pits full time, entertaining patrons before the first curtain, during entr'actes, and for accompanying incidental music to the plays. Many houses kept singers and dancers on their payrolls to provide entertainment during these entr'actes. And, the increasing leisure time resulting from new technologies drew more and more people into theaters.

At the same time, however, it is worth noting that our modern concept of musical theater as different from the "legitimate stage" (a form of drama that did not include music) had only just begun to emerge toward the end of the Gilded Age. For most of the nineteenth century, contemporary audiences and critics saw little distinction between the two traditions and our viewpoint, as theater historian David Mayer points out "was an aberration and clearly marked a change from long-standing tradition."[2] Well into the twentieth century, musical theater continued its varied, cross-fertilizing structures, which included variety, burlesque, vaudeville, musical comedy, and spectacle. Intrinsic to late nineteenth-century musical comedy was its spirit of spontaneity and dramatic flux, where the scripts typically functioned as a large umbrella for the various skits, singing, and dancing. The virtue of this structure is the dramatic flexibility, which allows for extraction and insertion of songs, holding only a tenuous connection to the plot. *Coherency,* to use a contemporary term, held little interest to writers of musical comedy. As two theater historians note, what did not really exist before *Showboat* was "a script in which the basic elements of the musical (star performances, choreography, spectacle, and songs) could be combined as an integrated whole within a more or less consistent narrative framework."[3] The only precedents in the nineteenth century were the operettas of Gilbert and Sullivan.

Serving as the magnet for all this bustling entertainment was the city of New York, which, after mid-century, had supplanted Philadelphia as the theater capital of the nation. The vibrant port was perfectly suited to become the center of the theatrical and musical world, with its dense population concentration on Manhattan, easily available capital, numerous theaters, and an endless supply of talented immigrant and first-generation talent, ready to try almost anything. New York had been the first stop for touring artists and traveling companies from Europe. Moreover, the rapidly expanding rail network made both city and hamlet throughout the country (including the Far West after the opening of the transcontinental railroad in 1869) readily accessible to the growing numbers of itinerant companies that presented everything from opera/operetta to variety and burlesque. During the final decades of the century, national theatrical syndicates out of New York, Chicago, or Boston controlled not only the local theaters but the itinerant companies visiting them. Finally, the singers, as well as the syndicate managers, worked together to hawk songs from popular shows that in turn drove the growth of Tin Pan Alley songs.

Sorting out these musical-theatrical forms now can be maddening; the same show might be advertised as a "farce-comedy," a "varieties," or an "extravaganza." And while the term we generally use today, "musical comedy," appeared early on—*The Pet of the Petticoats* (1866), *Evangeline* (1874), or *The Gaiety Girl* (1894) depending on which source one consults—not until well into the twentieth century was it understood to define a stage work based on a book and songs written for that production. Whatever terms one bestows on these works, they mark the coming of age of the American musical stage, as Katherine Preston so aptly puts it, "It was a gangly and untidy adolescent experiencing a magnificent growth spurt" that "would eventually mature into the twentieth-century American musical."[4]

EXTRAVAGANZAS AND SPECTACLES

One foreign importation that really ignited the American interest was the musical extravaganza. The success of foreign troupes inspired American theater managers to try others. London impresario Laura Keene put on several "grand burlesque spectacles" in the early 1860s with scandalizing costumes that exposed the women's legs. After the war, these types of shows grew in number and prominence, generally billed as an "extravaganza," "burlesque," or "spectacle." In 1866, an extravaganza called *The Balloon Wedding* opened at Wood's Theater but failed to catch on. About nine months later, however, on September 12, 1866, *The Black Crook* opened at Niblo's Garden at Broadway and Prince Streets, ran for 474 performances, and inaugurated the American musical theater as we now know it.

Advertised as "the most Resplendent, Grand and Costly Production ever presented on this continent," *The Black Crook* was an "eyes-a-poppin" hodgepodge of high ballet, low drama, and whatever else their producers thought they could get by with. Earlier that year a French ballet company performing *La Biche aux Bois* was stranded when the Academy of Music burned. At the same time, William Wheatley, the manager of Niblo's, had on his hands *The Black Crook*, "a knuckle headed melodrama by Charles M. Barras, who had once seen a performance of Weber's gothic opera *Der Freischütz* and had never gotten over it."[5] The men decided to join forces and produce an extravaganza of the most expensive and dazzling scenery, stage machinery, musical songs, dance, and costumes seen in the country. All the while, the story grew less black and less crooked. Whenever the story flagged, the nearly 100 bare-limbed girls in flesh-colored silk tights rushed on, delighting the audience, especially the men. Singer/actress Milly Cavendish notoriously wagged her finger at them, scolding, "you naughty, naughty men." Special effects included the "hurricane in the Harz mountains." Wheatley reportedly spent between $25,000 and $50,000. But it paid off and the producers grossed more than a million dollars.

With *The Black Crook* the Broadway musical was born. It differed from its predecessors; although it unashamedly played to the gallery with the tight-fitting silk tights, it elevated the evening above mere spectacle by threading the acts together with the bare bones of the *Faust* story, laughable as it was. Soon after the show's premier, 14 of New York City's 16 legitimate theaters had concocted their own versions. None of the ingredients was new, and *The Black Crook* was no less silly than the flimsy plots of Bellini and Rossini, but it was in English and incorporated American popular song, rather than European operatic music. And it spoke, sang, and danced with a uniquely American voice that birthed a new theatrical experience.

BURLESQUE

After *The Black Crook's* outrageous success, burlesque began to emphasize the sultrier side of the musical theater and slowly develop its own circuit.[6] It was cheap to produce, racy to see, and contained contemporary references, punchy one-liners, and dancing women—clad as scantily as the producers could dare. In an era of corsets, layered skirts, and neck-high fronts, any uncovered female flesh was a sensation. Ever the showman hoping to appeal to the mass tastes, in 1866, P. T. Barnum brought Lydia Thompson and her British Blondes from London and opened in the theater of Wood's Museum with *Ixion, or the Man at the Wheel* (1868), a travesty of classic Greece. It also scandalized the clergy and the literary guardians of morality. During the 1869–1871 tour, Thompson whipped the editor of the *Chicago Tribune* for his condemnation.

Attempting a "respectable" burlesque to counter the outcry of the bawdy genre, in 1874 Edward Everett Rice (1848–1924) and self-taught musician John Cheever Goodwin (1850–1942) wrote and produced a wildly successful burlesque in the same mold on Longfellow's poem *Evangeline; or the Bell of Acadie* (Niblo's Garden), described as a distinctly "American opera bouffe" in obvious deference to Offenbach.[7] As Preston points out, it is an excellent example of the stylistic intersection of late-century musical forms: spectacle provided colorful costumes, sets, and stage machinery, including a spouting whale; burlesque generated the rhyming text with puns; variety and minstrelsy offered skits and gags; and comic opera modeled the spoken dialogue; romantic plot; and a musical score brimming over with songs, dances, ensemble, and choruses. It was notable as the first time an American musical had a score of its own, written to order and for a specific occasion.

More successful, although less innovative, was Rice's 1884 hit *Adonis* at the Bijou Theater, billed as a "Delightful Perversion" of several well-known dramas. With music derived from numerous contemporary operetta composers, the show epitomized the standard nature of musical stage works of the time with its bare three-act plot that allowed for presenting the variety acts, musical numbers, and short skits. As burlesque theater managers pushed how much female flesh they could legally show, the genre drew fewer respectable crowds and commercialized sex as a major component of risqué stage entertainment.

VAUDEVILLE AND VARIETY

Contemporary with the passion for musical extravaganza was the emergence of vaudeville during the last third of the nineteenth century.[8] It had its roots in the British music hall show and the American minstrel show and was largely the product of one man, Tony Pastor (1837–1908). As a former circus ringmaster and singer, Pastor knew what would be popular and realized that to appeal to diverse crowd of men, women, and children, he had to bring variety entertainment out of the disreputable concert saloons, where singing waitresses were the chief attraction for the men. By the 1880s, variety theaters became increasingly popular and, like the opera houses, appealed to specific audiences. Its heyday spanned a brief 50 years, ending ingloriously in 1932 when union organizing failed and radio and film drew away audiences.

After drawing crowds in his Bowery location for some time, on October 24, 1881, Pastor opened Tony Pastor's Music Hall on East 14th Street where the entire family could enjoy a "straight, clean variety show" for a quarter. He lured the ladies not only by banning liquor and profanity and providing wholesome entertainment, but with added inducements such as door prizes. He also changed the name of the entertainment to the European term *vaudeville*. Shows usually consisted of eight or nine acts, beginning with a "dumb act" and built to a climax with a final act featuring a star. In between were a constantly changing potpourri of singers, comedians, animal acts, acrobats, jugglers, escape artists, magicians, and dancers, all announced by signs at the side of the stage.

The rapid growth of the country and New York City's ethnic mix meant that more and more Americans were flocking to the new theaters, causing other entrepreneurs to realize the enormous potential for profit in the popular theatrical form. Edward Franklin Albee and Benjamin Frankin Keith became the two most successful of these impresarios. Keith began running the shows continuously, and Albee spruced up the entertainment by getting rid of low comedy and the worst of the slapstick. By the 1890s, Keith and Albee, along with others such as Sullivan and Consodine, and Marcus Loew figured out the transportation network could radically increase the profits made in their New York productions. By that time, 200,000 miles of railroad tracks connected some 5,000 theaters in 3,500 communities throughout the country. These New York producers assembled chains of theaters across the country, creating vaudeville circuits. In the big cities these chains erected magnificent entertainment palaces, seating thousands in opulent auditoriums flaunting gold cherubs, winged angels, and wondrous frescoes. The opening of the Palace Theatre in New York in 1913 consummated the golden age of vaudeville, which gradually found itself eclipsed by the emerging technologies of radio, the phonograph, and the sound film. The largest theatrical association was Keith's United Booking Office, which controlled more than 1,500 theaters by 1915.

One notable variety performer who did much to shape the American musical was the Irish actor, lyricist, and playwright Edward Harrigan (1844–1911) who joined with the actor Tony Hart (Anthony Cannon, 1855–1891) to perform vaudeville sketches in Chicago and, from 1872, in New York where they were known as Harrigan and Hart. Harrigan teamed up with the English music hall theater composer Dave Braham (1834–1905) to produce, at first, extended skits and, later, complete comical musical plays. Harrigan wrote the material, which relied heavily on comic dialogue and burlesque, dance, and song, all caricaturing the urban New York German and Irish immigrants (like themselves), as well as African Americans, spiced up by ethnic jokes and quick pacing. The first skit titled *The Mulligan Guard* (1873) consisted of a 10-minute variety production involving three or four songs, dialogue, and "gags and business."

The show's wild popularity encouraged them to develop more extended shows and, by 1878, *The Mulligan Guard's Picnic* lasted 40 minutes.

The success of the show inspired Harrigan to continue expanding and tightening the show, which culminated on Monday, January 13, 1879, with *The Mulligan Guard's Ball*, the most fully formed comical musical play yet seen in this country.[9] Although billed as plays or farces with music, the shows by Harrigan and Hart included all the central elements necessary for musical comedy: a book, instrumental music, and songs by a single writer and separate composer, presenting a unified plot depicting a group of characters in conflict, happily resolved in the end. Although not as lavish as burlesque and spectacle, the plots were more substantial and the music more consistent. Moreover, the expanded amount of sung and danced music heralded the integration of music and drama that would characterize the mature American musical comedy.

MUSICAL COMEDY AND OPERETTA

In a fascinating cultural synchronicity, Wednesday of that same week of January 13, 1879, also saw the opening of W. S. Gilbert (1836–1911) and Arthur Sullivan's (1842–1900) *H.M.S. Pinafore* at the Standard Theater in New York after having a successful run in Boston, San Francisco, and Philadelphia. By February 8, the *Dramatic Mirror* wrote that "The constant spread of 'H.M.S. Pinafore has led to the report that every house in New York is to do the opera within two weeks."[10] By the end of the year more than 90 *Pinafore* companies were touring the country. Later that same year, Gilbert and Sullivan and the future D'Oyly Carte company crossed the Atlantic for the premiere of *The Pirates of Penzance* in New York to secure the American copyright. *The Mikado* followed in 1879, although neither of the later shows ever achieved the popularity of *Pinafore*. Deeply appealing to the growing middle-class audiences in this country was the more refined humor (as opposed to the low level of burlesque or vaudeville), the pointed satire of stuffy British society, and Sullivan's irrepressible melodies. Well into the next century the operetta's popularity pervaded American mass popular culture and determined the course and shape of the popular lyric stage in this country, cresting with *The Merry Widow* in 1907.

American operettas appeared in response to these imported British and Viennese works, even if most operetta and English opera companies more typically presented European imports. One early attempt was made by Julius Eichberg, a German immigrant who sought to build on the success of Offenbach with his *Doctor of Alcantara* in Boston in 1862. Other Americans tried their hand as well, including opera impresario Max Maretzek (1821–1897), with *Sleepy Hollow, or the Headless Horseman* (1879) and J. S. Crossey (*The First Life Guards at Brighton,* 1879). Willard Spencer's *The Little Tycoon* (1886) was one of the rare successes in the 1880s; his *Princess Bonnie* ran more than a thousand performances in Philadelphia in 1892. March king John Philip Sousa showed his indebtedness to Gilbert and Sullivan in his 15 operettas, although they were marred by weak librettos; his *El Capitan* (1896) ran for 112 performances, then toured the country for four years.

The year 1879 also saw the formation of one of the most famous, most musically skilled, and longest-lived English opera companies of the postbellum period.[11] Newly established concert manager Effie H. Ober (1844–1927) formed an operetta company in Boston, which she named the Boston Ideals, after they successfully produced *H.M.S. Pinafore* that year. This English troupe serves as an illuminating microcosm of the hundreds of itinerant troupes active in the United States during the Gilded Age. The Ideals performed up and down the East Coast and as far west as Denver and Colorado Springs, later traveling to the Pacific Coast. Their exhausting routes also illuminated the musical/theatrical activity connecting parts of the country. Moreover, they displayed a co-mingling of repertories typical of the period's stage entertainment and unheard of today. The group of singers were perfectly at ease performing an astonishing assortment of styles, which ranged from standard English-language operas (Balfe's *Bohemian Girl;* Wallace's *Maritana*), to translations of Italian and French standards (Donizetti's *L'elisir d'amour,* Flotow's *Martha,* Mozart's *Marriage of Figaro,* Auber's *Fra Diavolo*), and the most up-to-date and popular operettas. Among these were *The Chimes of Normandy* (Planquette), *Czar and Carpenter* (Lortzing), *Fatinitza* and *Boccaccio* (von Suppé), *Pinafore, The Pirates of Penzance, Patience, The Mikado* and *The Sorcerer* (Sullivan), *Barbe-Bleue* (Offenbach), and *Giroflé-Girofla* (Lecocq). This mixture of repertories typified English opera companies and marks the continued heterogeneity of late-century American musical life.

By the early 1890s, one can discern a subtle distillation of musical productions into operetta, musical comedy, and review, although the pattern is probably clearer in hindsight than to contemporary critics and audiences. Although American works were slowly gaining status, most houses still functioned as outposts of the London lyrical stage. Generally all composers—European and American—adhered loosely to a standard format that consisted of an overture, from 10 to 20 songs, and a few dance numbers. Most shows played out as a sequence of songs, comedy skits, and tableaux. The central musical unit was the single song, which only incidentally advanced the dramatic narrative. For Gilded Age audiences, the virtue of the Broadway musical was its flexibility and looseness, where songs could be easily added and extracted at the whim of the performer or audience. More important was that the song express the persona of the performers.

Two Americans appeared in this decade who showed that native composers could compete artistically with the European musicians. Reginald De Koven (1859–1920) was born in Connecticut, although his family moved to England. He studied music in Germany and France, where he gained mastery of orchestration and large-scale operatic forms. After returning here he wrote several operettas in the late 1880s, including *The Begum* (1887). He scored his major success in 1890 with *Robin Hood,* modeled closely on Gilbert and Sullivan, and whose fame outlived him. The show's big hit, "O Promise Me" lingers still as a wedding favorite.

Victor Herbert (1859–1924) soon eclipsed de Koven in popularity, becoming the most successful and skilled American composer of comic operas and operettas. Born in Ireland and educated in Germany and Vienna, Herbert possessed an unrivaled melodic gift, and as a conservatory-trained cellist he brought a professional level to Broadway orchestration unseen before. In his 40-plus musical scores he elevated the operettas into a serious theatrical experience that endures today in film and songs. His finest works include *Babes in Toyland* (1903), *Mlle Modiste* (1905), *The Red Mill* (1906), *Naughty Marietta* (1910), and *Sweethearts* (1913). He did little to alter the structure of the inherited theatrical elements, but in his better shows he thoroughly integrated the elements of comic opera, book, and song. At the same time, he demonstrated an unrivaled gift for synthesizing the European musical heritage with the exuberance of the American stage. Herbert soon found himself eclipsed by the Viennese imports and American successors to the operetta. In his day, however, his best works brought a maturity, dramatic depth, and lyrical gift to the American musical stage that never left it.

The heyday of American operetta also saw the emergence of one of the most influential figures for the stage musical in the Gilded Age, George M. Cohan (1878–1942). An American born aptly on July 4, 1878, to show-business parents, Cohan grew up in vaudeville, the best training possible for writing for American audiences. In his own productions, which he authored, composed, directed, and performed in, the Americanization of the musical was completed. Whereas operettas took place in faraway lands and were concerned with yearning romantic plots, star-crossed royalty, elegant lyricism, and refined, lush orchestration, Cohan's musical stage works brashly celebrated American Triumphalism, clear moral values, and untroubled isolation from the intrigues of the old country. If operetta served as a metaphor for a leisured, graceful American upper class, then Cohan's musicals spoke for everyone else who earned their money in hard, grinding jobs. Everything about his shows boasted confidence, verve, and down-to-earth characters the audience could identify with, all rushing around in a snappy tempo, wrapped in the American flag. Even the titles declared their theatrical independence from Europe: *Little Johnny Jones* (1904), *Forty-Five Minutes from Broadway* (1906), and *George Washington, Jr.* (1906).

Cohan's most enduring creation was his songs, which radiated "an energy and naturalness that grabbed the public on first hearing and seemed capable of sweeping away the cobwebs" of three-quarter time and aristocratic intermezzi. Whereas the graceful melodies of Herbert, Lehar, and others became popular mainly with more sophisticated listeners, everybody liked Cohan's music. As Oscar Hammerstein II put it, "Cohan's genius was to say simply what every-body else was subconsciously feeling." Songs such as "Give My Regards to Broadway," "The Yankee Doodle Boy," and "Mary's a Grand Old Name" were direct, unforgettable, and toe-tapping fun. The tunes were simple, but they stuck, and no one had heard lyrics like that before. "Cohan knew how to dress hackneyed ideas in a conversational tone," Ethan Mordden explains, "giving his work a lift rare for those times. Unlike most of musical comedy's inhabitants, Cohan's people sang over the footlights as if chatting in the street."[12]

After World War I, the styles and forms of Cohan's fast-paced, song-filled, homespun shows joined Victor Herbert's graceful, elegant operettas to bring the Broadway musical to maturity, appearing first in *Showboat* (1927). Later pieces such as *Oklahoma!, Sound of Music, West-Side Story, Hello Dolly!,* and even *A Little Night Music* are scarcely imaginable without the romantic orches-tration and lush scoring found in works like *Naughty Marietta* or the sassy characters, energetic pace, and catchy tunes of *Little Johnny Jones.*

AFRICAN AMERICAN MUSICAL THEATER

With emancipation after the Civil War, African Americans began to form their own minstrel troupes, such as the Georgia Minstrels, which was organized in Indianapolis and managed by a black performer, Charles B. Hicks.[13] As almost all black entertainers before the war had been minstrels, African Americans continued the practice of established white troupes: they black-ened their faces with burned cork, acted out farces such as *Mr. Jinks*, strutted through exaggerated dances, performed burlesques on popular operettas by Offenbach and others, and sang dialect, plantation, and minstrel songs as both solos and ensemble pieces. New to their productions was the race of the performers, presenting "genuine" plantation songs and dance.

Other black musicians chose to present their talents without the mask, asserting their independence from white stereotypes and traditions. The Hyers Sisters, Anna Madah (1855–1920s) and Emma Louise (1857–1899?), traveled with their own shows from the early 1870s into the 1880s, performing operatic excerpts, art and parlor songs, and jubilee songs and spirituals. The sisters mounted at least six original dramas and musical plays, including *Out of Bondage, Urlina, the African Princess,* and a dramatization of Harriet Beecher Stowe's *Uncle Tom's Cabin. Out of Bondage* maintained some of the outlines of the minstrel show, ending with the sisters and their co-stars singing operatic excerpts by Verdi, Flotow, Balfe, and others. *Urlina, the African Princess* focused on the popular theme of exotic Orientalism, which was becoming increasingly influential in American life during the 1880s. The 1880 production of *Uncle Tom's Cabin* abandoned the practice of having white actors in blackface play the major roles. In their cast, the sisters used white actors to play the white parts and black actors to play the black parts, a move that presented blacks (and whites) realistically before mixed audiences.

By the 1890s, the black minstrel show had become even more popular, with troupes touring not only throughout the United States but in England, Scotland, and Wales as well. These shows revealed a new type of minstrel show, championed by Sam Lucas (1840–1916), a seasoned African American musician/actor who strongly influenced black musical theater, and Sam T. Jack, a white theater owner. Their extravaganza, the *Creole Burlesque Co.,* added 16 young women in a snappy chorus line to the traditional all-male minstrel cast. Jack's advance man, John W. Ishram, formed his own company and went a step further in his 1895 show *Octoroons,* which maintained the typical three-part minstrel show format, but transcended that genre by eliminating many of the traditional minstrel show features. In its place was a musical extravaganza, "30 Minutes Around the Opera," during which the cast members performed popular operatic excerpts. Ishram's new production the next year, *Oriental America,* took another step, not only by taking place in a south Florida hotel, but by showcasing a cultivated society of African Americans as members of golf and lawn tennis clubs. Another major troupe also toured the country from 1896 to 1915, *Black Patti's Troubadours,* which ended with an appearance by Sisieretta Jones (1868–1933), the "Black Patti," who joined the cast in presenting her "operatic kaleidoscope."

The 1890s also saw the appearance of black actors and composers such as Robert Cole, Will Marion Cook, the Johnson brothers, Bert Williams, and George Walker, who experienced notable successes with their shows for New York theaters. In 1897, Robert Cole (1868–1911) and Billy Johnson (1858–1916) left Black Patti's Troubadours (which had white managers) and organized the first black stock company in New York, which began producing the musical *A Trip to Coontown* the same year. In April 1898, the show debuted in New York to critical acclaim and toured for four more years. Touted as the first full-length musical written and produced by blacks on Broadway, the show actually opened "Off Broadway" at an obscure Third Avenue house. More important was the fact that a black-produced show had finally succeeded in breaking into the New York circuit, the capital of the theater world. Three months after Cole and Johnson's opening, Cook produced his *Clorindy, or the Origin of the Cakewalk,* with a script and lyrics by Paul Laurence Dunbar (1872–1906) and Will Marion Cook (1869–1944), the most talented of the group of new black composers. *Clorindy* became the first black show to reach Broadway, although when it finally arrived there it played as a late evening entertainment on the roof garden of the Casino Theater. With *Clorindy,* the new ragtime "coon" songs with their catchy and slightly naughty cast were heard in a mainstream show. The cakewalk, too, proved so popular it became a central ingredient for most black shows. Broadway's next major black musical was the *Songs of Ham* (1901) by Bert Williams (1876–1922) and George Walker (1872–1911), the most renowned black comedy team of the era.

William and Walker's next production, *In Dahomey,* made theatrical history as the first full-length musical written and performed by blacks to appear on Broadway when it opened on February 18, 1903, at the New York Theatre.[14] After an enthusiastic reception there, the show played for seven months in London, then toured England and Scotland before returning to the United States. Although *In Dahomey* was far more integrated than the loose minstrel-show format, its strong roots in that tradition were apparent to audiences. Williams and Walker appeared as Shylock Homestead and Rateback Punkerton who pretend to be detectives in Florida in a con game after Cicero Lightfoot. The work is notable for a number of reasons. First, it has the most amount of extant music than for any other black show from the period. Second, most of the score was provided again by Cook, a superior musician. Finally, it gave voice to an important issue for the emerging African American social consciousness with the seriousness of the underlying romance of returning to Africa, a controversial subject of the time.

The songs in *In Dahomey* reflect the Tin Pan Alley structures of the end of the century, although Cook was especially creative in expanding and varying those styles. In contrast to other popular types, which depend on melodic and harmonic structures, the African American theater song genre centralized rhythm and timbre, as musicologist Tom Riis points out in his edition of the work. Rhythmic cleverness, specifically syncopation, became the distinctive fingerprint of the music. Riis continues, "Singers often sing about nothing of substance, but they do so with fervor and rambunctiousness, reveling in life for its own sake. Colloquial in language, yet always clean and clear, songs of aspiration and high spirits dominate the score."

No song captures this mood more pristinely than "Swing Along" from *In Dahomey.* Composed and written by Cook, the work integrates syncopated rhythm of the coon song, the cakewalk, and ragtime in a celebration of black dance and pride:[15]

> Swing along chillun, swing along de lane,
> Lif yo' head and yo' heels mighty high,
> Swing along chillun, 'tain't a-goin' to rain,
> Sun's as red as de rose in de sky.

Like the first, the second strain is cast in a 16-bar tune, but moderated from the first in 4/4 time instead of 2/4, which broadens the rhythmic motion. The first strain then returns, shortening its last phrase, building to the high-note climax.

Broadway book shows and revues by black composers prospered into the second decade of the century, but faltered after the death of Walker and Cole in 1911; Bert Williams joined Ziegfeld's *Follies*, often headlining the show until his death in 1922. Johnson worked with other performers, but failed to find a partner equal to Cole. The growing popularity of motion pictures drew crowds from the black productions, and many of the theaters began showing movies instead of live shows, closing a golden age in African American theater.

CHORAL MUSIC

Unlike the popular musical stage, however, choral music in the Gilded Age sought a morally higher plane, or at least claimed to. Many of the choral works composed between the Civil War and World War I set texts aimed at edification, uplift, religious devotion, or national pride. To counter what they saw as moral decay and personal irresponsibility, leading thinkers and commentators turned to High Art in the form of choral music, hoping that a sacralized culture would offer the edifying uplift needed to ameliorate these problems and improve the moral character of society. Louisa Cragin wrote, in 1870, that labor problems would improve if trade unions were transformed into choral societies and workers and their children were exposed to good music; soon "there will be fewer strikes, the grimy faces will be less haggard; under the unconscious influence of beauty, harmony, and rhythm, labor will be more cheerfully, more faithfully performed."[16]

These same impulses had precipitated the music-making in the sacred music reform movement in Boston instituted by Lowell Mason in the 1830s. Mason had taught secular singing with the same goal as that of psalmody instruction: to edify the singers and the audience, elevating their intellectual, moral, and spiritual lives. Central to this program of sacred music reform was the choir, but now its secular equivalent, the choral society, joined it as a bearer of this program for moral uplift. As Richard Crawford observes, this blend of sacred and secular elements proved a powerful musical attraction to Victorian Americans. The spiritual elements included typical performances in a church, Christian romantic texts, and sacred oratorio subjects, which drew many of the earnest evangelical Protestants to choral singing. The secular elements were the choral performance accompanied by organ and often orchestra, the price of admission, and the applause lauding the music. Crawford observes, "The concert brought sacred music to listeners who paid their way into the church, listened rather than sang, and responded by clapping rather than praying."[17] Speaking for many in 1887, the noted journalist Henry Krehbiel declared that "a more general, more zealous, wiser cultivation of choral music is the greatest of the socio-educational needs of the United States."[18]

The new choral music experience was *democratic*; average citizens could now sing music that was only slightly more difficult than traditional psalm tunes and simple anthems they sang in church, but in so doing could enjoy the thrill of participation in something that sounded like great music. These developments led, after mid-century, to a major shift in American life in the way secular choral music was performed. It began to be organized and institutionalized in new ways. The secular music was indeed a people's music, but a *high-class* grass roots music. Much of America's musical life took place "in the parlors, the club rooms, and the churches—the private, social, and spiritual sanctuaries of the American people." This movement produced a vigorous, nonprofessional flourishing musical life, which easily outpaced the visible, socially prominent concert world in investment and inclusiveness. As the writer for the *Musical Record* observed on May 3, 1879: "That the knowledge and love of music have prodigiously increased within the last few years cannot be doubted. Thousands now assist in choral societies and go to concerts and operas who a few years ago could only have been tempted to hear the simplest ballads and most common-place pianoforte pieces."[19]

Stimulated by the large waves of immigrants from Germany, after mid-century, mixed-voice choral societies sprang up throughout much of the country. Organized on English and German models, these rapidly increasing choral groups voiced some of the strongest elements of Victorian culture: the strong sense of duty, community participation, broad religious sentiment, rising nationalism, and enthusiasm for the new romantic musical styles. Soon, amateur groups sprang up in virtually every city with more than a thousand souls. The tide of German immigrants, which had been increasing steadily since the 1830s, formed singing societies as soon as they could get settled. Philadelphia probably formed the first *Gesangverein* with 12 singers in December 1815. New York saw the formation of the all-male chorus

Deutsche Liederkranz in 1847 and the rival *Männergesangverein* Arion in 1854. Large German-American communities in Midwest cities such as Milwaukee, Chicago, St. Louis, and Cincinnati established important choral societies as well. By the 1870s, a number of these groups had matured into large mixed choral societies. Chicago's Apollo Musical Club began as a small male chorus in 1872, added women in 1875, and eventually grew to a leading symphonic choral society of 250 voices.

English-language American singing societies evolved from the glee clubs based on English models. The leader here is the Mendelssohn Glee Club, which started in 1866 in New York with eight members; within two years the singers numbered 24. Chicago's Apollo Musical Club began as a small male chorus in 1872, added women in 1875, and eventually grew to a leading symphonic choral society of 250 voices. Philadelphia followed suit with the Orpheus Club in 1872. A visit by the Mendelssohn Club to Boston in April 1871 led to the founding of an Apollo Club in that city later that year with 52 men. In 1877, the Brooklyn Apollo Club, soon one of the most prominent such groups in the country, was organized with Dudley Buck as director.

The last half of the century saw the formation of choral societies in nearly every large city organized specifically to perform large-scale choral works with orchestra. Perhaps the best known group was the New York Oratorio Society, established in 1873 by Leopold Damrosch. Many of the large choruses imitated the Handel and Haydn Society by naming themselves after European composers, such as the Mendelssohn Club in New York. Chicago began its own Mendelssohn Society in 1858 and a Beethoven Society in 1873. Reconstruction Atlanta founded a Beethoven Society in 1872 with 45 members and performed in the recently rebuilt Georgia Railroad Depot with a small orchestra. Academic institutions also followed suit, including the Oberlin Musical Union of Oberlin College in 1860, the University Choral Union of the University of Michigan (1879), and the Madison Choral Union of the University of Wisconsin in 1893. By 1918, more than 400 official choral societies were listed in *Who's Who in Music;* 100 were designated oratorio class in 30 states.[20]

The tide of German immigrants rapidly accelerated the growth of male choral groups.[21] Nearly every town with a sizable German population had a *männerchor,* and large cities like New York boasted one on every other block it seemed. Suzanne Snyder lists an astonishing 950 German-American speaking choral societies that flourished in the United States sometime between 1835 and 1960. Perhaps the most important characteristic of the *männerchor* was its social, nonprofessional status, which meant it avoided getting mired in the whole class-polarizing high-culture/vernacular debate, yet it managed to maintain decently professional levels of musical performance.

American choral festivals, organized on English and German models, added considerable prestige to choral music in this country. In 1873, the first Cincinnati May Festival occurred, led by Theodore Thomas with a chorus of 800 and an orchestra of more than 100. The Handel and Haydn Society organized the first specifically American music festival in May 1856, with 600 singers and 78 orchestra players. Boston held the largest festivals of the century in 1869 and 1872 when Patrick S. Gilmore presented his Peace Jubilees. The 1872 Festival set the record for notorious extravagance with a chorus of 20,000 and an orchestra of 2,000. The bound copies of all the music for the festival choruses quickly formed the core repertory of nineteenth-century secular choral concerts in this country. By the 1880s, the festivals had caught on, with New York presenting its first on May 2–6, 1882, with a chorus of 3,000 and an orchestra of 300. The next year Pittsburgh, San Francisco, St. Louis, and other cities joined with their own celebrations. These concerts did much to strengthen and accelerate the spread of choral music in the country.

THE SECULAR CANTATA

Like several other genres of nineteenth-century choral music, the secular cantata has found no place in the standard narratives of American history. The rise of the secular cantata in the United States mirrored its popularity in England, where it occupied a position second only to the oratorio in importance. The mellifluous musical style and thinly disguised American Triumphalism of its text caused it to become a major exemplar of Gilded Age American culture. Triumphalism denotes the overriding conviction that the American way of life, thought, religion, economics, and politics would inevitably triumph over all other inferior historical systems and peoples. It was this fusion of triumphalism, romanticism, and liberal Protestant Christianity that connected so profoundly with American audiences.

The secular cantata became one of the major cultural expressions of national belief. Cast in the typical musical idiom of the day, the secular cantata rapidly became a favorite choral medium after the Civil War. The Victorian secular cantata, which typically lasted from 10 minutes to 1 1/2 hours, was scored for mixed chorus, male chorus, or, less frequently, female chorus, with solo or small vocal ensemble present in virtually every work. All composers used accompaniment, normally piano, small ensembles, or large orchestra. The prominent musicians of the period all penned numerous works in the form: Horatio Parker, John K. Paine, Frederick S. Converse, George W. Chadwick, Charles W. Cadman, Henry Hadley, Deems Taylor, Victor Herbert, and Dudley Buck.

As the enthusiasm for choral singing expanded, and as technological advances in printing lowered the price of music exponentially, composers began turning out torrents of secular cantatas. Even a cursory examination of scholarly catalogues, as well as publishers' listings of their own works during this period, reveals an astonishing amount of cantatas written during the period, mainly from the four main American publishers: G. Schirmer in New York, Arthur P. Schmidt and Oliver Ditson in Boston, and John Church in Cincinnati. When the British firm of Novello is included, an informed estimate puts the total at nearly 1,000 works! The critical figure in establishing the genre in this country was George F. Root (1820–1895), whose cantatas were intentionally composed for the secular theater.[22] His two final antebellum cantatas, *The Haymakers* (1857) and *Belshazzar's Feast* (1860), are probably his best works in the genre; and numbers from them, as well as his earlier cantatas, began finding performances at musical conventions and institutes.

By the early 1870s, the secular cantata had become a prominent musical entertainment in Victorian America, gradually assuming considerable cultural authority. The most gifted and successful of American composers was Dudley Buck, whose cantatas coincided with this period; from his first works in the early 1870s until 1898, he would turn out an extended sacred or secular choral work nearly every other year; by the turn of the century, he had completed 16 cantatas. Buck would eventually write six secular cantatas for mixed chorus, beginning with the *Festival Hymn* in 1872, and an additional six for male chorus, concluding with *Paul Revere's Ride* in 1898. Each work found publication within months of its premiere, mostly by G. Schirmer, with Oliver Ditson introducing two and Novello one in London. In the 40 years after the Civil War, Buck's secular compositions were among the most frequently performed works by American community choruses. Written in 1873, Buck completed the *Legend of Don Munio*, a "dramatic cantata," the libretto of which Buck adapted and versified from the *Spanish Papers* by Washington Irving; it proved his most popular work, finding performances well into the twentieth century. His *Centennial Meditation*, written for the 1876 Philadelphia Exhibition, confirmed Buck's stature as one of the most successful composers of American cantatas. The 15-minute work cogently presents the central American tenets of Christian romanticism, American Triumphalism, and pioneer heroism by incorporating those musical experiences common to all Americans: the Protestant hymn, the march, and the solo song.

THE PARTSONG

Like the secular cantata, the partsong, an unaccompanied secular choral composition of relatively short length, remains neglected in the standard narratives of American music history. Yet many American composers during the Gilded Age and the next wrote partsongs, including Amy Beach, George Chadwick, Arthur Foote, William Wallace Gilchrist, Henry Hadley, Margaret Ruthven Lang, Edward MacDowell, John Knowles Paine, and Horatio Parker.[23] We know that the American partsong has roots in two transatlantic traditions: that of the German *Männerchor* and the English glee club. The musical idiom of the partsong reflected its German legacy in its Mendelssohnian transparency and its British origins in its widespread popularity. Later in the century, many partsongs began to show an increasing chromaticism. Formally, works rarely departed from a straightforward ternary, modified strophic, or rondo-like design, with an inevitably homophonic and homorhythmic texture.

We also know that, by the 1820s, glee and glee singing rivaled the singing school in popularity and equaled sacred music in social status. Lowell Mason's Boston Academy of Music included glee singing in its curriculum. The first organized glee clubs in this country began about 1860. Singing at Yale is recorded as yearly as 1812 when 12 men who sang for chapel services designated themselves the Yale Musical Society. During the 1840s and 1850s, various informal groups began and dispersed until 1861 when the first organized Yale Glee Club started. The University of Michigan claims the second oldest male glee club in the country; records indicate the presence of a small singing group by 1846. By 1859, the singers joined with the banjo and mandolin groups and assumed the name the University Glee, Mandolin, and Banjo Clubs.

As choral groups increased dramatically, which spurred a growing market for partsongs, composers and publishers responded enthusiastically. According to a recent estimate, some 5,000 partsongs were published in this country between 1870 and 1885.[24] As in the secular cantatas, Dudley Buck contributed substantially to this tradition. Typically, Buck published most of these works in groups of five or six: an early set for mixed voices, three series for male voices, and a pair for treble voices late in his career.[25] Two of Buck's partsongs represent typical Victorian works in the genre, both set for male chorus. The first, "In Absence," comes from *Six Songs for Male Voices,* Op. 55 (Boston: Oliver Ditson, 1872; reissued in 1901), and the second, "The Signal Resounds From Afar," appears in *Five Four-Part Songs,* Op. 92 (New York: G. Schirmer, 1883).

"In Absence," set to a three-stanza text by Phoebe Cary (1824–1871), a New York poet, depicts a young man calling on the stars, the night, and the wind to remind his distant sweetheart that he loves her. The harmonic idiom is straightforward and triadic, with occasional chromatic coloring. A final composition, "The Signal Resounds from Afar," is both Buck's longest partsong (132 bars long) and the one showing the greatest formal complexity: a "Vocal March in Canon-Form," according to the composer. Buck himself seems to have written the militaristic text, whose spirit is reinforced by dotted figures and by generally diatonic harmony. The three sections include complicated contrapuntal lines involving a double canon weaving around Luther's *Ein feste Burg*.

TOURING VIRTUOSI

By mid-century, American concert life was undergoing a pervasive trans-formation as European virtuosos realized the considerable profit potential of the United States as a market for their talents. They understood that to succeed, however, they had to package their musical artistry as entertainment. And to deliver this entertainment, they needed the means, which technology provided in the form of a touring circuit that created a new musical market-place. The telegraph, invented in 1835 and actively used since the late 1840s, allowed artists to develop and change itineraries rapidly. Canals and railroads connected major cities as well. By the 1850s, track linked the Atlantic seaboard with the Midwest and, by 1860, total mileage grew to 30,000 miles. In the 1840s, growing leisure time for many Americans coupled with the spread of music teaching accelerated interest in music-making at home, centered on the parlor piano, which was becoming a required status symbol of middle-class propriety and affluence. In 1829, American firms manufactured an estimated 2,500 pianos, one for every 4,800 citizens; by 1852, 9,000 pianos were pro-duced, one for every 2,777 inhabitants; and by the 1860s, 21,000 pianos were manufactured, one for every 1,500 citizens. All of this also increased con-cert attendance in the growing number of opera houses, concert halls, and churches from village to urban city.

During the decade of the 1840s, all of these elements merged into a touring network for concert performers. Violinists Ole Bull and Henri Vieuxtemps (1820–1881) were among the first widely successful European artists. Vieuxtemps returned twice, in 1857, with Sigismund Thalberg and, in 1870, with soprano Christine Nilsson; Bull married an American and resided in Boston for a time. Pianists Leopold de Myer (1816–1883) and Henri Herz (1803–1888) enjoyed notable successes, especially Herz, who traveled for three years on the eastern seaboard before appearing in gold-rush California. These artists achieved widespread success with their virtuoso playing and diverse programming, which consisted of grand fantasies based on familiar tunes, often popular operas, established favorites, and dance music. The concerts of these traveling virtuosos connected back to the eighteenth-century tradi-tion where music was expected to entertain, amuse, and astonish. They also functioned completely within the marketplace and were expected to generate a profit without the patronage of wealthy subscribers.

It was the appearance of Swedish soprano Jenny Lind in her 1850–1852 tour, however, that proved to be a milestone in American concert life. Much of her success was due to the industry of her sponsor, impresario P. T. Barnum, who essentially invented mass concert marketing to promote her tours. And it worked—astonishingly. Her 93 concerts grossed $712,000 in a period when a net worth of $100,000 defined one as very rich. In addition to a celestial voice never encountered before by most Americans, she and Barnum wisely programmed her concerts to include a variety of pieces guaranteed to keep a musically unlearned audience's attention. After an overture, she opened with an Italian aria and continued with other operatic solos interspersed with orchestral numbers, including in the second half beloved American folk ballads such as "Home, Sweet Home" and "The Last Rose of Summer." Owing largely to her fame, Barnum became the most successful musical impresario of the century, and in so doing he firmly established the role, which today continues with the powerful concert promoters.

As the railroads opened up the American heartland, European impresarios tried seizing on Barnum's spectacular record. The most successful at mid-century were the Strakosch brothers Maurice and Max, Max Maretzek, and Bernard Ullman, all of whom managed tours into the 1880s. The artists they managed continually accused them of cynically being interested only in commercial gain to the detriment of artistic considerations. One of Ullman's own responses seems to confirm things. When asked by a New Orleans audience member what kind of music his artists were going to program, Ullman quipped: "Financial music." This quip most immediately applied to his pianist Sigismond Thalberg (1812–1871), who toured this country from 1856 to 1858 and who had been the only serious keyboard competition to Liszt in Paris in the 1830s. One concert in Boston drew more than 3,000 listeners.

The first American-born virtuoso to reap the advantages of the newly developed touring circuit was New Orleanian Louis Moreau Gottschalk (1829–1869). Born in the musical and ethnic melting pot of New Orleans, he toured continually from 1853 until his death, resting only from sheer exhaustion. After the director of the Paris Conservatory snubbed him without an audition, he studied piano with Camille Stamaty, a student of Frédéric Guillaume Kalkbrenner, the leading piano teacher and Liszt rival in Paris. Upon returning to this country in 1853, Gottschalk began touring the continental United States and later the Caribbean and South America. At the height of the Civil War, he toured this country from 1862–1865, presenting more than 900 concerts. By his own account he had journeyed an estimated 95,000 miles on the railroads by September 1865. During a tour of South America he died at age 40 in Rio de Janeiro of pneumonia aggravated by extreme exhaustion.

Gottschalk was also a prolific composer, penning nearly 300 pieces in his short professional career. He began composing in Europe as a student, where his pieces met with enthusiastic success, especially his *Bamboula,* subtitled *Danse des nègres,* based on a Creole tune. Likewise, *Le Bananier* and *La Savane* elaborated Creole songs, the former with its persistent octave drumming and open fifths, and the latter with its repeated diatonic melody above changing textures and harmonies pointed toward many later pieces. During the South American years, two of his most enduring pieces became the *Grand scherzo* and the *Grand tarantelle* for piano and orchestra. As a spirited supporter of the Union cause, he cast his sentiments into a rousing patriotic piano fantasy titled *Union,* paraphrasing and combining the three most popular northern airs: "Star-Spangled Banner," "Yankee Doodle," and "Hail Columbia." Two of his most popular pieces, *The Banjo* (1854–1855) and *The Last Hope* (1853–1854), illuminate the breadth of Gottschalk's appeal, from the fantastic to the sublime. *The Banjo* is actually labeled *Grotesque fantasie,* described as "An American Sketch," and closely emulates the popular music of the blackface minstrelsy with its brilliant paraphrasing of "Roll, Jordan, Roll" and Foster's "Camptown Races," which he seamlessly blended with virtuoso syncopations. Even though Gottschalk penned *The Last Hope* as a parody of a popular parlor piece, it became a constant favorite during his tours before finally being cleansed of its sensual origins and finding its way into the mainstream Protestant American hymnals as the hymntune MERCY.

Gottschalk did more than any other American in antebellum America to open the country up to concert music. Along with the touring European pianists, he presented a masterly assemblage of musics—popular, folk, classical—all played in a brilliant Lisztian style that few people in this country had ever heard, or even heard of. As late as 1915, no fewer than 55 of his compositions remained available in sheet music. Since the renewed interest in American music after the bicentennial, his works have returned to the concert stage. But it was in his demonstrating how exciting, wondrous, and downright fun great and not so great music could sound that he achieved his most enduring legacy. In so doing, he left American culture far richer than he had found it. He lived just into the dawn of the Gilded Age, where his younger contemporaries would richly reap the fruits of his pioneering work.

Another American who toured briefly during the 1850s was William Mason (1829–1908), son of the famous music educator Lowell Mason. After five years of studying in Europe, where he enjoyed the privilege of concentrated instruction from such legendary pianists as Ignaz Moscheles, Alexander Dreyschock, and Franz Liszt, Mason returned to the United States in 1854. Hampered by his homegrown American heritage, his ambitious but poorly attended concert tour that year was canceled midway and never again attempted. He relocated to New York City and began a multifaceted career of performing, teaching, and composing. Of special significance during this time was the formation of a chamber ensemble that included Mason and young violinist Theodore Thomas. During the next 13 years, the Mason-Thomas Quartette would present many world and U.S. premières of major chamber works. Mason was possibly the first pianist on these tours to play without assisting artists, performing many of the masterpieces of the European keyboard repertoire. In so doing, he did much to elevate the artistic level of concert pianism in the United States.

The outbreak of the Civil War interrupted the travels of the European pianists, who feared gunfire more than box-office failure. One exception to this was the appearance of Venezuelan pianist Teresa Carreño (1853–1917) who debuted in New York in 1862 when she was only eight years old. Although she did not enjoy the successes of her predecessors and had only a limited career in this country, she continued the artistic tradition of the earlier keyboardists.

After the cessation of hostilities in 1865, touring artists returned in full force. Expediting their travels was the expansion of the rail system from 35,083 miles in 1865 to 243,013 in 1897. The growing appetite for music rapidly accelerated interest in their performances. One thing in their presentations changed as concert life expanded and matured. Before the 1870s, pianists generally traveled in groups. Thalberg toured with violinist Vieuxtemps to great acclaim, and even Gottschalk had a retinue with him, generally a small troupe of opera singers who interspersed vocal music with his playing. Touring instrumental ensembles had been touring from the 1840s and the Thomas Orchestra travels had enjoyed enormous success.

With Mason things began to change and by the time the two European pianistic giants Anton Rubinstein (1829–1894) and Hans von Bülow made their tours in 1872–1873 and 1875–1876, respectively, they presented little but serious, original music for the piano, nearly always composed by the European masters. Their repertoire and the terms of their tour illuminate the crystallization of the concept of art music and how it is presented and packaged. Recall that Thalberg in his tours two decades earlier performed mostly his own pieces, often virtuoso fantasies on Italian opera arias, along with popular songs. And Gottschalk performed virtually anywhere at anytime. With Rubenstein, the imperative behind the entire tour had shifted from one of entertainment, whose success was measured by box-office returns, to one of High Art, where the success resided in the level and the quality of the works played, as well as the reverential tone of the experience. The enterprise was no longer driven by the market, but aspired to a higher calling, as clearly stated in his contract, "Rubenstein is not obliged to accompany in these concerts, nor to play in premises that are not dedicated to artistic purposes, such as garden concerts and smoking premises."[26] Seemingly unconcerned about audience comfort, his opening concerts in New York lasted from two-and-a-half to three hours, with 3,000 audience members sitting in stifling heat. In addition to playing a concerto (when an orchestra was available), he typically presented Beethoven sonatas; Mendelssohn works, especially the beloved *Songs without Words;* Chopin ballades, and Schumann pieces, along with popular transcriptions such as the Mendelssohn's "Wedding March" from *A Midsummer Night's Dream.* On one of his last concerts in New York in 1873, he played the last five sonatas of Beethoven, something that would have caused an uproar from audiences 20 years earlier.

Another major European traveling on these shores was Polish violinist Henryk Wieniawski (1835–1880) who began a two-year tour of North America in 1872. He gave 215 concerts the first year with Rubinstein, and both artists were near exhaustion at the end. Wieniawski remained for a second year and shared the stage with Paulina Lucca, earning a fortune but endangering his health. Critics extolled Wieniawski's pure and rapturous tone; his clean, crisp bowing; and his incredible technique. In contrast to Rubinstein's serious, almost grim visage on stage, Wieniawski's cheerful, relaxed personality made him more popular with audiences. His repertoire had a broader appeal as well, mixing the severely classical of Bach, Beethoven, and Mendelssohn with the bravura pieces by Paganini, and Vieuxtemps, in addition to his own works. With his more accessible works he could appeal to the most untrained audience member. His performances represent a transitional phase in the evolution of the Gilded Age concert program.

Completing the transition to High Art in the piano repertoire was Hans von Bülow's (1830–1894) tour of the United States in 1875–1876, where he gave 139 concerts, including the world premier of Tchaikovsky's *First Piano Concerto* to a full Music Hall in Boston, which, according to critic James Huneker, involved conductor, orchestra, and audience alike in a very public contretemps. Bülow represented the classic serious German professional pianist who brooked no infringements on either the works he played, the settings he played them in, or even the demeanor of the audience as he played them. More than once he was known to stop and glare at the audience when someone was whispering or entering with creaky shoes. Bülow was undeniably the best pianist to visit the United States. In the October 30, 1875 issue of his journal, Dwight found his playing "simply perfect.... He never fails; it seems impossible for him to fail."[27] Many reckoned him the best interpreter of Bach's music yet heard in America, as the complex contrapuntal textures of the Leipzig composer still struck many Americans as overly intellectual and sterile. On November 15, 1875, Bülow had the honor of inaugurating the splendid new Chickering Hall at Fifth and Eighteenth Street, to excellent reviews. With his authentic interpretations of the greatest piano music, Bülow contributed much to the professionalization of the musical concert in this country.

Bülow's tours, ending in 1876, completed the sacralization of the solo piano recital, where concerts now consisted of a single soloist (sometimes performing a concerto with an orchestra) performing the canonic masterpieces originally composed for the instrument, and received by an audience that listened in quiet, respectful reverence. They also proved that the solo piano recital could be viable financially, as well as artistically. In addition, the 1870s opened a golden age of piano virtuosos, including Leopold Godowsky (180–1938) in 1884, Josef Hofmann (1876–1957) in 1887, Moritz Rosenthal (1862–1946) in 1888, Ferruccio Busoni (1866–1924) in 1892–1893, and Ignacy Jan Paderewski (1860–1941) in 1891. With the enshrinement of the European masterworks as the most noble of High Art came discrimination against American artists. Only a handful managed to earn some success, particularly Julie Rivé-King (1854–1937), Amy Fay (1844–1928), and Amy Beach (1867–1944) who cut short a promising solo career for composition after her marriage. Listeners likewise abandoned the talking, outbursts of applause, and feet stomping that suited the superficial fantasies and variations of the early period in favor of quiet, rapt attention in pursuit of an intense aesthetic experience.

BANDS

The band became just as ubiquitous in American culture during the Gilded Age as the church choir. After the War of Independence, discharged military musicians formed the nucleus of civilian bands, which often took the names of the cities and towns they resided in. By the fourth decade of the nineteenth century, bands were already widely popular. As technology gave the general population more leisure time, civic functions increased considerably. By playing music accessible to everyone, and at a volume that could be enjoyed outdoors, a band proved exactly the right type of entertainment for American life. Towns as small as 200 people often supported a volunteer group, or even a semiprofessional band and considered it a civic duty to do so. As early as 1838, the *New Orleans Picayune* reported a "real mania in this city for horn and trumpet playing" complaining that it was impossible to turn a corner without running into a brass "blower."[28] In 1853, John Sullivan Dwight, the musical doyen of High Culture, expressed concern: "All at once the idea of a Brass Band shot forth: and from this prolific germ sprang a multitude of its kind in every part of the land, like the crop of iron men from the infernal seed of the dragon's teeth."[29] On the eve of the Civil War, more than 3,000 bands existed, boasting more than 60,000 musicians. During the postbellum period the number of bands increased dramatically, reaching an estimated 18,000 on the eve of World War I. A town band became a mark of affluence and social status: "A town without its brass band is as much in need of sympathy as a church without a choir," one writer observed in 1878.[30] A number of states passed "band laws," which enabled the levying of taxes to support free band concerts.

Also as in the church choir, the band brought a truly democratic musical experience to all Americans. Membership was open to all, offering access to public spaces for many otherwise denied it: children, women, ethnic groups, Native Americans, and African Americans. Many of the regimental bands during the Civil War were African American whose bandsmen did much to lay the groundwork for jazz in the following decades.

A number of factors contributed to the band's mass appeal, not only to listeners but to aspiring band members. First, technological improvements to brass instruments made them cheaper and much easier to play and to keep in tune, starting with the keyed bugle (1815), which played more expressively than earlier instruments. Ensembles generally consisted of cornets (a high soprano horn) and over-the-shoulder saxhorns, similar to French horns today. Saxhorns became a family of instruments and filled out the ensemble to create the uniquely brass-band sound. Band members only had to possess a modest technique, enough to keep a beat and maintain a melody line. Instruments also became inexpensive with mass production. The 1895 *Montgomery Ward Catalogue* displayed 11 pages of musical instruments, selling flutes for $1.65–$16.70, clarinets for $11–$28, trombones for $10.55–$16.70, and cornets for $5.10–$26.[31]

Most important, bands provided a true music for the people. As in nineteenth-century theater, which cross-fertilized the various genres throughout the period, the clear distinction we make today between bands and orchestras did not hold. Bands and orchestras regularly shared musicians, who simultaneously played wherever they could obtain positions. The groups also shared repertories that included music from all strata of the musical spectrum: overtures, operatic arias, hymns, waltzes, polkas, fantasies, symphony movements, and the ever popular march. Operatic music provided as rich a source for band performances. In 1861, a band played music from *Rigoletto* for President Lincoln's inauguration, and union soldiers marched to the "La Traviata Quickstep." Likewise, even the staunchest orchestra evenings inevitably involved marches.

The Civil War greatly accelerated the existing popularity of brass bands. The Union Army, with more than two-and-a-half million men, had 500 bands and 9,000 players; Confederate regiments were usually similar.[32] After the war, the large numbers of players and directors returned to civilian life, where they ushered in the golden age of the American band. Irish immigrant Patrick S. Gilmore (1829–1892), considered the father of the symphonic band, had served in the war when his group, Gilmore's Band, joined the 24th Massachusetts Volunteer Regiment. The group was later mustered out and Gilmore traveled to New Orleans where he organized a giant musical celebration for the inauguration of a new governor. After returning to Boston he began organizing monster musical extravaganzas in 1864, culminating in the 1872 Boston World Peace Jubilee, which boasted an orchestra of 1,000, a band of 2,000, and a chorus of 20,000. More important, the high performance standards of the visiting European bands at the Jubilee stimulated him and others to improve the quality of band performance.

During the 1870s, however, as Richard Crawford points out, the Boston jubilees marked a major milestone in the growing debate over art versus entertainment. The view that had prevailed in American life that such diverse elements as edifying music, entertaining music, and grandiose spectacle could democratically mingle together ceded ground to the notion that edifying music deserved venues all its own. As European music gained increasing cultural authority, it gradually deigned to justify and support itself in the marketplace. Orchestras began to seek patronage while bands had to make money, or at least pay for themselves, something Gilmore clearly understood.

Declaring himself "through with tornado choruses," in 1873 Gilmore assumed leadership of the New York's 22nd Regiment Band, promptly renaming it the "Gilmore Band." With his radiant personality, infectious enthusiasm, excellent musicianship, and shrewd business sense, he led it to become the finest professional wind and brass ensemble in the country. He immediately expanded the band's size and repertoire, adding transcriptions of the great orchestral classics. He also innovatively changed the band's instrumentation, transforming the traditional brass band sound by infusing it with woodwinds; trombones were also added. In 1878, Gilmore's Band had 35 woodwinds, 27 brass, and 4 percussion players. With none of the country's four professional orchestras having a full season, the best players in the country joined his band, which toured every autumn and spring, spending summer and winter in New York. The professional level of playing, blended instrumentation, and eclectic programming of his group exercised a lasting influence on the level of the band performance and literature.

By 1889, *Harper's Weekly* estimated there were more than 10,000 "military" bands in the country. For many smaller communities, and especially frontier towns, the local band provided the only music. Even though many bands were uniformed, they retained their civilian status, such as the New York 7th Regimental Band. Professional and amateur groups alike played virtually everywhere: parades, Sunday afternoon concerts, picnics, dances, political campaigns, meetings, funerals, weddings, bar mitzvahs, and much more. The large bands had their resplendent conductors; the smaller ones typically followed the solo cornetist, who led from the solo cornet part, which served also as the conductor's cue sheet.

The year that Gilmore died, 1892, John Philip Sousa (1854–1932) inherited Gilmore's mantle, becoming the most important figure in the history of American band music. As conductor, he thrilled audiences by combining superb musicianship and showmanship. As a prolific composer for stage and concert, he forged such perfect marches that he became the "March King," as well as the single most well-known American composer. By the time he ended his performing career in 1931, the heyday of the professional band closed as well, supplanted by the school band and the university wind ensemble.

In 1880, at age 25, Sousa assumed leadership of the Marine Band, forging it into the world's most famous band during his 12-year tenure. In 1892, he formed his own band and after Gilmore's death gained some of the latter's most talented musicians, gradually increasing the membership from 46 to an average of 70 players. They toured North America for more than half of each year, becoming a powerful attraction at fairs and expositions. He typically programmed an exhausting seven days a week and often twice a day.

Few American audiences had ever heard anything like Sousa's band performances. Outfitted in military-style uniforms and playing gleaming instruments, the band performed with granite precision, led by Sousa brandishing his baton like a Prussian Field Marshall. Contributing perhaps even more to Sousa's success was his keenly intuitive programming, which drew on both orchestral and band repertoire. He ingeniously programmed collages of sound at each concert, mixing and matching classical and popular, loud and soft, solo and ensemble, vocal and instrumental, responding to the mood of the particular audience and occasion—all interspersed with encores, which he chose on the spot, keeping not only the audience in suspense but the musicians as well. As he told an interviewer in 1911, Shakespeare found nothing incongruous in following a tragic scene with a comic one, so why shouldn't he combine in a program clever comedy with symphonic tragedy, rhythmic march, or waltz with sentimental tone poems?

Sousa's great theme was patriotism, the source of his most unforgettable music. In the closing decades of the century, patriotic nationalism had supplanted religion as the driving force behind American character, which Sousa instinctively tapped into. The most vibrant symbol of that patriotism was the American flag, which Sousa's best-known march exalts, *The Stars and Stripes Forever* (1897). Sousa invested his marches with fervent artistic and ethical power, articulated by a crisply precise "military" beat.

Sousa possessed a melodic gift that elevated him above nearly everyone else of his generation. He wrote 136 marches, three-fourths of which form a standard musical pattern of an introduction, followed by three or four strains, each of which has a new melody. Unlike dance music, which is continuously repeatable, Sousa's marches build to the final climactic strain in a new key. Opening quietly and simply, the march builds as new instruments are added, growing into a full sound at the end, replete with unforgettable tunes and counterpoint.

Other directors of the day deserve a mention, many of whom worked with the great Sousa, first as soloists who then went on to form their own bands. Herbert L. Clarke (1867–1845) had been a star cornetist with both Sousa and Gilmore, as had Alessandro Liberati (1847–1927), who formed the Liberati Grand Opera Company, which presented abridgements of grand operas. Arthur Pryor (1870–1942) became not only Sousa's leading trombone soloist but his assistant conductor; he later directed the Sousa Band in many of its recordings. Many other professional bands made good livings, often by touring, such as circus and family bands—including wives and daughters! Thousands of amateur ensembles filled American cities and towns with music as well, such as Shriner bands, railroad bands, industrial bands, and children's bands. Bands composed of ethnic groups proliferated, composed of Italians, Irish, Germans, Native Americans, and of course African Americans. New Hampshire native Helen May Butler (1898–1937), a violinist and cornetist, directed the professional Ladies' Military Band through the first decade of the century, performing "Music for the American people, by American composers, played by American girls." The high quality and financial success of her group affirmed growing sentiments that women could compete in the all-male band world and make a go of it.

As the Gilded Age drew to a close, so the did the popularity of bands, which faced increased competition from radio, phonograph, and motion pictures. Growing automobile use drew people away from amusement parts and fairs where bands had been a staple of entertainment. Band music such as polkas, waltzes, and even marches diminished in favor of the new dance music, especially ragtime and jazz. Fittingly, Sousa's death in 1932, after the Crash of 1929, marked the end of the Golden Age for American bands as the leadership for the band and wind ensemble passed from the professional band master to the educator.

"After the Ball," "Come On and Hear," and Other Songs They Sang

In the two decades after the Civil War, songwriters and audiences sought a respite from the fever pitch emotions that had resulted in so much bitterness, death, and destruction. George F. Root observed that at the end of the war, sales of "war songs stopped as if they had been shot," for "everybody had had enough of war."[1] Seeking to avoid contemporary issues, composers looked back to older songs for their musical inspiration and structure. Poets and songwriters complacently produced songs depicting romantic love, nostalgia, or moralizing admonition reminiscent of the sentimental American songs earlier in the century. For the first time, something not seen before entered American popular song—escapism.

Turned out by the hundreds, songs followed an unimaginative prescribed formula—the ballad form of antebellum popular music—with verse-and-chorus used by Stephen Foster and his contemporaries. The kernel of the song consisted of a brief, catchy musical phrase, generally four bars long, repeated throughout the piece. Songs imitated the evangelical hymn pattern of harmonically related eight-bar phrases, divided into introduction, verse, and refrain. Postbellum songs presented the main phrase in the introduction, the verse—or usually verses—the chorus, often arranged for four voices, and the piano tag. Imperative was a comforting familiarity.

These songs metaphorically reflected the surface glitter of the Gilded Age, which unfolded in a self-aggrandizing pursuit of material wealth while suppressing any discussion of the mounting social ills of crime, poverty, and economic disparity. Favorites like "Silver Threads Among the Gold" (1873) remained popular alongside songs that glorified drinking such as "The Little Brown Jug" (1869) and "There Is a Tavern in the Town" (1891). "Silver Threads Among the Gold" with music by H. P. Danks on a poem by Eben Rexford typifies the genteel songs that dominated the postwar years. Danks unwisely sold the song to C. W. Harris, who published it to great profit. It soon appeared in the repertoire of virtually every singer in vaudeville, boosting its sales to well over two million copies of sheet music. The four verses valorize romantic married love and nostalgia, expressing a hope that the speaker's love will never fade, ending with "Since I kissed you, mine alone,/You have never older grown." The four-bar introduction preimitates the main statement: a pair of two-bar phrases curving first upward then descending. The chorus text repeats the four lines that opened the first stanza, which produces a repeating structure that emphasizes love as a stabilizing force, like home itself: a haven sheltering partners from the ravages of time (and the rapacious caprice of the emerging capitalist market).

In the decade of the 1880s, however, American popular song began to change profoundly, affected by a number of forces. First was the emergence of a business culture that thrived on the cult of the new. Aggressive marketing techniques created a flourishing demand for the new lyrically compelling music produced in mass quantities on sheets and, later, sound recordings. Second was the emergence of New York as the capital of the American entertainment industry, both in performance and popular-song publishing. The term *Tin Pan Alley* became the catchall title for the new, brash song publishers who emerged in New York after 1880. Finally, not only was the music elegant and accessible, but it provided a powerful emotional release for a culture increasingly pressured into social conformity by the Protestant market economy, which eschewed expression of personal emotions.

The Tin Pan Alley formula rarely varied. Unlike the earlier Civil War and postbellum songs such as those of Stephen Foster, which contained a four-part chorus, the Tin Pan Alley song typically replaced that with a solo "chorus." It was the chorus that the song came to be known by, and the verse came increasingly to be used as a narrative introduction. The hymnlike 4/4 meter was supplanted by the more alluring, sensual 3/4 waltz rhythm. All followed a fixed formula: a major key, a short piano introduction, followed by a verse and chorus.

The songs of Stephen Foster had marked a major shift in the way popular music in America was produced. Before his work, sheet music had proclaimed on its covers "as sung by" and was mainly a performer's music. During the

Civil War, however, music publishers had begun seeking and commissioning composers, which found its final development in the songs of Tin Pan Ally. Now popular songs had become a composer's music.

Out of 16 of the most popular songs written in the years 1892–1905, only two were not published in New York and all but "Daisy Bell" are by Americans. The 16 include works that remain in the repertory into the early twenty-first century, including "After the Ball" (1892), "Daisy Bell" ("A Bicycle Built for Two"; Englishman Harry Dacre, 1892), "The Band Played On" (Charles Ward, 1895), "My Wild Irish Rose" (Chauncey Olcott, 1899), "A Bird in a Gilded Cage" (Arthur Lamb and Harry von Tilzer, 1900), "In the Good Old Summer Time" (Ben Shields and George Evans, 1902), "Meet Me in St. Louis" (Kerry Mills, 1904), and "My Gal Sal" (Paul Dresser, 1905).

Tin Pan Alley never appeared on any map. It became a nickname for the New York City neighborhood where the early popular sheet-music publishers gathered, first around Union Square at 14th Street and Broadway, and then, after the turn of the century, on West 28th near Fifth Avenue. Journalist and songwriter Munroe H. Rosenfeld is credited with coining the term. Harry Von Tilzer relates that when Rosenfeld was visiting him on West 28th, listening to Von Tilzer's piano, which had been muted with paper, he quipped, "It sounds like a tin pan." Another story attributes it to the sound of the cacophony produced by the sound of Von Tilzer's piano, played with an open window, competing with all the other pianos in the neighborhood. Rosenfeld soon used the nickname "Tin Pan Alley" in one of his newspaper articles to the publishing district that emerged in New York around 1890, and the new popular music it produced. By end of the decade, nearly every major music publisher had moved their office on or near West 28th Street.

Before the 1880s, song publishing was a sideline to the two major producers of music in the United States: music shops and major music publishers. Both institutions viewed their work as a noble calling, producing serious, edifying classical and religious music and instructional materials; popular songs seemed almost a frivolous business necessity. The men who founded the major publishing houses were somber and earnest gentlemen of a puritan bent: Oliver Ditson in Boston; Chicago's Root and Cady and Lyons and Healy; John Church in Philadelphia; and J. L. Peters, William A. Pond, and G. Schirmer in New York. They saw no need to promote or advertise their songs, selling the modest number of titles to people who entered their stores.

Before about 1880, New York had been no more important than Boston or Philadelphia in the field of popular song, although the city had already become the theatrical capital of the nation; by 1890, however, virtually all of the popular music business had migrated there. Leading this change were the brothers

Alex (1856–1901) and Tom Harms (1860–1906), who opened their music publishing business, T. B. Harms, in 1881. When one of their first songs, "Wait Till the Clouds Roll By" (Wood/Fulmer) was a hit in 1881, they realized they were on to something. They revolutionized the music publishing industry by concentrating their efforts on popular songs that had been introduced in the minstrel shows and variety theaters. They also used the primitive methods of introducing and plugging songs that showed any promise.

As the first Tin Pan Alley publishers began their work in the 1880s, the distinction between genteel and stage songs remained: sentimental, often moralizing ballads for the parlor continued to be written and published alongside more worldly, sensual, urban songs performed in minstrel shows, vaudeville, and the first musical comedies. As the popularity of Tin Pan Alley songs exploded, the sheet music of stage songs increased the respectability of the popular stage. The new style of music appealed to the more sophisticated, musically literate middle class, who owned pianos, bought the music, and sang the songs—by the millions.

The precipitating event that launched the music of Tin Pan Alley into America's mainstream occurred when M. Witmark and Sons established their firm on East 14th Street in 1888, the Union Square area, which had become the entertainment capital of America. Anchored by 14th Street from Third Avenue into the Square, the entertainment district housed the most famous music palaces in the country: vaudeville in Tony Pastor's Music Hall, opera in the Academy of Music, burlesque in the Dewey Theater, as well as numerous other places. This would become the first home to America's burgeoning popular music industry.

After Julius Witmark was paid only $20 for a song and then dismissed by Willis Woodward, he and his brothers opened M. Witmark & Sons, in 1885, using their father's name, as they were all under legal age. Soon they proved so successful at plugging and selling songs that they were receiving as many as 1,000 manuscript submissions a month. Sensing the potential in the new energies coming out of African American theater, they also became early publishers of ragtime.

Corset salesman Edward B. Marks (1865–1945), one of the most successful song publishers of the period, also understood where the real market lay. He opened his memoirs *They All Sang: From Tony Pastor to Rudy Vallee* by asserting that "The best songs came from the gutter in those days."[2] In 1894, he and necktie salesman Joe Stern joined forces and founded the music publishing firm of Joseph W. Stern & Company in a rental office on 14th Street with a dollar's worth of used furniture and only $100 in the bank. When their maudlin waltz song "The Little Lost Child" sold an astonishing million copies, they were off and running.

As mentioned earlier, Tony Pastor played a central role in the establishment and popularization of the variety show. His new theater on 14th Street quickly became the most popular musical stage in the city as he began showcasing in his variety shows the most famous entertainers of the age—Harrigan, and Hart, Lillian Russell, George M. Cohan, May Irwin, Weber and Fields, and Vesta Victoria, among others. Following his lead, Keith and Albee later organized a circuit of vaudeville houses all over the country, rapidly exposing most of the country to the new sounds of Tin Pan Alley. The hundreds of performers traveling across the country ushered in the first mass market era of American popular music in the 1880s and 1890s.

Singers became the mainstay of variety shows, performing a wide diversity of songs that soon became popular: genteel ballads, parlor songs, selections from opera and operetta, songs in foreign languages, novelty songs, ragtime and "coon" songs, sacred songs, spirituals, and minstrel songs. Each performer possessed his or her own style of singing, and many came to be identified with a certain style or genre. Even though the songs were composed and published, they became performers' music that provided a departure point for the singer to embellish and elaborate according to his or her own talents.

Thus the singer became the crucial link between the songwriter and successful sheet-music sales. The old-line firms like Ditson and Schirmer were content to publish music they deemed worthy and let it gradually find its own market, with very little advertising. The early group of popular-song musicians became some of the most-well-known publishers because they wanted to reap the profits themselves. Harry Von Tilzer, Edward Marks, Kerry Mills, Joseph Stern, and Charles Paul Dresser all started out as composers. Dismayed at the paltry payments they received for their early songs, which usually ranged from a one-time fee of $10 to $25 with no royalty rights, they decided to publish their music themselves.

They soon realized that to get their songs to the public they had to first be plugged, which became the publishers' main activity. Nothing was beneath them—from bribing performers, managers, conductors, and reviewers; planting seat pluggers in the audience who would rise and join the singer in the new song after the first verse; to passing out the music to the departing theatergoers. In his memoirs, *After the Ball: Forty Years of Melody*, Charles K. Harris described it, "A new song must be sung, played, hummed and drummed into the ears of the public, not in one city alone, but in every city, town, and village, before it ever becomes popular."[3] Until about 1900, the songs were typically plugged by blackface minstrels, who remained popular into the new century and in the variety houses and drinking houses. After 1900, musical comedy and vaudeville began to supplant those venues as the major force in the popularization of songs. Edward B. Marks in his autobiography, *They All Sang*, relates the process:

In the nineties, a publisher had to know his way about night spots. It was important to get his wares before the bibulous public; so he had to spend a large part of his time making the rounds for plugs and more plugs. Sixty joints a week I used to make. Joe Stern, my partner, covered forty. There songs were started where liquor flowed and released the impulse to sing.... The way to get a song over was to get it sung in the music halls by a popular singer.... I bought beer for the musicians and jollied the headliners.[4]

THE MAJOR SONGWRITERS

It was on 14th Street that Charles K. Harris opened his office after his first smash hit in American song history, "After the Ball." Harris was one of the three most significant of the hundreds of songwriters/publishers straddling the turn of the century who embodied the spirit and talent of the late Gilded Age. The other two were Paul Dresser and Harry Von Tilzer.

Born in Poughkeepsie, New York, Charles Harris (1867–1930) earned his living as a teenager in small variety theaters in Milwaukee singing minstrel show tunes and accompanying himself on a banjo. At 18 he opened his own publishing house and hung a sign outside his door reading "Songs Written to Order." With that phrase American song expanded from a marginal cottage enterprise and became big business. The genius of composers like Harris and the many that followed him lay in their shrewd insight in identifying and appealing to their buyers, a new emerging mass market. This new breed of songwriters began to understand how much potential there was in songs written for the millions of immigrants pouring into this country, as well as the growing number of American workers. The vehicle was sheet music, which by the 1890s spewed forth in torrents by the publishing houses springing up from Union Square north to Harold Square. They realized the money was in songs that sold not in thousands of copies but in the millions.

"After the Ball" (1892) became a cultural icon not only for early Tin Pan Alley but for the twilight years of the Gilded Age. The song arose from an idea that occurred to Harris after leaving a dance: "Many a heart is aching after the ball," he thought. He set out a story in three extended verses of 64 bars, interspersed with a repeating 32-bar chorus. Angry over his previous experience with New York publishers, whose minuscule royalty payments he found insulting, he published the song himself. After his initial efforts to get the song performed, it seemed as if it would be quickly forgotten until he persuaded a well-known baritone to highlight it in a vibrantly successful musical called *A Trip to Chinatown* currently playing in Harris's hometown of Milwaukee. After the song drew a five-minute standing ovation, Harris promised the singer $500 and a share of the royalties to sing it in every performance.

Set in a catchy *tempo di valse*, the song tells how an old man recounts to his little niece the heartbreaking story of his love lost many years after a ball. "I had a sweetheart years ago," he remembers. After seeing her kiss another man, he left the ballroom in sorrow and never saw her again. Only long after, when she was dead, did he learn that the "other man" was her brother.

The song broke lots of hearts besides that of the niece. After musical idol May Irwin introduced it to New York at Tony Pastor's, Oliver Ditson & Co. wired Harris an order for 75,000 copies. The song quickly reached sales of $25,000 a week, sold more than two million copies in only several years, and eventually achieved a sale of some five million. In an era of mass immigration not only on an international scale, but as Americans moved from country towns to large cities, families found themselves separated, and the theme of lost love and absence struck a resounding chord among audience members. Even today, the sadness of the chorus can still touch hearts:

> After the ball is over, after the break of morn—
> After the dancers' leaving; after the stars are gone;
> Many a heart is aching, if you could read them all;
> Many the hopes that have vanished after the ball.

As Richard Crawford suggests, it is the music that brings a genuine emotional atmosphere to a song that otherwise might be little more than a moralizing admonition. The music intensifies the emotional drama of the text by separating the exterior narrative of the verse from the reflective cast in the chorus. The lilting melody presents the ball's public, exterior face, masking personal tragedies. At the same time, the elegant, unruffled lyricism presents the illusion of calm control, underneath which personal and tragic human emotions are played out. The long melody of the verse is unified by a four-bar rhythmic motive that continues through its 64 measures. The chorus recalls that motive with a memorable tune on its own new four-bar rhythmic phrase, which it repeats until its last section. Harris then abandons that figure and returns to the verse, blending the song's two sections fittingly, concluding with the title of the work.

Soon the race was on to create tear jerkers that would tug at the heart of the public and hopefully enrich the songwriters. The broad range of the songs deliberately played to the gallery, aiming for the sentimental and often the maudlin. Some seemed to emerge from genuine sentiment, such as in the works of Paul Dresser, but the majority seemed contrived to appeal shamelessly to emotionalism. Another subject central to Victorian American life and thought was death, which dominated some of the country's most popular songs. None could have ever exceeded the sadness and pathos of "The Fatal Wedding" (1893). One of the most depressing songs ever written, this song tells the horrifying tale of a wedding interrupted by a wife and her child who unmasks the bigamist-to-be. The baby dies in her arms; the groom commits suicide; and finally, there's a double funeral after which the two women go to live with one another. Very heavy emotional stuff indeed. The song was introduced in a minstrel show and remained popular in vaudeville for several years. Just as baldly manipulative was "In the Baggage Coach Ahead" where the "baby's cries can't waken" the body of the dead mother being carried in the same train to the funeral.

Paul Dresser (1857–1906) was born in Terre Haute, Indiana, by the banks of the Wabash, the river he immortalized in song. His brother was Theodore Dreiser, the important novelist. After spending time in minstrel shows, he eventually settled in New York, where he came out with some of the earliest Tin Pan Alley hits. He never adjusted to life in the big city, remaining lonely and lost, dying alone. His gift lay in his ability to essentialize his grief, lost happiness, and hope in a manner that still can be genuinely moving. In this he was the only rightful successor to the gentle, expressive spirit of Thomas Moore and Stephen Foster. Dresser's songs acted as an enduring counterpart to the raucous, noisy, and often flippant spirit of much of Tin Pan Alley.

His brother Theodore Dreiser argued that Paul was moved to tears by the sadness of some of his songs, which epitomized the sentimental ballad of Victorian America. In his earliest hit, "The Letter That Never Came" (1886), he portrays an abandoned young woman asking the mailman each day, "A letter here for me?" In "Just Tell Them That You Saw Me" a schoolmate from earlier years encounters the protagonist on the streets of a big city and wants to take a message to her family "in a village far away." The answer in the chorus immediately burned itself into common usage: "Just tell them that you saw me/She said, they'll know the rest." We'll have to guess I suppose.

In "My Gal Sal," his biggest hit that appeared in 1905 just before his death, the lovers were parted by death, as told by "Jim," who is remembering his friend. The way Dresser depicts Sal marks a shift in the way women were portrayed in Tin Pan Alley and would not have been successful 15 years earlier:

> They called her frivolous Sal,
> A peculiar sort of a gal, With a heart that was mellow,
> An all 'round good fellow, Was my old pal;
> Your troubles, sorrows, and care,
> She was always willing to share,
> A wild sort of devil, but dead on the level,
> Was my gal Sal.

Here Sal comes across not as an idealized romantic interest but as "the best pal I ever had," to whom as she lay dying he "softly whispered 'Goodbye, Sal.'" As Jim described her as frivolous and wild, the audience smugly delighted in imagining her indulging in libertine antics of drinking and wayward sex. Edward Marks talks about "sniffly songs for the strayed sister, whom her virtuous co-females delighted to pity." "In these numbers dishonor was always presented as the equivalent of death" (p. 44).

Harry Von Tilzer (1872–1946) and Arthur Lamb's "A Bird in a Gilded Cage" expressed the same moral. Tilzer had been singing in circus and burlesque shows since the age of 14. He became a vaudeville performer in Chicago after a stint in the circus, and in 1891 found his way to New York with $1.65 in his pocket where he became a saloon pianist. Soon, he decided to try his hand at the songwriting business, and when his song "My Old New Hampshire Home" became a big hit, the publishing firm of Shapiro and Bernstein invited him to become a partner. In 1902, Von Tilzer left the firm and organized his own publishing house on 28th Street, producing seven major hits in his first four years. He also made an uncanny find by hiring the 16-year-old Irving Berlin as a song plugger. Unlike Harris and Dresser, who preferred writing sentimental ballads, Von Tilzer proved not only versatile but prolific. He reportedly composed and published more than 100 songs, which sold more than a half-million copies each, as well as a number of multimillion copy works.

In 1900, he penned the music that became the anthem not only for Tin Pan Alley, but for the entire Gilded Age. Songs about women either bought or betrayed were central issues in Victorian America. The titles of some gained such enduring cultural force that they remain in our social discourse: "She May Have Seen Better Days" (1894), "Mother Was a Lady" (1896), "She Is More Pitied Than to Be Censured" (1898), and of course the moral ideal of an era obsessed with female purity, "Only a Bird in a Gilded Cage." In the song a woman betrays her gender by marrying for wealth, which not only automatically sentenced her to be unhappy, but to die early as well:

> A tall marble monument marked the grave
> Of one who'd been fashion's queen;
> And I thought, "She is happier here at rest,
> Than to have people say when seen:
> (Chorus): A beautiful sight to see ...
> And her beauty was sold for an old man's gold
> She's only a bird in a gilded cage.

Von Tilzer went on to compose songs such as "Down Where the Wurzburger Flows" (1902), which began a craze for drinking songs; "On a Sunday Afternoon" (same year), a waltz; "Good-bye, Eliza Jane" (1903), one of several ragtime influenced songs; "Wait Till the Sun Shines Nellie" (1905), still a hit with barbershop quartets; and "I Want a Girl Just Like the Girl That Married Dear Old Dad," which once again extolled the virtues of Mother; and a number of coon songs such as "Down Where the Cotton Blossoms Grow" (1901).

Lines from these songs quickly entered social consciousness as well. *And the Band Played On* became the title of a well-publicized book and movie about the appearance and early indifference to AIDS in the United States. The imagery of "A Bird in a Gilded Cage," which was first about prostitution and then altered, still holds a compelling image for marriages of financial convenience: "her beauty was sold for an old man's gold." "Sweet Sixteen" and "Take Me Out to the Ball Game" remain part of common conversation more than a century later. Many Americans can still sing or hum some of these works.

The first years of Tin Pan Alley also saw the emergence of a more sophisticated type of popular song, with more intricate melodies and complex harmonies imitative of European vocal music. Enduring still as a perennial wedding favorite is Reginald De Koven's "O Promise Me" (1889) from the opera *Robin Hood*. Nothing in this song suggests syncopation, a waltz, or a march. Its style harkens back to the songs of Robert Schumann and Franz Abt with its repeated chords in the right hand and a harmonic vocabulary far richer that Charles K. Harris or Harry Von Tilzer. Even more popular during the period were the songs of Victor Herbert, discussed previously, most notably "Ah! Sweet Mystery of Life." Herbert became one of the rare Gilded Age composers who managed to write in an idiom popular enough to appeal to millions while containing enough depth for more sophisticated audiences. Not surprisingly, his songs, which originated in Broadway operetta, were marketed by the Tin Pan Alley firm of M. Witmark & Sons. Ethelbert Nevin (1862–1901) enjoyed a brief career as a concert pianist. His "The Rosary" (1898) gained prominence as a popular parlor song, a recital piece for opera singers, and a favorite religious song. Like De Koven, Carrie Jacobs-Bond (1862–1946) continues to have an audience with wedding goers in her "I Love You Truly" (1906), which surpassed many of the Tin Pan Alley favorites in popularity.

COON SONGS

The coon song, along with the cakewalk, and ragtime first appeared in vaudeville and musical comedy and soon entered the mainstream of American culture during the 1890s. Derived mostly from the minstrel show—both black and white—the new brash, catchy sounds increasingly appealed to Americans from all walks of life. Even though the minstrel show would soon be eclipsed by vaudeville and musical comedy, it remained popular in the 1890s. After

1880, its plantation and minstrel songs, sung in dialect, powerfully influenced American popular song. During that decade, a new character had appeared in these shows that became enshrined in the repertoire of Tin Pan Alley: the "coon," a lazy, irresponsible black male, often hostile as well. The music of the coon song could take any form, from waltz to ragtime, but the texts were uniformly based on disparaging racial stereotypes The term entered mainstream consciousness when several songs used the word in their titles: "New Coon in Town" (Paul Allen, 1883), "The Whistling Coon" (Sam Devere, 1888), and "Little Alabama Coon" (Hattie Star, 1893), all written by whites. More than 600 coon songs appeared in the 1890s, and some sold astonishingly well, such as Fred Fisher's "If the Man on the Moon Were a Coon," with more than three million sales.

The coon song was a genre of American novelty song that flourished from about 1880 to the end of World War I. Musically, it reflects the verses-chorus form of contemporary Tin Pan Alley Songs, with the main melodic material in the chorus. It is generally sung at a lively tempo, often with syncopations. Even though it predates ragtime, it became associated with the rhythmic energy of ragtime. After ragtime entered national prominence in the 1890s, elements from it were grafted onto the coon song, boosting its popularity enormously.

Coon songs served Victorian society on a number of levels. Their appeal came not just from the catchy music, but the fact that they dealt with topics banned by the repressive Victorian culture, topics that were rarely voiced explicitly in Tin Pan Alley songs. Most obviously, they affirmed Jim Crow segregation, currently being enacted in the South. By extension, the same economic/class apartheid could apply to the millions of southern European immigrants flooding into the Northeast at the same time, many of whose sole advantage over African Americans was that they were white. On another level, the coon song's focus on sexuality, violence, gambling, and libertinism was presented behind the cloak of the burnt-cork mask, a strategy tolerated by whites as blacks were seen as more shiftless, sexual, and violent. One can argue, however, that the instinctive powerful forces of sexuality, poverty, and crime in American culture, refusing to remain suppressed, were pushing up from the collective unconscious through the coon songs into the general public awareness. Song such as "I Got Mine," "Pump Away Joseph," and "A Red Hot Member" often typified the "red hot" coon and his "honey" with sexual titillation and bawdy behavior. Seeing blacks in this inferior light also helped justify the growing racism as segregation, social restrictions, and lynchings spread in the United States. In addition, projecting these qualities onto African Americans enabled white Americans to maintain their own denials about the realities of racism, prostitution, venereal disease, and social inequities.

White female "coon shouters" became favorites of the vaudeville stage in the years straddling the century, most prominent of whom was May Irwin (1862–1938). Blond, full-figured, and buxom, she learned her trade in vaudeville, becoming a favorite at Tony Pastor's theater before striking out on her own. Her rendition of Charles E. Treviathan's "The Bully Song" in *The Widow Jones* in 1895 did much to popularize the genre and the stereotype of the razor-carrying, jealously hostile black male. The song expounds all the common racist imagery of coon songs, telling of an urban black bully who brandishes a razor and steals watermelons. Other hits of hers such as "Leave Your Razors at the Door" (1899) and "I'm the Toughest, Toughest Coon" (1904) kept her in the limelight for more than 30 years.

Black composers also penned coon songs. Most well known was minstrel songwriter Ernest Hogan (c.1860–1909) who had been the sidekick to Bert Williams in minstrel shows before Williams teamed up with Walker. Hogan's big hit in 1896, "All Coons Look Alike to Me," sold like wildfire and did much to extend the popularity of the ragtime coon song. The demeaning message was unmistakable:

> All coons look alike to me
> I've got another beau, you see
> And he's just as good to me as you, Nig! Ever tried to be.
> He spends his money free ...
> So I don't like you no-how.
> All coons look alike to me.

The work became the test piece for the finals of the Ragtime World Competition in New York in January, 1900. The piece also contained the earliest association of the word "rag" with instrumental music. The second chorus of the song has the option "Choice Chorus, with Negro 'Rag' Accompaniment, Arr. By Max Hoffman." Conventional coon song accompaniment involved simple um-pah movements, whereas "rag" accompaniment used an accented syncopation. Other black showmen harshly criticized Hogan for the work and he later regretted having written it.

RAGTIME

The same years that saw the appearance of composers, such as Hogan and Haney, and black actors, such as Robert Cole, Will Marion Cook, the Johnson brothers, and Bert Williams, also gave rise to a distinctive style of black entertainment music—ragtime. This new music more directly expressed the individuality of black life and personality than the white-dominated Broadway musicals. Emboldened by the energy and vitality of the music, Cook in his 1898 song, "Darktown is Out Tonight," went so far as to predict that African American music would spread throughout American culture in the twentieth century:

> Never min', for the time
> Comin' mighty soon
> When the best like the rest
> Gwine a-be singin' coon.

The shifting mores of Gilded Age culture indeed made it seem like soon everyone would be "singin' coon." Fueling this shift was the work of the rising generation of black musicians such as Cole, Cook, and others who had been born in freedom and felt unconstrained to develop and peddle the new black secular music.

By the time Cook composed his song, ample evidence already existed to support his claim. The first known printed use of the term *rag* had appeared in black Kansas newspapers from 1894, referring to both dance, piano, and vocal styles. When distinctively syncopated songs were published with the "ragtime" label in 1896, the styles was already familiar to many. Other early references to rag-music players describe anonymous drifters in the South and Midwest who played the piano in cheap riverside dives, eating places, honky-tonks, and saloons, working for cheap wages or sometimes only for tips. As canny entertainment business owners began to see that they could substitute a cheaper pianist for a dance band, the practice spread. The fact that the early ragtime piano players read music as well as played by ear stimulated the new styles, especially when the musicians began to catch on to the profits possible in publishing sheet music.

The new music grew spontaneously out of the African American experience. The style of piano-rag music had emerged first in the dance-music practices of slaves, where the percussive element for antebellum fiddle and banjo playing had been the foot stomping and patting of the onlookers. When young itinerant black pianists found employment in the saloons and black entertainment places, they transferred this musical energy to the keyboard. In piano-rag music, the left hand assumed the task of the stomping and patting while the right hand played the syncopated melodies. With the black minstrel troupes emerging after emancipation, this new style of ragged music naturally made its way into the minstrel shows. By the late 1880s, marches for the shows with syncopated, ragtime-like rhythms found publication in New York. At the same time, blackface minstrels throughout the country began ragging tunes, especially coon songs. For the fall season of 1898, ragtime songs began appearing on the musical stage. Instrumental ragtime began circulating in mechanical reproductions, piano rolls and cylinder recordings, in addition to sheet music.

It was the combination of the syncopated coon song with the instrumental cakewalk that produced the rhythmically invigorating music. With roots in African tradition, the cakewalk had been a competition during slavery times when couples danced to show the fanciest strutting, with the winners receiving a cake or some other prize. By1890, the cakewalk had migrated to the musical stage, electrified by the new driving syncopation, which accompanied the cakewalking, now called ragtime. Until then the published cakewalks had been unsyncopated, but after mid-decade, white songwriters incorporated the rag-style syncopation in their songs. Today we identify ragtime almost exclusively with music for the piano, but during its heyday it was a flourishing branch of Tin Pan Alley's songs. A survey of more than 200 ragtime-related books and articles published between 1896 and 1920 reveals only 21 that refer to piano music.[5] Ragtime historian Rudi Blesh argues that perhaps less than 10 percent of what Gilded Age listeners understood as ragtime was piano music. By 1898, the seductive rag rhythms had begun pushing the previously popular ballads and waltzes out of the spotlight, and ragtime songs began finding their way into Broadway revues and musical comedies. Popular song writers, trying to cash in on the new craze, inundated America with ragtime, usually in forgettable songs remembered more for their novelty titles than musical interest, such as "Dish Rag," "Turkish Towel Rag," and "Wagner Couldn't Write a Ragtime Song." Through the second decade of the new century, the publishers of Tin Pan Alley issued thousands of songs in the spirit, if not the style, of ragtime.

Many writers of the day give Benjamin Robertson Harney (1871–1938) credit for bringing ragtime and ragtime songs to New York. While growing up in Kentucky, he undoubtedly heard the new vibrant ragtime music in saloons before he finally appeared at Tony Pastor's in 1897, billed the "Inventor of Ragtime." His *Ragtime Instructor* appeared the same year as the first method book for teaching the new syncopated piano style. His most famous songs included "You've Been a Good Old Wagon But You Done Broke Down" (1895), "Mr. Johnson Turn Me Loose" (1896), and perhaps his most popular song, "The Cakewalk in the Sky" (1899), widely accepted as the first ragtime song.

If we accept the common definition of early ragtime, sometimes called the "cakewalk figure," as the use of a syncopated treble melody over a study beat of the piano's left hand, however, then we have a terminological misfit with ragtime songs. The problem is that none of these three songs by Harney have any more syncopation in their melody than many contemporary minstrel, cakewalk, or George M. Cohan songs. Nor do the three big enduring ragtime hits,

"A Hot Time in the Old Town Tonight" (Theodore Metz, 1896), "Hello! Ma Baby" (Joe Howard, 1899), and "Bill Bailey, Won't You Please Come Home?" (H. Cannon, 1902). "Hello! Ma Baby" is not identified on the cover as a ragtime song, but when it came out in a piano version it was labeled "Rag-Time March," and permanently linked to ragtime by contemporary writers. What identified the song as ragtime to many contemporaries was its energy and subtle allusion to black women as "honey." Also characteristic of ragtime is its opening syncopation in the melody, which follows the pattern short-long-short and subsequently displaces the following notes in the treble from sounding on the downbeat of the measure. What we see now is that this song and all the other well-known ragtime songs merely suggest the rhythmic spirit and culture of ragtime, which makes it difficult to separate songs described as ragtime songs from coon songs found in minstrel and vaudeville shows.

Some of the most enduringly popular songs of the era appeared then, such as Theodore A. Metz's "A Hot Time in the Old Town Tonight" (1896), Kerry Mills's "At a Georgia Camp Meeting" (1897), Howard and Emerson's "Hello! Ma Baby" (1899), and H. Cannon's "Bill Bailey, Won't You Please Come Home?" (1902). Black composers produced such hits as James T. Brymn's "Cuban Cake Walk," Cook's "Bon Bon Buddy," and "Darktown is Out Tonight," Cole and Johnson's "When the Band Plays Ragtime," and Fred Stone's "My Ragtime Baby." By 1900, more than 100 cakewalks were published, most labeled with terms such as "cake walk march," "two-step," and "ragtime cake walk."

RAGTIME PIANO

Like ragtime songs, instrumental ragtime music emerged out of the same fertile cultural mix that produced ragtime songs. It was first heard in the bustling frontier towns of the central Midwest, which were rapidly growing and thriving from the commerce up and down the Mississippi. St. Louis was the economic and musical center of all this new musical activity. Young black musicians were drawn there by the numerous opportunities for entertainment and work in the sporting sector of town filled with pleasure houses and honky-tonk saloons on Chestnut and Market Streets. Dominating this jumping underworld was the Silver Dollar Saloon, operated by the notorious "Honest John" Turpin. The Silver Dollar typified the places found in many cities where "the joints rang with the archaic, jangling, jig-piano syncopations that in only a few years would be a developed music to be dubbed ragtime."[6]

Around 1885, a talented young man of 17 named Scott Joplin (1868–1917) arrived in St. Louis and began frequenting Honest John's Silver Dollar Saloon. Born on the Texas side of Texarkana, he inherited his musical talents from his parents. His mother played the piano and his father, an ex-slave, played the violin, performing popular nineteenth-century dance music, as well as traditional fiddle tunes. Scott benefited from free piano lessons from Julius Weiss, a German émigré in Texarkana, who instilled in him a love for European and more artistic musical styles. Scott soon developed into a proficient pianist and was playing in the neighborhood; he also sang in a vocal quartet as well as a touring minstrel troupe. After working in St. Louis, he traveled in 1893 to the World's Columbian Chicago Exposition where he found ample opportunity to perform among the many ragtime musicians. When the fair ended in October, he returned to St. Louis and then moved to Sedalia in central Missouri, where he lived until 1901.

When Scott Joplin moved to Sedalia in 1894, it was a thriving railroad community of 15,000. The citizens and many visitors found a vibrant town of 13 schools, 20 churches, 28 secret and benevolent societies, an orchestra and a band, five newspapers, and saloons, pool halls, dance halls, and brothels. Music played in these places knew no racial barriers and cross-pollinated among players and styles. Even though the city was officially segregated, Sedalia was much more relaxed and moderate in its racial attitudes, which only further fueled the musical crosscurrents. Wood's Opera House allowed both blacks and whites (segregated by areas) to see the same traveling minstrel troupes, wind bands, singers, and operetta companies.

Joplin became the most talented, enduring composer of ragtime piano, a style of music that had probably been known to the pianists of the St. Louis/central Missouri region since he had moved there in the mid-1880s. Not until the Chicago World's Fair, however, did it break out into the wider American public. Even so, not until the end of the century did any of these rags get published. In 1897, William Krell's *Mississippi Rag* was the first instrumental rag to be printed, one year after the initial ragtime coon songs appeared. Later that year, with Honest John's son Tom Turpin's *Harlem Rag*, a black composer found publication of an instrumental rag. This piece demonstrates an artistic maturity and sophistication well ahead of contemporary cakewalks, indicating that the performer's ragtime had been well established for some time. Joplin had published two songs and three piano pieces in 1895, but they revealed little of the infectious creativity of his mature rags.

Soon another critical figure for the history of ragtime enters the narrative. John Stark (1841–1927) was an ex-farmer and pioneer who had earlier moved to Sedalia and opened a music store, where he also published music. When he heard Joplin play his piano rags at the Maple Leaf Club, Stark sensed here was new music with considerable economic potential. In 1899, he offered Joplin a royalty contract, paying him one cent per copy, an unusual business arrangement, as most popular compositions were sold outright for not more than 25 dollars. The first year the work sold only about 400 copies. By 1909, however, the public had eagerly purchased more than half a million copies, earning Joplin the reputation as "King of Ragtime" until the title passed later to Irving Berlin. Joplin became one of a trio of the three major piano ragtime composers, including James Scott (1886–1938) and Joseph Lamb (1887–1960).

Ragtime music supposedly takes its name from the "ragging" of the rhythm—the idiomatic syncopation or displacement of the musical stresses from the duple meter's alternating strong and weak beats. A more recent theory, however, suggests that ragtime derived its name from the practice of black dancers raising handkerchiefs (rags) to begin a dance—ragtime. Joplin later objected to the demeaning idea in his *School of Ragtime:* "What is scurrilously called ragtime is an invention that is here to stay." He asserted, slightly defensively, "Syncopations are no indication of light or trashy music, and to shy bricks at 'hateful ragtime' no longer passes for musical culture."[7] Joplin penned his *School* to define what had originated as an oral music tradition and only recently had assumed written form. Now, ragtime's "weird and intoxicating effect" could be achieved by any pianist willing to master the notation through careful practice. In a series of easily grasped exercises, Joplin demonstrates how syncopation involves traditional notation where the sixteenth notes are connected by a tie against a strict beat in the left hand. In his examples, Joplin removed the ties and added dotted lines between the staves, which enabled the pianist to see exactly the proper alignments between notes when observing the ties, which would give "each note its proper time." These comments and others, as Richard Crawford points out, helped bridge the distance between styles of an oral tradition and classic ragtime, which is composers' music, as opposed to performer's music.[8]

Soon Stark began to advertise his publications as "classic rags" to distinguish the artistic quality of Joplin, Scott, and Lamb from the ragtime songs and piano novelties published by Tin Pan Alley. This term, originally a marketing device for Stark's publications, sought to express Joplin and other's aspirations to link their works to the sacralized, hallowed tradition of European classical music. The term also came to denote music whose artistic quality aimed to transcend the marketplace. The publications attempted to obscure ragtime's African American origins. Nowhere is this more in evidence than the shift in cover art for the rags. The cover for the *Maple Leaf Rag* had depicted two strutting black couples, but the cover of *Gladiolus Rag* (genteel titles themselves seeking some Victorian respectability) pictures an attractive young white woman clothed in a flowered necklace over a flowing gown draped in blossoms.

Joplin insisted that ragtime not be played too fast, "Play slowly until you catch the swing, and never play ragtime fast at any time." An inscription on the *Gladiolus Rag,* like most of them published by Stark insisted: "Not fast, not fast, not fast." So, as Crawford observes, sheet-music buyers could enjoy the thrill of slightly naughty music that combined flowers, dancing, female charm, and a slight sensuality—all properly restrained by a strict tempo. It seems quite clear that Joplin intended to convey the idea that artistic beauty and elegance could be found in black music as well as classical.[9]

In these classic rags Joplin and others sought to soften the racial cast of ragtime and find acceptance in the world of white Eurocentric music. This loosening of the artistic boundaries gradually accelerated during the twentieth century between popular and classical when musicians of the cultivated and folk spheres contested the artistic elitism of classical composers and performers. This crossover activity, as it came to be known, gained impetus in the 1920s when Gershwin performed his music in the concert hall and later when opera singers began making popular albums. The African American origins of jazz and ragtime further intensified the whole debate, inserting a racial component into the controversy. Although the supporters of classical music viewed this contamination with alarm, the popular musicians began to gain some respectability not seen before. Scott Joplin, like Will Marion Cook, was at the forefront of this development: "a black composer-performer earning a living in the popular sphere, steeped in the traditional sphere, and seeing his music's acceptance in the classical sphere."[10] Joplin asserted that black music contained the same artistic dignity, and thus merit, as European music, and deserved to be respected as such.

A *rag* such as Joplin composed—strictly speaking—is an instrumental, syncopated composition following the formal conventions of a march. *Ragtime* is a much more inclusive term and generally applies to almost any syncopated music. Like the march, ragtime has a duple time signature, and many rags (Joplin's *Maple Leaf Rag* included) are marked *"tempo di marcia"* or "in slow march time." The music's roots lay in the performer's music of earlier in the nineteenth century when black musicians grafted African syncopations onto the existing conventions of the duple-meter march and the two step. Eubie Blake recalled hearing bands as a child in Baltimore: "I used to hear colored bands going to the funerals. On the way over they'd play the funeral march straight, but coming back they'd rag the hell out of the music. So I started playing my music like that."[11] Jelly Roll Morton (1855–1941) similarly described ragging a Sousa march. Harlem Renaissance poet Paul Laurence Dunbar (1821–1906) wrote as well:

> But hit's Sousa played in ragtime, an' hit's Rastus on Parade,
> W'en de colo'd ban' comes ma'chin' down de street.[12]

The four-bar phrases, sectional repetitions, and 16-bar strains provided a sturdy structure that Joplin and many other musicians filled with the engaging lyricism and infectious rhythms of African American folk tradition.

Joplin's *Maple Leaf Rag* proved a milestone in American music history. John Stark published it in 1899 in Sedalia, and, even though it sold slowly at first, sales reportedly grew to more than a million. Soon after its appearance ragtime pianists from all over were playing it to great applause from whites as well as blacks, producing a national craze. Based on the black oral tradition, the *Maple Leaf Rag* became one of the first enduring crossover compositions, securing a beloved niche in the inner sanctum of Victorian America, the parlor, and did much to spread the toe-tapping, rhythmically elegant music throughout the country. In the 1970s, the piece also spearheaded the classic ragtime revival.

The quality that elevated Joplin's rags above similar works by his contemporaries lay somehow in his synthesis of rhythmic and melodic interplay. The formal structure inherited from the familiar march provided a sturdy and predictable framework that allowed Joplin and others to give reign to the infectious rhythmic energy. The pitches establish their own musical displacement in addition to the syncopations. The left hand offers an unbending anchor supporting the right hand's intricacies while the beat marches on inexorably, propelled forward by the harmonic motion. The *Maple Leaf Rag* contains four strains, each 16 bars long, each repeated at least once, which became the standard format for rags afterwards. But the musical details reveal an artistic imagination that accounts for much of the work's popularity.

Joplin followed the *Maple Leaf Rag* with a number of successes such as *The Easy Winners* (1901), *Elite Syncopations* (1902), and *The Entertainer* (1902), in which he produced works that he called "real ragtime of the higher class." Like classic works in any genre, they belie the notion that ragtime is a carefree, frivolous music, fit only for rowdy saloons or background cocktail music. Joplin adroitly blends the refined elegance of the Eurocentric musical tradition of moderate tempos and restrained moods with the deep sadness of the African American slavery experience. What comes through much of this music is an elegant sophistication tinged with sadness, a feeling saved from sentimentality by its strong rhythmic pulse.

Even though Joplin holds the undisputed title of King of Ragtime, others contributed significantly to its popularity. While working as a window washer at age 16 for a music store in Carthage, Missouri, James Sylvester Scott (1886–1938) began playing the piano. The owner soon was printing his rags when he met Joplin and then Stark, who became his principal publisher. In works such as *Frog Legs Rag* (1906) and *Grace and Beauty* (1909), he expanded on Joplin's virtuosity and musical sophistication, incorporating black elements such as blue notes and call-and-response patterns, as well as ingenious chromatic voice-leading. Scott's later rags are among the most demanding of all published piano ragtime.

That Joseph F. Lamb (1887–1960) succeeded as well as he did with his rags is a credit to his talent and perseverance, for little about his background, location, career, or race prepared him for becoming a major ragtime composer. Not only did he live in Brooklyn, he never formally studied music, worked in Manhattan's garment district, and was white. While still a teenager, he got in contact with Joplin and Stark, who published Lamb's first rag, *Sensation*. His works reflect the influence of Joplin, although Lamb's rags have an untypical restraint and introspective gentility. Lamb fashioned the rag into a more intimate composition, such as in the *Alaskan Rag* (published posthumously), where gracefully arching arpeggios expand on the chromatic harmony. Two of his most successful rags were *American Beauty* (1913) and *Ragtime Nightingale* (1915).

Like Lamb, Artie Matthews (1888–1959) lived to see ragtime recede from American musical life and start to make a comeback. Raised in the ragtime country of Springfield, Missouri, at age 16 he discovered his passion for the invigorating new music at the St. Louis World's Fair of 1904. He returned there three years later as a professional ragtime performer and would make his living as a performer and composer. Matthews established his reputation with a series of five *Pastime Rags* (1913–1920) published by the Stark Music Company of St. Louis. His classical orientation is indicated by the directions "don't fake" and "not fast." The pieces display an astonishing variety of rhythm and chromatic texture, including tango, habanera, and barrelhouse, as well as dissonant tone clusters.

RAGTIME BREAKS OUT

As the piano ragtime craze spread during the first decade of the new century, it cross-fertilized and stimulated three other areas in America's musical life: the piano, ensemble music, and the songs of Tin Pan Alley. Not surprisingly, piano sales rose steeply in the heyday of ragtime and Tin Pan Alley. In 1870, one of every 1,540 Americans bought a new piano; in 1890 one of 874; and cresting in 1910, the heyday of the instrument as well as of Tin Pan Alley, 350,000 pianos were produced, one for every 252 citizens. But many who attempted to play ragtime from the music found themselves stymied by the difficulty of the works, so they turned to mechanical reproduction, the player piano, which was introduced in 1897. For this reason, much of ragtime entered the American parlor first in piano rolls, which were either recorded from pianists, often by the composer himself, or arranged by punching the paper rolls. Indeed, many rags, including one by Joplin, never found publication in sheet music form but were issued only in piano rolls.

Of course the compelling, spirited music invoked the wrath of the defenders of Victorian gentility, who saw in the new sounds degradation and licentiousness. The *Musical Courier* of New York in 1899 thundered: "A wave of vulgar, filthy and suggestive music has inundated the land. The pabulum of theater and summer hotel is 'coon music.' Nothing but ragtime prevails, and the cakewalk with its obscene posturing, its lewd gestures."[13] As moralists of every generation, it feared for the purity of the young. "Our children, our young men and women, are continually exposed to the contiguity, to the monotonous attrition of this vulgarizing music. It is artistically and orally depressing and should be suppressed by press and pulpit." Ivan Narodny, writing in the *New York Evening Post* later, in 1916, claimed it evoked "the odor of the saloon, the smell of the backyard and subways. Its style is decadent." The controversy only swelled the enthusiasm.

The first years of the new decade saw the appearance of the next generation of piano ragtime players, who began to transform classic ragtime into jazz. For a time the two terms were used indiscriminately. The most important of these pianists were Ferdinand Joseph "Jelly Roll" Morton (1890–1941, né La Menthe), James P. Johnson (1891–1955), and James Hubert "Eubie" Blake (1883–1983). Born as a New Orleans Creole, Jelly Roll Morton started playing professionally in the notorious Storyville District in 1902 when he was only 17. Growing up in the rich musical gumbo of the city, his music and career drew on the splendid variety of ragtime, blues, gospel, and early jazz, stewing them all together in his own performing and compositions. For these reasons he serves as central figure in the new emerging jazz idiom. He later clearly distinguished between the new style and the older ragtime. His historic recordings, with commentary, made for the Library of Congress in the late 1930s, provide valuable insights into these distinctions and remain a valuable source of insight into the evolution from ragtime to jazz. After performing at the St. Louis World's Fair in 1904, he played all over the country, returning to Chicago, where he made his first recording in 1922. Most of his works, variously titled, "rags," "blues," and "stomps" date from the post-ragtime era, but as a performer he played a critical role in the dissemination of the rag styles. His best-known rags are *Frog-I-More Rag, Kansas City Stomp*, and *King Porter Stomp*.

Eubie Blake was born in the red-light district of Baltimore to a pious mother who called ragtime the music of the devil. It is ironic that she bought Eubie piano lessons so that he could play in church. Instead, he snuck out each night over the back fence and got a job about age 15 in one of the bawdy houses. After composing some early rags such as *Charleston Rag* (1898), he went on to a long and successful career that embraced performing, composing, lecturing, publishing, and touring. He not only wrote many piano rags, but more than 300 songs, and a number of Broadway shows, including *Shuffle Along*, with words by the singer Noble Sissle whom he met in 1915. The show is credited with helping inaugurate the Harlem Renaissance in the 1920s.

James P. Johnson (1894–1955), like Eubie Blake, grew up on the East Coast in Brunswick, New Jersey, and like Blake enriched classic ragtime with the more jazz-oriented aspects such as the blues and the driving left-hand style known as stride piano. By blending ragtime elements such as stride piano with syncopated right-hand figurations, James P. and others energized ragtime, transforming it into early jazz with its faster tempo, driving beat, and an elaborated melodic line. Among his early ragtime works are *Caprice Rag* (1914) and *Harlem Strut* (1917).

Bands and orchestras also jumped on the ragtime craze. All types and sizes of brass ensembles and orchestras added the vigorous new music to their programs, often drawing on the new stock arrangements publishers quickly turned out to meet the demand. Many sheet music rags advertised the availability of the piece as "published for band, orchestra, mandolin, guitar, accordion" and more. Sousa was one of the first to see ragtime's potential for enriching his repertoire and added it to his programs in the early 1890s. His band introduced ragtime to many European audiences in his tour of 1900 with arrangements of works such as "Smokey Mokes," and "Bunch o' Blackberries." He was also one of the first to record ragtime for band with his version of Kerry Mill's popular ragtime song "At a Georgia Camp Meeting" in 1908.

Aptly, the death of Scott Joplin in 1917 signaled the end of vogue for ragtime music as the new jazz began to supplant it. By the time the jazz era burst into full swing after the war, ragtime—mainly a composer's art—with its restraint, polish, and elegant rhythms quickly began to recede from the stage, soon to vanish from public awareness until the revival of the 1970s. It was in the New York songs of a brash new émigré that ragtime would find its most complete transformation.

The Gilt Fades

The émigré mentioned at the end of chapter 6 turned out to be an unknown 23-year-old Russian Jewish immigrant, Irving Berlin (1888–1989). Berlin, like millions of others, moved to New York, which more than ever was *the* musical and entertainment capitol of the country. Here the Gilded Age had found its music published and here the dawning jazz age would break into general consciousness. The appearance in 1911 of his "Alexander's Ragtime Band" became the swan song of ragtime and the Gilded Age, even if it did briefly boost interest in the new music. That song made Berlin the most celebrated songwriter of his day and musical spokesman for ragtime. He more than any other composer effected a major shift in the way ragtime was perceived, which ushered its language and spirit into the mainstream of American popular song.

Raised in Manhattan's Lower East Side, Berlin had been eking out a living since age 16 plugging songs for Harry Von Tilzer and writing ragtime songs of his own—ragtime as sung through Tin Pan Alley eyes. He probably never heard true ragtime played by the great black pianists of his day, but he was well acquainted with the popular ragtime songs that ripped off superficial elements of ragtime rhythm and pasted them onto otherwise standard popular songs.

Berlin's early songs, composed in the years 1907–1917, serve as a fascinating microcosmic mirror of the shift from the elegance of Tin Pan Alley songs into the heady new spirit of ragtime, broadening out with the music of the Jazz Age after World War I. These songs contain an array of styles, encompassing older Victorian ballads, novelty songs, ragtime songs, and show songs.

The traditional songs symbolized the spirit of the Gilded Age, and others captured the emergence of a new, liberated society. Old fashioned waltzes and ballads such as "Dreams, Just Dreams" and "I Love You More Each Day" are mixed with comic novelties such as "If You Don't Want My Peaches (You'd Better Stop Shaking My Tree")" and "Yiddle, on Your Fiddle, Play Some Ragtime." Berlin's early songs include not only coon songs, but German, Italian, and Jewish protagonists, not surprising given Berlin's own Jewish heritage. In "Sweet Marie, Make-a Rag-a-time Dance Wid Me" (1910, with Ted Snyder), the narrator Tony feels desperate to get his beloved Marie to dance ragtime: "If you love-a Tony nice-a fine, Make-a noise-a like-a rag-a time," he sings in the standard pseudo-Italian dialect. Ragtime also raised immigrant consciousness by bringing ethnic songs into mainstream American musical life. For millions of immigrants, ragtime became their passport into American life.

Until 1911, ragtime songs were inexorably identified with African American life and culture, including "Alexander's Ragtime Band." Richard Crawford describes the subtle racial connotations in the song that would have been clear to contemporary audiences. The name Alexander was well known as a black minstrel character; the song's energetic, rousing mood was associated with the excitement of black performances. Soon, however, Berlin made a critical turning point in his songs. In "That Mysterious Rag," published in August after "Alexander's Ragtime Band," there is no black protagonist and none appear in any later Berlin songs. The piece also avoids the crude racial language of early ragtime songs. Moreover, at about the same time, Berlin began preferring the word "syncopated" over "ragtime" to describe his songs. Now, syncopated rhythm from black folk culture was assimilated from ragtime into the musical language of Tin Pan Alley song. Ragtime no longer was portrayed as a caustic racial joke, but as a song of irresistible instinctual power, ready to seize control of the singer or dancer and throw them into bawdy behavior. The verse explains that the infectious, unforgettable rhythms invade even sleep, bewitching the character like a drug. The chorus offers a stern warning:

> That mysterious rag.
> While awake or while you're a-slumbering.
> You're saying,
> Keep playing
> That mysterious drag,
> Are you listenin'?
> Are you listenin'?
> Look! Look! You're whistlin'
> That mysterious rag.
> Sneaky, freaky, ever melodious
> Mysterious rag.

Through these early songs, Berlin uses ragtime to narrate how a diverse immigrant population can come together to forge an American nation, where all are liberated from the restrictive social mores and legal barriers of the old world. Ragtime invites, indeed, pulls everyone to "Come on and hear" this exciting new music. Listening to Alexander's band starts everyone's toes a tap-pin', bubbling over with high spirits; it does not recognize or respect class or ethnic distinctions; it is the great equalizer, enticing the commonest laborer with the same joyful rhythms as the most dignified Manhattan socialite. This new, intoxicating music came to represent the spirit of social liberation, first in New York, then elsewhere.

CLASSICAL MUSIC

New York also became the birthplace for modernism in art music. In 1915, Edgard Varèse (1883–1965), already a modernist, avant-garde radical, arrived there from France. In the 1920s, he would produce a series of innovative com-positions influential in their rhythmic complexity, use of percussion, free atonality, and forms not relying on harmonic progression or thematic develop-ment for their organization. Even before World War I, he began using the term *organized sound* for his works rather than *music*. The only other serious Ameri-can composer writing contemporary music was Leo Ornstein (1893–2002), who emigrated from Ukraine to New York in 1907. In 1913, he wrote his first modernist compositions, *Dwarf Suite* and *Wild Men's Dance (Danse sauvage)*. His series of four recitals at the Bandbox Theatre in 1915 quickly led to Orn-stein becoming a major voice of the new music.

Modernism was breaking into the visual arts as well. In 1903, Alfred Stieglitz introduced a quarterly publication called *Camera Work*, which ran for 50 issues, defining the new art in photography. More influential was his Gallery 291 on Lower Fifth Avenue that he opened in 1905 and that became ground zero for modernist activity. The exhibitions included the first shows in the United States of the work of Henri Matisse, Henri de Toulouse-Lautrec, Paul Cézanne, and Pablo Picasso. The Gallery was also a gathering place for the new dadists. A decisive event in the development of American art occurred with the exhibition in 1913 at the Sixty-ninth Regiment Armory, which exposed the American pub-lic for the first time to European modernism. Beginning with J.A.D. Ingres and Eugène Delacroix, the exhibition displayed works by impressionists, symbolists, postimpressionists, fauves, and cubists. Diaghilev's Ballets Russes had a cele-brated American tour in 1916, sans *The Rite of Spring*. New poets Carl Sandburg, T. S. Eliot, and Ezra Pound were being published and read. Even more fascinat-ing, many Americans were just discovering the "talking cure" of Freud.

All of this modernist activity in New York quickly displaced Boston as the center of American art music. Dismissing the Gilded Age mandate to compose and perform works comfortably within the structures of inherited tradition, composers slowly began embracing modernism. Most important here was the adamant rejection of cultural authority, a revolt against convention, antiromanticism, fragmentation, modest experimentation, and new theories of art such as naturalism, symbolism, impressionism, futurism, neoclassicism, and expressionism. Artists sought to nurture individuality and resist external, academic controls, which were seen as sterile tradition or psychological/sexual repression. As Edith Wharton noted, there was a "dread of doing what has been done before," a "fear of being unoriginal."[1]

No American concert composer of the period approached the radicalism of Eliot, Pound, or Stieglitz. The real push for new music came from Europe, and by the mid-1910s new European works, alongside their American counterparts, began to appear on selected programs. Between 1908 and 1911, New York heard Mahler's First, Second, and Fourth Symphonies under the composer's baton. Debussy's *Pelléas et Mélisande* was performed first in New York, then in Boston, in 1912, which received it more graciously. In 1914, the Boston Symphony Orchestra gave Schoenberg's *Five Pieces for Orchestra* its American premiere, which outraged Boston's critics with its atonal harmonic system and its sterile emotional atmosphere. In 1922, Stravinsky's path-breaking works began appearing on American concerts. New York saw two of his ballets, the *Firebird* and *Petrouchka,* as well as the suite from *Pulcinella* and chamber works. In contrast, new French music by Debussy, Ravel, and Erik Satie found positive receptions here.

Contemporary musicians and critics were keenly aware that an era was passing. In 1907, George Chadwick wrote an article that recalls the years 1890–1897 as a kind of golden age (as well as a gilded one). He expressed fond memories of the group of composers of which he was a part, which historians have called the Boston Classicists, especially Paine, Foote, Parker, MacDowell, and Loeffler. They all moved in the same social and musical circles, forming a supportive and engaging artistic salon. After a symphony concert they often were "seen gathered about the same table" in the Tavern Club, reviewing the night's music, "rejoicing in each other's successes, and working for them too." Always ready to deflate overheated egos or puncture puffery, they worked to keep everyone artistically honest. Chadwick wistfully remembers the group as a community of equals who constructed an "invigorating atmosphere of mutual respect and honest criticism," in which "they worked with joy and enthusiasm, knowing that if only their work was good enough it would be pretty sure of a hearing sooner or later."[2]

Critics predictably resisted the new music. Philip Hale, in Boston, granted the "strangely beautiful effects of color" in the Schoenberg pieces, but expressed overall dismay at the sterile, unanchored sounds. New York's Henry Krehbiel most completely articulated and reasserted the boundaries of Gilded Age aesthetics. He rejected the music of Schoenberg and Stravinsky and found Debussy's *Pelléas et Mélisande* monotonous. For him, Richard Strauss was only an opportunist. In Krehbiel's *Chapters of Opera,* he dismissed Strauss's opera *Salome,* where the composer outraged "every sacred instinct of humanity," seeking only effect: "Strauss, to put it mildly, is a sensationalist despite his genius."[3] He insisted that true art must follow the Victorian imperative of sweetness and light, avoiding the vulgar, offensive, and the dissonant, which of course put him at odds with the new music.

Around 1913, the clear genres of American classical music that held during the Gilded Age began to fracture into the multiple musics, genres, and factions that persist today, each with its own practitioners, fans, stars, publicity materials, and institutions. These arose, as we have seen, from clear racial, ethnic, and economic classes during the postbellum period. One only has to list the great names in American classical music, versus the jazz greats, versus the Broadway stars and producers to see how watertight the class divisions were through the first decade of the twentieth century. The classical composers were virtually all white, Protestant males; the ragtime and jazz performers black; and the Broadway stars largely Jewish.

After about 1910, these boundaries began to dissolve. Accelerating this dissolution was the outbreak of World War I, which spawned a wave of anti-German feeling in America. The war rapidly discredited the genteel tradition and ended the optimism of the Gilded Age. The gas warfare, barbed wire, and machine gun, combined with the German atrocities, appalled Americans even before they entered the conflict. The moralism of Gilded Age culture, which had insisted that art serve an edifying, uplifting function, could not be sustained in the face of the carnage and horror.

The effect of all of this on classical music was obvious. Gilded Age musical culture was essentially a German transplant. Nearly all American musicians had studied in German conservatories and virtually all the repertoire was Germanic. For the first decade of the new century Wagnerism reigned supreme. After 1915, the number of German compositions on programs dropped considerably or were banned altogether. Wagner disappeared from the Metropolitan Opera, even in translation, along with other German operas. German composers performed by the Boston Symphony fell from 62 percent in 1916–1917 to 29.7 percent in 1918–1919. The New York Philharmonic abandoned all music by living German composers.

The results of this anti-German movement were twofold. First, it accelerated the rise of American composers in place of the banished German composers. And second, American arts and letters began replacing the historical German orientation with French culture. Standing in the wings to take advantage of these developments was a generation of American classical composers who would transform Gilded Age music. These men were born in the 1870s and early 1880s and worked into the third decade of the twentieth century. Trained like their predecessors in the styles of German academic romanticism, as they matured they sought inspiration from other places such as Russian music; French composers César Franck, Claude Debussy, and Maurice Ravel; and, for the first time, popular American music, folk music, Indian music, and ragtime. The two leading musicians of this group were Arthur Farwell and Charles Tomlinson Griffes. Unlike the composers of the New England School, they wrote fewer abstract chamber works and more narrative, descriptive tone poems and keyboard music. The new group of composers saw themselves as unabashed modernists, although they all honored the past and refused to go down the road of radical experimentation that Ives and Schoenberg trod. In the first decades of the century, modernism largely meant French to most Americans.

The musical developments during the Gilded Age had prepared the way for this transition. Since the Civil War art music had proliferated throughout American life. New orchestras appeared every year and interest in opera increased, spurred by the new recording technology. Opera singers, with their large, focused voices recorded some of the first widely successful disks. New conservatories were founded and by the prewar years, extracurricular high school bands and orchestras, as well as classes in music appreciation, became increasingly common in public schools. In 1907, the Music Education National Conference was founded. Performing institutions and networks likewise spread, making concert touring even easier. All these developments consolidated the trends from the previous century and broadened access and hearing of new works.

During the first two decades of the new century, the leaders of Gilded Age art music either died or retired from active creative work. Three of the most prominent, John Knowles Paine, Edward MacDowell, and Dudley Buck had died in 1906, 1908, and 1909, respectively. The last of the old generation of nineteenth-century symphonic composers, William Gilchrist and Silas Pratt, died in 1916. Joplin, as mentioned, died in 1917, taking ragtime with him for all practical purposes. Horatio Parker died in 1919. Ives had suffered a heart attack the year before, by which time he had completed most of his creative work. Charles Tomlinson Griffes died in 1920 at age 36, leaving much promised unfulfilled. At the same time, Henry Cowell, Ives's closest disciple;

George Gershwin; Irving Berlin; and W. C. Handy all were assuming the spotlight, while Aaron Copland, Virgil Thompson, Roy Harris, and other American symphonists were entering their serious student years.

Art music, like popular music, was evolving along a number of different lines and seeking to find its own American voice and distance itself from its European models. In the process, these young composers were fermenting a rebellion in American arts that would come to fruition in the 1920s, producing an avant-garde milieu that was at odds with the music of the Gilded Age. It was as if a line had been drawn across American culture separating the Victorian decades from the twentieth century.

The composers effecting the first stage of this transition had virtually all been born in the 1870s and 1880s. Of these, Arthur Farwell (1872–1952) and Charles T. Griffes (1884–1920) were the most important. These men expanded their inspirational sources beyond the Germanic models of their predecessors to include the native musics of America, especially New England psalmody, ragtime, blues, jazz, and folk music in addition to French and Asian influences.

Farwell worked as a center of the group through his establishment of the Wa-Wan Press in Newton Center, Massachusetts, between 1901 and 1912, which devoted itself to publishing the music of about 40 younger progressive American composers that other publishers had spurned. Farwell symbolized the spirit of the new century, which prized openness and exploration, in opposition to the formal constraints and narrow stylistic character of Gilded Age works. He did not reject the music of the Boston classicists, but, like others of his group, he viewed it as just one approach among many to composition. These men found the unquestioned classicism of Chadwick, Parker, Foote, Paine, and Buck outdated and stifling and were committed to the development of an American music.

Charles Tomlinson Griffes was perhaps the most important composer of the period and one of the few whose works continue in the repertoire today. Griffes died in 1920 from lung abscesses, but his work pointed toward the profusion of musics that would proliferate during the first half of the twentieth century. After studying at the Stern Conservatory in Berlin in 1903, he returned to this country in 1907 and taught music at the Hackley School for the rest of his life. Even though his early style breathed the air of German romanticism, after about 1911, he seems, like many of his generation, to have turned to France for his musical inspiration, especially the works of Claude Debussy and Maurice Ravel, which focus more on sound and color, formal dissolution, and an atmosphere of allusion, image, and inference—all qualities inherent in French impressionist painting and poetry. His *Pleasure-Dome of Kubla Khan* (1912) reflects these new stylistic models and was performed by the Boston

Symphony Orchestra in 1919. After about 1916, Griffes expanded his sound palette further by composing music inspired by Asian cultures, such as in *Shojo,* a one-scene pantomime with shimmering harmonies and muted orchestration. Griffes continued his stylistic explorations in two abstract pieces in late 1917 and 1918, with his one-movement *Piano Sonata* and the *Poem for Flute and Orchestra.* Griffes became a model for subsequent American composers through his efforts to integrate non-Western musical ideas into Eurocentric symphonic, vocal, and instrumental genres.

MOTION PICTURES, RECORDING, AND AUTOMOBILES

Motion Pictures

Motion pictures first flickered on October 6, 1889, when Thomas Edison opened The Kineographic Theater in West Orange, New Jersey. On April 4, 1894, he exhibited the kinetoscope in New York. By 1896, flickers, or moving pictures, could be seen in penny arcades through a viewer after inserting a coin, which offered about a minute of film. About a year later, technological improvements enabled theaters to project the pictures on a screen, enabling large audiences to view the films. Vaudeville added films to their entertainment after Benjamin Franklin Keith first used one in 1896 at the end of a live show. By the 1890s, penny arcades demonstrated how much appeal devices showing short films contained. Soon drug stores, hotel lobbies, railway stations, and department stores were installing the machines. For a penny, viewers—mostly men—could thrill to waves crashing on the shore or more titillating shorts like *Little Egypt, How Girls Undress,* or *The Birth of the Pearl.* In 1904, in Pittsburgh, Harry Davis opened the first theater with a projected film and audience seating, charging a nickel. Firms such as Edison, Essanay, Vitagraph, and Biograph were soon making hour-long films for showing in makeshift rooms and converted storefronts. Soon nickelodeons were everywhere, numbering nearly 10,000 by 1908. Originally intended for working-class audiences, one-reel motion pictures soon became respectable entertainment for middle-class patrons. In 1910, 26 million viewers per week went to the movies. By 1914, multireel feature films began commanding higher prices. Feature films added to the respectability of motion pictures, as they drew many stories from middle-class novels and plays, which also brought concomitantly higher demands from their patrons.

Movies soon discovered the profit in pushing Victorian prohibitions regarding sex and class, where single women could mingle with working-class men in darkened theaters. Couples could steal away unchaperoned for an afternoon at the nickelodeon. Films soon shocked more proper Americans with their sexual innuendo, scantily clad women, and, most distressing, a live screen kiss. Flying in the face of Gilded Age mores, the movies encouraged passion, epitomized by the titillation of an onscreen kiss, which was exactly what the guardians of culture feared.

Exhibitors soon realized that they could make greater profits by building stand-alone movie theaters in the form of grand movie palaces, which seated between 2,500 and 6,000 patrons at a time; "de luxe" palaces presented glamorous stage shows, permanent orchestras, first-run films, and an array of customer services unknown to today's cinema goers. The Regent was America's first motion picture palace. In 1913, it opened in a New York City working-class neighborhood uptown from the "legitimate" theater district. The majestic grandeur of the place and the new medium convinced the better classes to attend anyway. The social decorum and gentility of these new audiences brought film a social respectability it had not held before. The commercial success of these movie palaces quickly dismantled the barriers erected by Gilded Age nabobs between class and race entertainments, enabling working- and middle-class Americans to enter into a fantasy version of European high culture and aristocratic privilege. In rapid succession the Strand, Rialto, and Rivoli picture palaces opened, finally taking their place alongside legitimate theater.

Movie palaces typically featured marble, mirrored foyers, plush seats, oil paintings, and personal lounge attendants, smoking lounges, restrooms, and powder rooms as lavishly appointed as the lobby and auditorium. With their luxurious interiors offering a fantasy escape from the daily working world, the movie palaces had to show features rather than shorts to attract large audiences at premium prices. These palaces inevitably contained grand theater organs to accompany the silent films when the theater orchestras were not playing. The lobby of San Francisco's Fox Theater (1929) featured throne chairs, statuary, and a pair of vases once owned by the royal family of Russia. Viewed in these magnificent buildings, motion pictures quickly eclipsed vaudeville. Movie historian Ben Hall described the movie palace as "an acre of seats in a garden of dreams."

Technology improvements and the development of a classical narrative style in such film epics by D. W. Griffith as *The Birth of Nation* (1915) and *Intolerance* (1916) rapidly accelerated attendance at the movies. More than any other entertainment development, the emergence of film foreshadowed the end of the Gilded Age era of vaudeville and the cabaret, which had been the central purveyors of Tin Pan Alley. By the early 1920s, 40 million Americans, half of them minors, attended the movies each week.

Phonograph and Radio

Thomas A. Edison developed another technological competition to live entertainment when he filed his patent application for a phonograph machine on December 15, 1877, to be used for office dictation. In 1887, Emile Berliner developed the flat disk revolving on a turntable, which proved a more practical and efficient method of mass production than Edison's cylindrical disks. Ten years later May Irwin and Lottie Gilson recorded coon songs for the Universal Phonograph Company. In 1902, Caruso's disks appeared, which became a sensation, firmly establishing the financial viability of recorded music. In 1910, Sophie Tucker became the hottest of the red-hot mommas with her Edison recording of "That Lovin' Rag." By the start of World War I, the run was on as stage stars Eddie Cantor, Fanny Brice, and others entered American living rooms through records. In 1911, the year of Berlin's hit song "Alexander's Ragtime Band," sheet music continued to be the most profitable way to make money from published music, but that would soon change. After the phonograph and recording industries began to develop more rapidly, they would permanently alter the way Americans experienced music. Sheet music sales began declining as Americans listened to records and then the radio rather than playing new songs

In 1919, the Victor company recorded "Mary," which sold 300,000 disks in three months. That same year, Victor also produced the first dance disk to sell an estimated million copies, and the next year Paul Whiteman hit the two-million mark with his "Whispering." By 1920, a song was seen as a success if it sold several hundred thousand copies. At the same time, a success began to be measured more by the number of records a song sold than by copies of sheet music. By the middle of that decade, 130 million records were sold annually.

Automobiles

Probably no single development physically moved America out of the Gilded Age more directly and quickly than the automobile. Austrian engineer Siegfried Marcus built and drove a cart with a one-cylinder engine in the 1860s that was the forerunner of the modern automobile. In 1876, Nikolaus August Otto invented a successful four-stroke engine, and, in 1883, Sir Douglas Clerk put together the first successful two-stroke engine. Two years later, Gottlieb Daimler invented what is considered the prototype of the modern gas engine, and by 1890, Wilhelm Maybach was testing the first four-cylinder, four-stroke engine. Two years later Charles and Frank Duryea constructed the first "car" in this country, which successfully won a 50-mile marathon in 1895.

Soon Henry Ford installed the assembly line and began turning out automobiles that looked much as we know them. Numerous technological improvements rapidly increased sales. The all-steel vehicle rode on four wheels covered by fenders and turned using a steering wheel. An internal combustion, piston engine that ran on a mixture of gasoline and air provided power, detonated by an electric spark and transmitted to the wheels through a transmission and a differential. Brakes at the wheels slowed the vehicle. Soon nearly everyone could afford a car. By World War I, Henry Ford was turning out millions of the things, boosting car ownership in America to more than two million vehicles by 1915. Primitive as it was, the Ford Model T literally put America on wheels.

DANCE AND STAGED MUSICALS

Since the 1890s, New York had been the promised land for ragtime and jazz musicians. Even though jazz remained unknown to most Americans, they still heard about it and worried lest the new ragtime sounds would corrupt their kids with this music that came from Negro brothels. When the prewar press talked about the new popular music, it did so with a great deal of consternation and condemnation, lumping everything together as ragtime. In October 1915, Hiram Moderwell, the astute music critic for the *New Republic*, one of the growing liberal, progressive voices, accused critics and composers of neglecting "the one original and indigenous type of music of the American people." Ragtime was one of the most vibrant, visible, and visceral elements of the American character; it voiced the personality of the new bustling American street, the jerk and rattle of American cities.

The furor over ragtime paled with the excitement over the Dance Craze. Before 1913, social dancing had been formal, genteel, and carefully regulated by church, school, and community leaders. The dance halls in working-class neighborhoods had often been connected to African American saloons and houses of prostitution and shunned by well-bred middle- and upper-class whites. This attitude began to soften when the professional ballroom dance couple, Vernon and Irene Castle, started gaining attention with their stylish, refined interpretations of dances already popular among working-class whites and African Americans. As Vernon Castle remarked, "When a good orchestra plays a 'rag' one has simply *got* to move."[4] After success in Europe the Castles returned to New York, where they starred in the musical *The Sunshine Girl* (1913), which caused a sensation with their artistry in dancing the tango and the turkey trot. Their style and elegance demonstrated that these earthy, sensual dances could be done with taste, grace, and decorum.

Soon, respectable public dance halls, along with hotel ballrooms, cafes, restaurants, and cabarets with dance floors began appearing in large numbers. In the cabarets, bands played for dancing before, during, and after the dinner hour. Seized by the new, alluring rhythms, diners often dropped their forks and whirled around the floor, joining right in the dancing frenzy. Drawing the new middle- and upper-class dancers were a flood of new dances. One contemporary observer estimated that between 1912 and 1914, "over one hundred new dances found their way, in and out of our fashionable ballrooms."[5] And Jesse Lasky later observed that in 1911, "it was still scandalous to dance in a public place. Only a year or two later that prejudice was swept aside, and then nightclubs blossomed like magic."[6] This was not your grandmother's quadrille. Earlier social dances like quadrilles and waltzes with their genteel formality and careful physical distance between partners gave way to exuberant syncopation in new dances with outlandish titles such as the turkey trot, grizzly bear, bunny hug, fox-trot, lame duck, and the seductively enticing tango. The dance bands began adopting the brassier instrumentation of saxophones, clarinets, and trumpets used by dance leaders such as James Reese Europe and W. C. Handy, rather than strings and softer winds.

Ragtime joined cabarets, movies, and sound recordings in creating a new popular culture, increasingly divorced from the strict confinements and prohibitions of Victorian morality. And like ragtime, many of these dances had African American origins, often from red-light districts. With an astonishing rapidity, the painstakingly maintained racial barriers separating white and black music, social and dirty dancing, and proper musical entertainments began to leak. Even more, the very names of the dances came from the barnyard, directly connecting the dances by white people to the natural processes of animal behavior, notably their sexuality. And by drawing on the working-class entertainments, black culture, and red-light districts for their music and dances, overly socialized urbanites could find release from the stifling Victorian conformity and emotional weightlessness.

In 1914, the Castles hired James Reese Europe (1880–1919) to conduct their accompanying band. Since the 1910s, James Reese Europe's Clef Club Orchestra had been playing fast ragtime dances, which they recorded for Victor in 1913. Yet when a group of white New Orleans musicians called the Original Dixieland Jazz Band recorded "Livery Stable Blues" and "Dixie Jass Band One-Step" in 1917, the torrid tempos and improvised passages were heard as something new and thrilling.

Europe's "Society Orchestra" performed W. C. Handy's the *Memphis Blues* for the Castle's fox trot. The 1919 recording of *Memphis Blues* offers a clear insight into this style and how startling it must have sounded to contemporary listeners, accustomed to the elegance of "On the Banks of the Wabash" or a sentimental parlor piano piece. Europe's recording plays with a driving insistence energized by aggressive syncopation, howling trombone licks, grumbling trumpet notes, and a surprising trombone break at the end. The music now was rhythmic and physical rather than vocal and passive, which redefined popular music as music to be danced, rather than heard. With the liberating rhythm, dancers no longer adhered to the proper, proscribed steps of the nineteenth century, but moved, jerked, hopped, and whatever else struck them in time to the beat. Irving Berlin again led the way with his "Everybody's Doin' It Now" of 1911 with its irregularly accented ragtime beat, depicting couples swaying, swooning, and movin' together.

It seemed everyone was caught up in the dance mania, which alarmed the custodians of morality and culture, who looked on with horror at the collapse of public morality and social decorum. They remained powerless as the people from all classes and backgrounds flooded the dance floors—Lower East Side immigrants, Upper West Side society matrons, housewives, staid businessmen, and of course young people, lots of young people, ecstatic to finally be liberated from the social seclusion of Victorian mores. One journal in 1914 wrote that "suddenly in the midst of this money-getting machine-made age, we throw all our caution to the wind; we give up some of our business hours, and we not only dance in the evening, but in the afternoon and in the morning."[7]

Songwriter, poet, novelist, journalist, critic and prominent figure of the Harlem Renaissance James Weldon Johnson (1871–1838) observed wryly:

> It is to this music that America in general gives itself over in its leisure hours.... At these times, the Negro drags his captors captive. On occasions, I have been amazed and amused watching white people dancing to a Negro band in a Harlem cabaret; attempting to throw off the crusts and layers of inhibitions laid on by sophisticated civilization; striving to yield to the feel and experience of abandon; seeking to recapture a state of primitive joy in life and living.[8]

At the same time James Reese Europe was leading his ensemble, Jelly Roll Morton, James P. Johnson, J. Russell Robinson (1892–1963), and other pianists in New York City were expanding the ragtime piano tradition with a style that came to be known as *stride*. This new sound mainly involved a steady beat in the left hand usually played in alternating bass patterns, supporting more intricate and rhythmically diverse patterns in the right hand. Stride further differed from ragtime in using a larger variety of left-hand patterns while the right hand moved in more rhythmically active figurations. Another stylistic difference from ragtime was that stride incorporated the 12-bar blues into its harmonic language, and it was played at lightening fast tempos. Finally, ragtime was (and is) essentially a composed, notated music, but jazz continued to be an improvisatory performer's art.

These three developments during the second decade of the century—the orchestral/dance ragtime of James Reese Europe, the small group style of the Original Dixieland Jazz Band, and the new stride piano style—accelerated the transition from ragtime to jazz. The shift at first was primarily one of terminology. There was no musical distinction during this period; many ragtime musicians such as Jelly Roll Morton and J. Russell Robinson simply began calling themselves jazz musicians. Well into the 1920s, few musicians or listeners could have defined the difference between ragtime and jazz, but they knew something new was afoot. Gunther Schuller aptly observes that jazz did not so much evolve from ragtime as within ragtime. By the time the boys came home from the war, the jazz era was into full swing and ragtime, with its restraint, polish, and moderate rhythms quickly receded from the stage, soon to vanish from public awareness until the 1970s.

These new developments in popular culture completed the separation between High Culture and mass culture and, in so doing, presaged the dominance popular culture would assume by the end of the twentieth century. Whereas legitimate theater and Shakespeare, musicals, instrumental concerts, and opera had enjoyed broad appeal throughout much of the nineteenth century, as the Gilded Age faded, these arts became increasingly distinct and found themselves appealing to a narrowing group of elite Americans. At the same time, the more accessible and cheaper forms of entertainment such as vaudeville, burlesque, musicals, sheet music, and motion pictures drew a larger percentage of Americans, who felt themselves looked down on by the leaders of elite culture.

BROADWAY

New York remained the home of the staged musical. George M. Cohan opened the century in 1904 with his landmark work, *Little Johnny Jones,* which had a tightly crafted book, immediately accessible tunes, and an American brashness unseen before. His story captured the universality of American life, not just the New York experience, by showcasing sentimental Irish waltzes, energetic syncopated marches, and ragtime rhythms. These songs reflected the thriving Tin Pan Alley style that was now dominating American popular music. He continued his successes with *Forty-Five Minutes from Broadway* (1906), which introduced "Mary's a Grand Old Name," and *George Washington, Jr.* (1906), which produced "You're a Grand Old Flag." These were the first skillfully crafted books and music related to and growing out of the dramatic situations. With Cohan's informality, brazen sexual innuendos, toe-tappin' melodies, and unabashed Americanism, the American musical entered the threshold of modernity. Indeed, one can argue that the American musical comedy was born with George M. Cohan.

The final separation between High Art in the form of opera and a more accessible musical drama occurred with the New York performance of two very different musical stage works in 1907. One foreshadowed the modernism of the twentieth century and one culminated all the elegance, glamour, and refinement of the Gilded Age. That year Richard Strauss's notorious operatic setting of *Salome* had its American premiere at the Metropolitan Opera. Taken from a biblical story and retold by the dishonored English poet Oscar Wilde, *Salome* epitomized all the decadence and depravity that modernism's critics had been raving about. The work outraged critics and audiences alike, bringing instant fame to the work.

That same year, a Viennese import by the Austrian band director and composer Franz Lehár made its New York debut, *The Merry Widow*. From that date until the opening of World War I operetta dominated the American musical stage. Viennese works had been increasingly popular since the 1890s with musicals such as Johann Strauss' *Die Fledermaus*. *The Merry Widow* soared above all of them as it captured all the romance, nostalgia, royal glamor, infectious melodies, and beguiling waltzes of the Gilded Age. Soon all of America, it seemed, was singing and dancing the heartfelt melodies. The work burst onto the theatrical circuit; during the 1907–1908 season alone, 5,000 American performances were given. It seemed to be everywhere.

Operetta proved to be the exactly right entertainment for Gilded Age audiences. It drew its emotional tone from opera and needed operatically trained singers. But whereas the musical numbers burst forth when the characters no longer could contain their emotional intensity, the plot moves forward through speech. The central characters are high-born aristocrats, often in disguise and always in distress. Operetta could also always be counted on to contain full-bodied romance and passion, but stopped short of the murderous intrigue and despair of serious opera. Of course, there was the luscious, elegant, and bewitching melody.

Irish-born Victor Herbert (1859–1924) was an American cellist and composer who successfully rivaled Lehár and the English team of W. S. Gilbert and Arthur Sullivan. He composed more than 40 operettas between 1894 and his death in 1924. Some of his most popular works epitomized the American side of Gilded Age Romance, including *Babes in Toyland* (1903), *The Red Mill* (1906), *Naughty Marietta* (1910), and *Sweethearts* (1913).

In 1914, an American would move the musical stage in another direction, Jerome Kern (1885–1945), who succeeded Cohan as the leading composer of American musical comedies. He achieved his first stage success that year with

The Girl from Utah and first song hit with "They Didn't Believe Me" (Herbert Reynolds), which sold two million copies in sheet music. Kern was a native New Yorker, studying piano and music theory at the New York College of Music. After studying in Europe he turned from composing classical music to the popular musical stage and worked for several Tin Pan Alley publishers as a song plugger.

For nearly a decade Kern's songs were interpolated into the scores of other composers. Between 1905 and 1912, about a hundred of Kern's songs appeared in Broadway musicals. Finally, in 1912, he wrote a whole show, *The Red Petticoat,* which failed. He finally succeeded on April 20, 1915, with the opening at the intimate Princess Theater of *Nobody Home,* which ran for 135 performances, followed by the even more successful *Very Good Eddie,* lasting for more than a year. Both shows established a new genre in American musical theater that broke with the extravagant, hells-a-poppin' rowdiness that had characterized much of Broadway such as in the musicals of Cohan. They also founded the Princess Theater Show as a Broadway style of writing. The two shows were concise, low key, relaxed, and looked forward to the intimate comedies of Noel Coward. By the time the Princess Theater closed in 1918, a shift away from the brash, bawdy, dramatically weak shows of the Gilded Age had come about. The Princess Shows pointed the way to a new kind of musical stage production in which the musical numbers grew convincingly out of the drama.

Another type of musical show appeared as Kern was beginning his work, produced by Florenz Ziegfeld. Ziegfeld's *Follies,* which opened in 1910, was an expansion of the revue, a type of vaudeville entertainment. By combining vaudeville, extravaganza, and burlesque with sumptuous sets and elaborate costuming, the first producer George W. Lederer could charge higher prices. Ziegfeld's *Follies* became the revue *par excellence* and dominated the genre for the first two decades of the twentieth century. He thought and planned grandly and boldly, presenting his shows in Broadway houses, not vaudeville theaters. Right from the start in the *Follies of 1910,* Ziegfeld introduced two performers that would hold the limelight for years, the black star Bert Williams and the 19-year-old singer/comic Fanny Brice, who Ziegfeld discovered in a burlesque house. The *Follies* quickly came to symbolize the glamour, excess, and titillating allure of the new musical era. When that era crashed with the stock market, so did the *Follies.*

Irving Berlin had also brought his songwriting talents to Broadway in 1914 with his first complete show, *Watch Your Step,* starring the newly famous Vernon and Irene Castle. Berlin energized his show with ragtime and syncopated songs including a sequence set at the Metropolitan Opera House featuring "ragged" versions of popular operatic arias. The next year his hit show *Stop!*

Look! Listen! gave two enduring tunes to American song, "The Girl on the Magazine Cover" and "I Love a Piano." By 1921, his series of *Music Box Revues* confirmed him as one of the country's most successful writers for the musical stage.

The season of 1916 saw a new name on Broadway that would complete the transformation of Gilded Age musical comedy, George Gershwin, only 17 years old, who contributed "The Making of a Girl" to the *Passing Show* revue. Brooklyn born in 1898 to immigrant Russian parents, Gershwin studied with Charles Hambitzer, who recognized Gershwin's genius and took him to concerts. In 1914, however, Gershwin abandoned his study, dropped out of high school, and began working for Tin Pan Alley publisher Jerome H. Remick & Co. as a song plugger. There he quickly learned much of the song repertoire including the songs from Broadway, as well as hundreds of Tin Pan Alley pieces. His early songs showed influences from all the traditions he played, including the ragtime, the blues, parlor songs, and of course jazz. In this way Gershwin served as the most visible artist of the new era. In 1916, Harry Von Tilzer published the first song with Gershwin's name on it; and in 1919, he composed his first complete Broadway show *La, La, Lucille,* which ran for more than 100 performances, assisted by the appearance of his hit "Swannee." With the opening of *Lady, Be Good* on December 1, 1924, Gershwin came of age as one of the country's foremost writers for the musical stage. The score included some of his finest songs, all to lyrics by his brother Ira, including "Fascinating Rhythm," "The Man I Love," and "So Am I." Gershwin, along with Cohan, Kern, and Berlin, had assembled all the necessary ingredients for the Golden Age of the American musical from the 1920s to the end of World War II. Finally, in 1924, Gershwin brought the jazz age fully into the middle-class, white mainstream with the premiere of his *Rhapsody in Blue* on February 12, 1924, in New York's Aeolian Hall with Paul Whiteman's Palais Royal Orchestra. With this piece Gershwin combined three important strands of American music: the popular blues song form, jazz as an instrumental music, and the acceptance of classical modernism, all in one piece.

The Gilded Age was a memory.

Appendix: Timeline

1864	Theodore Thomas organizes his orchestra
	Stephen Foster dies
	William Henry Fry dies
1865	Civil War ends
	Abraham Lincoln assassinated
	Oberlin Conservatory established
1866	Tony Pastor opens his Opera House in New York
	The Black Crook opens at Niblo's Garden, New York
1867	Reconstruction begins
	President Andrew Johnson impeached
	Vanderbilt takes control of the New York Central Railroad
	New England Conservatory established
	J. K. Paine conducts his *Mass in D* in Berlin
	Amy Marcy Cheney (Beach) born
	Slave Songs published
1868	U.S. Senate fails to convict President Johnson
	Ulysses S. Grant elected president
	Charles "Buddy" Bolden born, New Orleans
	Scot Joplin born
	Peabody Institute established, Baltimore
	J. P. Sousa enlists as apprentice in the Marine Band
	J. K. Paine's *Mass in D* performed, Boston Music Hall

1869   Transcontinental railroad completed
        Fisk and Gould try to corner the gold market
        Patrick Gilmore's Peace Jubilee, Boston
        Louis Moreau Gottschalk dies
1870   Population of United States reaches 39.8 million
        Rockefeller forms Standard Oil
1871   Chicago fire
        The Fisk Jubilee Singers tour the northern states
        Edward Harrigan and Tony Hart form their partnership
1872   Boston fire
        Grant reelected
        Boss Tweed jailed
        Johann Strauss conducts in Boston
        Arthur Farwell born
        Anton Rubinstein tours the United States
        J. K. Paine appointed instructor at Harvard
1873   Moody-Sankey revival tours begin
        W. C. Handy born, Florence, Alabama
        Patrick Gilmore appointed conductor, 22d Reg. Band, New York City
        Daniel Gregory Mason born
        Panic on Wall Street
1874   Massachusetts mandates 10-hour workday for women and
            children
        Mark Twain publishes *The Gilded Age: A Tale for Today*
        Charles Ives born
        Leopold Damrosch founds New York Oratorio Society
1875   J. K. Paine appointed Professor of Music at Harvard
        Dwight L. Moody returns from Europe to begin Brooklyn revival
        Ira D. Sankey's *Revival Hymns* published
        Tony Pastor's Opera House relocates from Bowery to Broadway
1876   Rutherford B. Hayes elected president
        Alexander Graham Bell invents the telephone
        Custer killed at Little Big Horn
        Centennial Exposition opens in Philadelphia
        Philip B. Bliss dies
        J. P. Sousa publishes his first march (*The Revival*)
        Edward MacDowell begins European study
1877   Reconstruction ends
        Cornelius Vanderbilt dies, leaving $100 million
        National Railroad strike
        Theodore Thomas appointed director of the New York Philharmonic

G. W. Chadwick begins European study

Thomas Edison patents the phonograph

1878   George M. Cohan born

Gilbert and Sullivan's *HMS Pinafore* performed, Boston

Edison Speaking Phonograph Co. formed

Fisk Jubilee Singers tours Europe

Leopold Damrosch founds New York Symphony

1879   Yellowstone designated the first national park

D'Oyly Carte Company tours America

Gilbert and Sullivan's *HMS Pinafore* and *Pirates of Penzance* performed, New York

1880   U.S. population reaches 50 million

James Garfield elected president

J. P. Sousa appointed leader of the Marine Band

Metropolitan Opera formed

G. W. Chadwick returns from Europe to Boston

Lillian Russell debuts in New York

Sarah Bernhardt debuts in New York

1881   Garfield assassinated; Chester A. Arthur becomes president

Gunfight at OK Corral, Tombstone Arizona

Tony Pastor opens Casino Theater in Tammany Hall

Rudolf Friml born

Boston Symphony Orchestra established

Dwight's Journal of Music ceases publication

Charles Martin Loeffler arrives in America

1882   Casino Theater opens in New York, specializing in operetta

G. W. Chadwick joins New England Conservatory faculty

Horatio Parker begins European study

1883   Brooklyn Bridge opens

T. B. Harms publishes its first major work

Metropolitan Opera House opens with Gounod's *Faust*

American Conservatory established, Chicago

1884   Grover Cleveland elected president

Charles T. Griffes born

M. Witmark & Sons established, New York

Dvorak's "New World" Symphony premiered, Brooklyn

1885   Washington Monument completed

Grant dies

Ferdinand "Jelly Roll" Morton born

Leopold Damrosch dies

Walter Damrosch appointed director of the New York Symphony

National Conservatory established in New York
Harrigan and Hart dissolve their partnership
Jerome Kern born
Joseph "King" Oliver born

1886   100,000 strike for an 8-hour workday
Chicago Haymarket bombing
Samuel Gompers heads American Federation of Labor
Statue of Liberty dedicated
M. Witmark & Sons established in New York
Mapleson withdraws from opera production, New York Academy of
Music

1887   Emil Berliner invents disk recording
Sigmund Romberg born

1888   Benjamin Harrison elected president
Great New York blizzard (March 12)
Witmark moves to "Tin Pan Alley," 14th Street in New York,
Irving Berlin born
Edward MacDowell returns from Europe to Boston
Theodore Thomas disbands his orchestra
J. P. Sousa publishes *Semper Fidelis*

1889   Johnstown, Pennsylvania flood
Jacob Riis publishes *How the Other Half Lives*
Matthews and Howe publish *A Hundred Years of Music in America*
J. P. Sousa publishes *Washington Post March*

1890   U.S. population reaches 63 million
Lakota massacred at Wounded Knee, South Dakota

1891   Carnegie Hall, New York, opened
Tchaikovsky conducts concerts in New York
Theodore Thomas retires from New York Philharmonic
Thomas organizes Chicago Symphony

1892   Grover Cleveland elected president
Ellis Island opened
Walt Whitman dies
Steel strike, Homestead, Pennsylvania
Charles K. Harris publishes "After the Ball"
Patrick S. Gilmore dies
J. P. Sousa organizes his own band
Dvořák becomes director of National Conservatory in New York
Oscar Hammerstein opens Manhattan Opera House

1893   Stock market crash, depression begins
Scott Joplin and other ragtime pianists at Chicago World's Fair

Witmark moves "Tin Pan Alley" to theater district, East 28th
   Street
J. S. Dwight dies
Theodore Thomas directs music at Chicago World's Fair
Saint-Saëns and Paderewski in United States
Dvořák's "New World" Symphony performed, New York
Parker's *Hora Novissima* performed, New York
Victor Herbert succeeds Gilmore as director of 22d Reg. band

1894   Pullman strike, Chicago, Illinois
   Parker appointed music department head at Yale
   Ira Sankey's cumulative *Gospel Hymns* published

1895   Dvořák returns to Europe

1896   William McKinley elected president
   Vitascope moving pictures introduced in New York
   MacDowell appointed professor of music at Columbia, New York

1897   New Orleans officially establishes Storyville
   Krell's "Mississippi Rag" published
   Sousa publishes *Stars and Stripes Forever*
   A. W. Thayer dies

1898   New York City becomes five boroughs
   Maine explodes in Havana harbor starting war with Spain
   Admiral Dewey at Manila Bay
   Theodore Roosevelt and Rough Riders at San Juan Hill
   Treaty of Paris ends hostilities of Spanish-American War
   Walter Damrosch resigns from New York Symphony
   Frank Damrosch begins Young People's Concerts

1899   Thorstein Veblen publishes *Theory of the Leisure Class*
   Scott Joplin publishes "Maple Leaf Rag," *Original Rags*

1900   U.S. population reaches 75.9 million
   William McKinley reelected president
   Galveston, Texas, hurricane kills 8,000
   E. S. Votey patents "pianola" player mechanism
   Sousa's band tours Europe
   Paderewski establishes $10,000 fund for American composers
   Symphony Hall opens in Boston

1901   McKinley assassinated; Theodore Roosevelt becomes president
   Panic in Wall Street over Northern Pacific Railroad
   Rudolf Friml in America
   Victor Talking Machine Co. formed
   Arthur Farwell establishes Wa-Wan Press
   Florodora closes after 505 performances

1903	Ford Motor Co. formed
	Wright Brothers flight at Kitty Hawk, North Carolina
	Herbert's *Babes in Toyland* opens
1904	Theodore Roosevelt elected president
	St. Louis Louisiana Purchase Exposition opens
	D. D. Emmett dies
	George M. Cohan's *Little Johnny Jones* opens, New York
	Richard Strauss in New York
1905	Theodore Thomas dies
	Juilliard School founded, New York
	Nickelodeon movies spread
1906	Upton Sinclair publishes *The Jungle*
	San Francisco earthquake and fire
	Manhattan Opera House opens
	J. K. Paine dies
	Keith Albee forms vaudeville United Booking Office of America
1907	Charles "Buddy" Bolden committed to institution
	First Ziegfeld Follies opens
	Lehar's *Merry Widow* opens in New York
	Music Educators National Conference established
1908	William Howard Taft elected president
	General Motors formed
	Ford introduces the Model T
	Toscanini conducts in New York
	Ira D. Sankey dies
	Gustav Mahler conducts Wagner's *Tristan* at Metropolitan Opera
	Edward MacDowell dies
	Gatti-Casazza becomes general manager of Metropolitan Opera
	Hammerstein opens the Philadelphia Opera House
1909	Congress passes the Copyright Act
	Peary reaches the North Pole
	Dudley Buck dies
	Pavlova debuts in New York
	First broadcast from Metropolitan Opera
	Rachmaninoff begins American tour at Smith College
	New York Philharmonic reorganized
	Stokowski becomes director of the Cincinnati Orchestra
	Boston Opera Company established
	Sigmund Romberg arrives in America
1910	Mahler returns to Vienna
	Hammerstein withdraws from classical opera production

Mark Twain dies

Hammerstein produces Victor Herbert's *Naughty Marietta* in
New York

Chicago Grand Opera established

1911   Scott Joplin completes opera *Treemonisha*

James A. Bland dies

1912   Woodrow Wilson elected president

Strike at Lawrence, Massachusetts, textile mills

Titanic sinks

W. C. Handy publishes "Memphis Blues"

Stokowski director of New York Philharmonic

Parker's *Mona* performed at Metropolitan Opera

G. Schirmer acquires Farwell's Wa-Wan Press

Schubert brothers open theater

Friml's *The Firefly* opens in New York

1913   Armory art show opens in Chicago

1914   World War I begins in Europe

Panama Canal opened

American Society of Composers, Authors and Publishers (ASCAP)
formed

1915   *Lusitania* sunk by German U-boat

Joplin's *Treemonisha* performed in Harlem

Schirmer establishes *The Musical Quarterly*

Princess Theater musicals open with Kern and Bolton's *Very Good
Eddie*

1916   Wilson reelected president

Federal child-labor law passed

Diaghilev's dance company arrives in New York

1917   U.S. enters World War I

Jascha Heifitz debuts in New York at age 16

Scott Joplin dies

New Orleans closes Storyville

Victor releases first jazz recording

Supreme Court upholds ASCAP

1918   World War I ends

Influenza epidemic

Princess Theater series of musicals end

Eastman School established, Rochester, New York

New Orleans *Times-Picayune* calls jazz a "musical vice"

Notes

INTRODUCTION

1. *The New Grove Dictionary of American Music*, s. v. "Centennial Exhibition"; John Mass, *The Glorious Enterprise. The Centennial Exhibition of 1876 and H. J. Schwarz-mann, Architect-in-Chief* (Watkins Glen, N.Y.: American Life Foundation, 1973), 41.

2. Steven Baur, "Music, Morals, and Social Management: Mendelssohn in Post-Civil War America," *American Music* 19, No. 1 (Spring 2001): 68.

3. Stewart H. Holbrook, *The Age of Moguls* (Garden City: Doubleday, 1954), 8–9. The Rockefeller quote is reported, among other places, in Aline B. Saarinen, *The Proud Possessors* (New York: Random House, 1958), 87.

4. Lewis A. Erenberg, *Steppin' Out. New York Nightlife and the Transformation of American Culture, 1890–1930* (Chicago and London: University of Chicago Press, 1981), 5–25.

5. ———, *Steppin' Out*, 17.

CHAPTER 1

1. Material on the Peace Jubilee is widespread and accessible, among other places, in H. Wiley Hitchcock, *Music in the United States: A Historical Introduction*, 4th ed. (Englewood Cliffs: Prentice Hall, 1999), 117–18; Charles Hamm, *Music in the New World* (New York: W. W. Norton, 1983), 309–10; Ronald L. Davis, *A History of American Life, Vol. II: The Gilded Years, 1865–1920* (Huntington, NY: Robert Krieger, 1980), 2–3; Richard Crawford, *America's Musical Life: A History* (New York: W. W. Norton, 2001),

289–91; Lawrence W. Levine, *Highbrow, Lowbrow: The Emergence of Cultural Hierarchy in America* (Cambridge: Harvard University Press, 1988), 105–07; the July 3, 1869 issue of *Dwight's* was devoted to the Jubilee. See also Irving Sablosky, *What They Heard: Music in America, 1852–1881. From the Pages of Dwight's Journal of Music* (Baton Rouge: Louisiana State University Press, 1986), 58–70.

2. Lawrence W. Levine, *Highbrow Lowbrow*, 107–11, provides examples, including a sign advertising an 1848 "Grand Concert of Music" in Baltimore by the Germania Society, a highly disciplined and professional chamber orchestra, along with "An African Monkey and Several Chinese Dogs. Come One Come All." On P. T. Barnum and Jenny Lind, see Milton Goldin, *The Music Merchants* (London: Macmillan, 1969), 21–43.

3. Richard Crawford, *America's Musical Life*, 309; Dizikes, *Opera in America*, 152.

4. Ronald L. Davis, *A History of Music in American Life*, 6. William Mason, *Memories of a Musical Life* (New York: The Century Co., 1901), 261.

5. Philip Hart, *Orpheus in the New World: The Symphony Orchestra as an American Cultural Institution* (New York: W. W. Norton, 1973), 5–6; Vera Brodsky Lawrence, *Strong on Music: The New York Music Scene in the Days of George Templeton Strong. Vol. 1: Resonances, 1836–1849* (Chicago: University of Chicago Press, 1988), 156–58.

6. Neil Butterworth, *The American Symphony* (Aldershott: Ashgate, 1998), 4–6; Goldin, *Music Merchants*, 123.

7. ———, *American Symphony*, 6; Levine, *Highbrow Lowbrow*, 109; Harold Schoenberg, *The Great Conductors* (New York: Simon and Schuster, 1967), 149–54; George P. Upton, ed., *Theodore Thomas: A Musical Autobiography* (Chicago: A. C. McClurg, 1905; repr. New York: Da Capo Press, 1964), 26–27; Vera Brodsky Lawrence, *Strong on Music, Vol. 2: Reverberations, 1850–1856* (Chicago: University of Chicago Press, 1995), 356–68.

8. Philip Hart, *Orpheus in the New World*, 11–13; Mason, *Memories*, 195–98; Sablosky, *What They Heard*, 223–24.

9. William Mason, *Memories*, 200; Charles Edward Russell, *The American Orchestra and Theodore Thomas* (New York: Doubleday, 1927; repr. Westport, Conn.: Greenwood Press, 1971), 24–26; Hart, *Orpheus in the New World*, 14–15. Joseph Musselman, *Music in the Cultured Generation*, 144; D. W. Fostle, *The Steinway Saga* (New York: Scribner's, 1995), 165.

10. Charles Edward Russell, *American Orchestra and Theodore Thomas*, 48–66.

11. Philip Hart, *Orpheus in the New World*, 16–19; Goldin, *Music Merchants*, 116–18; 96.

12. Harold Schoenberg, *Great Conductors*, 196–97; Russell, *American Orchestra and Theodore Thomas*, 91, 98–103.

13. Lawrence L. Levine, *Highbrow Lowbrow*, 116–18; Russell, *American Orchestra and Theodore Thomas*, 133.

14. ———, *Highbrow Lowbrow*, 118; Butterworth, *The American Symphony*, 8–9.

15. Ezra Shabas, *Theodore Thomas: America's Conductor and Builder of Orchestras, 1835–1905* (Urban: University of Illinois Press, 1989), 206.

16. ———, *Theodore Thomas*, 1–3, 213–14.

17. Philip Hart, *Orpheus in the New World*, 25; Richard Schickel, *The World of Carnegie Hall* (New York: Julian Messner, 1960), 18–19; W. L. Hubbard, *History of American Music* (New York: Irving Square, 1908), 277–79; Levine, *Highbrow Lowbrow*, 112.

18. Richard Schickel, *World of Carnegie Hall*, 19; Schoenberg, *Great Conductors*, 345; George Martin, *The Damrosch Dynasty: America's First Family of Music* (Boston: Houghton Mifflin, 1983), 28.

19. Richard K. Lieberman, *Steinway and Sons* (New Haven: Yale University Press, 1995), 56–7; Schabas, *Theodore Thomas*, 67, 122; Schickel, *World of Carnegie Hall*, 19–20.

20. Richard Schickel, *World of Carnegie Hall*, 21.

21. George Martin, *Damrosh Dynasty*, 45–6.

22. Ezra Schabas, *Theodore Thomas*, 91.

23. W. L. Hubbard, *History of American Music*, 220; Martin, *Damrosch Dynasty*, 34–47; Schickel, *The World of Carnegie Hall*, 21; Russell, *American Orchestra and Theodore Thomas*, 116, 136; Levine, *Highbrow Lowbrow*, 110.

24. Richard Schickel, *World of Carnegie Hall*, 24–36.

25. ———, *World of Carnegie Hall*, 36–48; Martin, *Damrosch Dynasty*, 111–19.

26. George Martin, *Damrosch Dynasty*, 144–50, 166–71.

27. ———, *Damrosch Dynasty*, 185–95.

28. Philip Hart, *Orpheus in the New World*, 52–54.

29. Mark A. DeWolfe Howe, *The Boston Symphony Orchestra: An Historical Sketch* (Boston: Houghton Mifflin, 1914); Martin Green, *The Problem of Boston* (New York: W. W. Norton, 1966), 110–11; Goldin, *Music Merchants*, 119–26; Hart, *Orpheus in the New World*, 54–55.

30. Nicholas Tawa, *From Psalm to Symphony: A History of Music in New England* (Boston: Northeastern University Press, 2001), 121.

31. Milton Goldin, *Music Merchants*; Levine, 120–24; Hart, *Orpheus in the New World*, 55–61. Max Fiedler conducted the orchestra during the intervening period, 1906 to 1912.

32. Philip Hart, *Orpheus in the New World*, 72–75; Schoenberg, *Great Conductors*, 309–10.

33. George Martin, *The Damrosch Dynasty*, 247–252; Goldin, *The Music Merchants*, 132–34.

CHAPTER 2

1. Cited in Joseph Horowitz, *Classical Music in America* (New York and London, W. W. Norton & Company, 2005), 122.

2. Among many sources, see Eric Homberger, *Mrs. Astor's New York: Money and Social Power in the Gilded Age* (New Haven: Yale University Press, 2002), 230–37; and Jerry D. Patterson, *The First Four Hundred: Mrs. Astor's New York in the Gilded Age* (New York: Rizzoli, 2000), 20–21.

3. Richard Crawford, *The American Musical Landscape* (Berkeley: University of California Press, 1993), 73–74.

4. ———, *The American Musical Landscape*, 73–74.

5. Vera Brodsky Lawrence, *Strong on Music. Volume II. Reverberations 1850–1856* (Chicago and London: University of Chicago Press, 1995), 165, 168.

6. The main sources for much of this chapter can be found in: Lawrence W. Levine, *Highbrow Lowbrow: The Emergence of Cultural Hierarchy in America*, 88–97; Karen Ahlquist, *Democracy at the Opera: Music, Theater and Culture in New York City, 1815–1860* (Urbana: University of Illinois Press, 1997), 78, 117–30, 166; and Katherine K. Preston, *Opera on the Road: Traveling Opera Troupes in the United States, 1825–1860* (Urbana: University of Illinois Press, 2001); and "Between the Cracks: The Performance of English-Language Opera in Late Nineteenth Century America," *American Music* 21:3 (Fall 2003), 349–74. Although not necessarily in the original language, Italian opera companies sang French opera, and even Wagner's German music dramas, in Italian; and conversely, German companies sang Verdi in German translation.

7. Joseph Musselman, *Music in the Cultured Generation: A Social History of Music in America, 1870–1900* (Evanston: Northwestern University Press, 1971), 125.

8. Richard Crawford, *America's Musical Life: A History* (New York: W. W. Norton, 2001), 309; A major source for much of this chapter is John Dizikes, *Opera in America: A Cultural History* (New Haven: Yale University Press, 1993), 147–73, 216–21, 243–45, 253, 281–95, 312–23, 330–35, 355–69, 406–10.

9. Julian Mates, *The American Musical Stage Before 1800* (New Brunswick: Rutgers University Press, 162), 147–48; John Ogasapian, *Music in the Colonial and Revolutionary Era* (Westport, Conn.: Greenwood Press, 2004), 131–33, 161–64.

10. A number of references are found in Milton Goldin, *The Music Merchants*, 5–16, 52–56, 87–115, 137–58. The most recent biography is April Fitzlyon, *Maria Malibran, Diva of the Romantic Age* (London: Souvenir Press, 1987).

11. *Letters from John Pintard to His Daughter Eliza Noel Pintard Davidson, 1816–1833*, v. 4 (New York: The New-York Historical Society, 1941), 135, 158. Pintard's tastes ran more to church music; and in any case, he was by this time quite deaf and probably unenthusiastic about music or theater of any kind.

12. Allan Nevins (ed.), *The Diary of Philip Hone* (New York: Dodd and Mead, 1927), 104, 183.

13. Katherine K. Preston, "Between the Cracks," 350.

14. Lawrence W. Levine, *Highbrow Lowbrow*, 100; Lawrence, *Strong on Music: Reverberations*, 544–45.

15. Max Maretzek, *Sharps and Flats* (New York: American Musician Publishing Co., 1890), 12–15; Maretzek, *Crochets and Quavers* (New York: S. French, 1855), 330–40; both reprinted with original page numbers in *Revelations of an Opera Manager in 19th Century America* (New York: Dover Publications, 1968). See note 9.

16. Preston, "Between the Cracks," 351; Good, Edwin M. "William Steinway and Music in New York," *Music and Culture in America, 1861–1918*, ed. Michael Saffle (New York: Garland Publishing, 1998), 16–17.

17. ———, "Between the Cracks," 351.

18. Henry Pleasants, *The Great Singers: From the Dawn of Opera to Our Own Time*, (New York: Simon and Schuster, 1966), 209, including the quote from Fink; Frances Alda, *Men, Women and Tenors* (Boston: Houghton Mifflin, 1937; repr. New York: AMS Press, 1971), 48.

19. Paul Eisler, *The Metropolitan Opera: The First Twenty-Five Years, 1883–1908,* (Croton-on-Hudson, N.Y.: North River Press, 1984), 4–6. There is little question that the men who incorporated the Metropolitan and underwrote the subscriptions were far less interested in the enterprise than were the women in their families, for whom social status was a matter of great concern.

20. Johanna Fiedler, *Molto Agitato: The Mayhem Behind the Music at the Metropolitan Opera* (New York: Doubleday Anchor, 2001), 5–6; John Briggs, *Requiem for a Yellow Brick Brewery: A History of the Metropolitan Opera* (Boston: Little, Brown and Co., 1969), 7.

21. Joseph Horowitz, *Classical Music in America,* 135.

22. Eisler, *The Metropolitan Opera,* 90–95; Fiedler, *Molto Agitato,* 6; Goldin, *Music Merchants,* 98–100; George Martin *The Damrosch Dynasty,* 73–85.

23. Johanna Fiedler, *Molto Agitato,* 7; Briggs, *Requiem,* 34–35; Musselman. *Music in the Cultured Generation,* 143, 146.

24. Joseph Horowitz, *Classical Music in America,* 140–41.

25. Dizikes, *Opera in America,* 243.

26. ———, *Opera in America,* 221.

27. Johanna Fiedler, *Molto Agitato,* 8–9.

28. John Kobler, *Otto the Magnificent: The Life of Otto Kahn* (New York: Charles Scribner's Sons, 1988), 30.

29. Joseph Horowitz, *Wagner Nights* (Berkeley and Los Angeles: University of California Press, 1994), 338; Giulio Gatti-Casazza, *Memories of the Opera* (New York: Vienna House, 1973), 15, 168–69; Kobler, *Otto the Magnificent,* 31; Fiedler, *Molto Agitato,* 11.

30. Johanna Fiedler, *Molto Agitato,* 11–13; Kobler, *Otto the Magnificent,* 52–54.

31. John Frederick Cone, *Oscar Hammerstein's Manhattan Opera Company* (Norman: University of Oklahoma Press, 1966), 277.

32. John Briggs, *Requiem,* 324–25.

33. Gatti-Casazza, *Memories,* 10, 175. Dizikes, *Opera in America,* 312–16, 365.

34. Frances Alda, *Men, Women and Tenors,* 21.

35. Alda, *Men, Women and Tenors,* 21; Fiedler, *Molto Agitato,* 21; Schoenberg, *The Great Conductors,* 258.

36. John Frederick Cone, *Oscar Hammerstein's Manhattan Opera,* 4–5, 32. The numeral designation is often applied to distinguish him from his better-known grandson and namesake, the lyricist half of the Rodgers and Hammerstein team who bestrode the Broadway musical stage during the mid-twentieth century.

37. ———, *Oscar Hammerstein's Manhattan Opera,* 46–47. As already noted, in spite of his position and generosity, the Morgan faction at the Metropolitan denied Kahn the ownership of a box because he was Jewish. Not until 1917, four years after Morgan's death, was Kahn offered his own box. By that time he was accustomed to his seat in the orchestra, and although he did accept the box, he seldom used it.

38. Giulio Gatti-Casazza, *Memories,* 168. Cone, *Oscar Hammerstein's Manhattan Opera,* 102–16, 123, 177, 261–63, 267–77.

39. Emanuel Rubin, "Jeanette Meyer Thurber (1850–1946): Music for a Democracy," *Cultivating Music in America: Women Patrons and Activists Since 1860,* ed. Ralph P. Locke and Cyrilla Barr (Berkeley and Los Angeles: University of California Press, 1997), 138–44; Catherine Parsons Smith, "Inventing Tradition: Symphony and Opera in Progressive-Era Los Angeles," *Music and Culture in America, 1861–1918,* ed. Michael Saffle (New York: Garland, 1998), 305–307.

40. Joseph Horowitz, *Classical Music,* 139–45.

41. ———, *Classical Music,* 139–45.

42. ———, *Classical Music,* 139–45.

CHAPTER 3

1. John Dizikes, *Opera in America,* 152; Mark N. Grant, *Maestros of the Pen: A History of Classical Music Criticism in America* (Boston: Northeastern University Press, 1998), 36; Louis Menand, *The Metaphysical Club: A Story of Ideas in America* (New York: Farrar, Strauss and Giroux, 2001), 248. The standard biography is still George Willis Cooke, *John Sullivan Dwight: Brook-Farmer, Editor and Critic of Music* (Boston: Small, Maynard & Co., 1898; reprinted, New York: Da Capo Press, 1969). See also Ora Frishberg Soloman, *Beethoven's Symphonies and J. S. Dwight: The Birth of American Musical Criticism* (Boston: Northeastern University Press, 1995).

2. Philip Hart, *Orpheus in the New World: The Symphony Orchestra as an American Cultural Institution* (New York: W. W. Norton Co., 1973); 51–52; Chmaj, "Fry versus Dwight: American Music's Debate over Nationality," *American Music* 3:1 (Spring 1985), 68; *Dwight's Journal of Music,* 4 (February 4, 1854), 141; Grant, *Masters of the Pen,* 200, 265; Henry Krehbiel, *How to Listen to Music* (New York: Scribner's, 1876).

3. John Sullivan Dwight, *Dwight's Journal of Music,* (May 16, 1864): 318.

4. Mark N. Grant, *Maestros of the Pen,* 94–95; 80–83; 99–102; and 109–23 and Matthews, *A Hundred Years,* 364–70. In addition to his own autobiography, *Steeplejack,* the main biography is Arnold T. Schwab, *James Gibbons Huneker, Critic of the Seven Arts* (Stanford, Calif.: Stanford University Press, 1963).

5. Quoted in Grant, *Maestros of the Pen,* xix.

6. Steven Ledbetter, "Higginson and Chadwick: Non-Brahmins in Boston," *American Music* 19:1 (Spring 2001), 61; Hitchcock: *Music in the United States,* 135–38; Hughes and Elson, *American Composers,* 210–21, 477–79; Tawa, *Coming of Age,* 103–30. The standard work on Chadwick is Victor Fell Yellin, *Chadwick: Yankee Composer* (Washington: Smithsonian Institution Press, 1986).

7. Hughes and Elson, *American Composers,* 174–175, 407–408; Tawa, *Coming of Age,* 164, 167.

8. ———, *American Composers,* 174–179; Tawa, *Coming of Age,* 157–169. The major study of Parker is William K. Kearns, *Horatio Parker, 1863–1919: His Life, Music and Ideas* (Metuchen, N.J.: Scarecrow Press, 1990).

9. ———, *American Composers*, 221–34; Tawa, *Coming of Age*, 169–77. The major work on Foote is Tawa, *Arthur Foote, A Musician in the Frame of Time and Place* (Lanham, Md.: Scarecrow, 1997). Foote left two autobiographical pieces: "A Bostonian Remembers," *Musical Quarterly* 23 (1937), 37–44; and *An Autobiography* (Norwood: Plympton Press, 1946).

10. Nicolas Tawa, *Coming of Age*, 131–56; Hughes and Elson, *American Composers*, 34–57. There is a fairly ample bibliography on MacDowell, including an old but nevertheless valuable biography—Lawrence Gilman, *Edward MacDowell* (New York: Lane, 1908)—and a recent study, Alan Howard Levy, *Edward MacDowell: An American Master* (Lanham, Md.: Scarecrow Press, 1998).

11. Hughes and Elson, *American Composers*, 426–432; Tawa, *Coming of Age*, 177–86. The definitive study on Beach is Adrienne Fried Block, *Amy Beach, Passionate Victorian* (New York: Oxford University Press, 1998).

12. Joseph Horowitz, *Dvorák in America* (Chicago: Cricket Books, 2003), 71–72.

13. ———, "Dvorák in Boston," *American Music* 19:1 (Spring 2001), 9–11; Adrienne Fried Block, "Dvorák, Beach and American Music," *A Celebration of American Music: Words and Music in Honor of Wiley Hitchcock*, ed. Richard Crawford, R. Allen Lott, and Carol J. Oja (Ann Arbor, Mich.: University of Michigan Press, 1990), 257–61.

14. Quotes from Joseph Horowitz, *The Post-Classical Predicament*, (Boston: Northeastern University Press, 1995), 63; and Sablosky, *American Music*, 107–108.

15. Alan Howard Levy, *Musical Nationalism: American Composers' Search for Identity* (Westport, Conn.: Greenwood Press, 1980), 11–12, 16, 19; *Musical Courier* 32:6 (February 5, 1896), 23. MacDowell quoted from Charles Hamm, *Music in the New World* (New York: W. W. Norton, 1983), 414.

16. Thomas Stoner, "The New Gospel of Music: Arthur Farwell's Vision of Democratic Music in America," *American Music* 9:2 (Summer 1991), 183.

17. Henry and Sidney Cowell, *Charles Ives and His Music* (New York: Oxford, 1955), 66–70. There is a massive bibliography on Ives, especially noteworthy among which are J. Peter Burkholder, *Charles Ives: The Ideas Behind the Music* (New Haven: Yale, 1985), and Burkholder (ed.), *Charles Ives and His World* (Princeton: Princeton University Press, 1996); Vivian Perlis, *Charles Ives Remembered: An Oral History* (New Haven: Yale, 1974); Jan Swafford, *Charles Ives: A Life with Music* (New York: Norton, 1996); Gayle Sherwood, *Charles Ives: A Guide to Research* (New York: Routledge, 2002), and Crawford, *America's Musical Life*, 495–523.

18. Charles E. Ives, *Memos*, ed. John Kirkpatrick (New York: W. W. Norton, 1972), 196.

19. All quotations in this paragraph are from Charles E. Ives, *Essays before a Sonata*, ed. Howard Boatwright (New York: W. W. Norton, 1970) xxv, 11, 41–42.

20. ———, *Essays before a Sonata*, 130.

21. Gilbert Chase, *America's Music, from the Pilgrims to the Present*, rev. 2nd ed. (New York: McGraw-Hill Book Co., 1966), 408.

22. Tawa, *Coming of Age*, 3–4, 16, 40.

23. Emanuel Rubin, "Jeanette Meyer Thurber," 308–10; Horowitz, *The Post-Classical Predicament*, 65.

CHAPTER 4

1. Alexis de Tocqueville, *Democracy in America,* ed. J. P. Mayar. Trans. by George Lawrence (Garden City, N.Y.: Doubleday, 1969), 295, 292–93.

2. T. J. Jackson Lears, *No Place of Grace* (Chicago: The University Press of Chicago,1994), 32.

3. Steven Baur, "Music, Morals, and Social Management: Mendelssohn in Post-Civil War America," *American Music* 19, No. 1 (Spring 2001): 83.

4. Leonard Ellinwood, *A History of American Church Music* (New York: Morehouse-Gorham, 1953; repr. New York: Da Capo Press, 1970), 73–74.

5. *The American Musical Directory* (New York: Thomas Hutchinson, 1861), 215–33.

6. Stanley Robert McDaniel, "Church Song and the Cultivated Tradition in New England and New York" (DMA dissertation, University of Southern California, 1983), 346, 357–58.

7. McDaniel, "Church Song and the Cultivated Tradition," 343–46, 370.

8. See William K. Gallo, "The Life and Church Music of Dudley Buck (1839–1909)" (PhD diss., Catholic University, 1968); and N. Lee Orr, "Dudley Buck: Leader of a Forgotten Tradition," *The Tracker* 38:3 (1994): 10–21.

9. Dudley Buck, *Illustrations in Choir Accompaniment* (New York: G. Schirmer, 1877), 29; Elwyn A. Weinandt and Robert H.Young, *The Anthem in England and America* (New York: Free Press, 1970), 330–31.

10. *The National Cyclopedia of American Biography,* s.v. "Buck, Dudley."

11. Cited in Ellinwood, *The History of American Church Music,* 134.

12. N. Lee Orr, "Dudley Buck," 18–19.

13. E. Jane Rasmussen, *Musical Taste as a Religious Question in Nineteenth-Century America* (Lewiston, NY: Edwin Mellen Press), 335–38; Clifford Nelson, *The Lutherans in North America* (Philadelphia: Fortress Press, 1980), 210–51; Ralph Gerald Gay, "A Study of the American Liturgical Revival" (PhD diss., Emory University, 1977), 98–99; 116–39.

14. *American Musical Directory,* 216–19, 220–24.

15. Stanley Robert McDaniel, "Church Music and the Cultivated Tradition," 558–61.

16. *The Parish of the Advent in the City of Boston: A History of One Hundred Years* (Boston: Parish of the Advent, 1941), 42–3, 124–26; Edward Hodges, "Choristers," *New York Musical World* 16: 294 (November 22, 1856): 627.

17. *American Musical Directory,* 247–48. John Ireland Tucker's Holy Cross Church in Troy, New York, was by this time singing daily services; in fact, as will be noted presently, both Trinity and Advent had used Holy Cross as their model.

18. E. Jane Rasmussen, *Musical Taste,* 356–62, 549; Ellinwood, *History of American Church Music,* 77–78.

19. Francis F. Bierne, *St. Paul's Parish, Baltimore: A Chronicle of the Mother Church* (Baltimore: St. Paul's Parish, 1967), 126–32.

20. Watkins Shaw, *The Succession of Organists* (Oxford: Clarendon, 1991), 189.

21. John Ogasapian, "The Restoration of Sacred Music in Romantic Germany," *Journal of Church Music* 30:3 (March 1988): 9–12, 30.

22. Leonard Ellinwood, *History of American Church Music*, 99–107; Mathews and Howe, *A Hundred Years of Music in America*, 280–282. The main source is Ronald Damian, "A Historical Study of the Cæcilian Movement in the United States" (Ph. D. diss., Catholic Univ., 1984).

23. Ronald Damian, "Cæcilian Movement," 38.

24. *The Sun's Guide to New York* (New York: *Sun*, 1892), 265–266.

25. Ronald Damian, "Cæcilian Movement," 84–86.

26. D. W. Krummel and Stanley Sadie, eds., *Music Printing and Publishing* (New York and London: W. W. Norton & Company, 1990), 114–24; 217; 409; 521.

27. Carlton R. Young, *Companion to the United Methodist Hymnal* (Nashville: Abingdon Press, 1993), 18–33.

28. *The New Grove Dictionary of American Music*, s.v. "Hymnody."

29. Ann Douglas, *The Feminization of American Culture* (New York: The Noonday Press, 1977), 218–20.

30. Albert Christ-Janer, Charles W. Hughes, and Carleton Sprague Smith, *American Hymns Old and New* (New York: Columbia University Press, 1980), 279.

31. All quotations in this paragraphs are from Nicholas Temperley, *The Music of the English Parish Church*, 2 vols. (Cambridge: Cambridge University Press, 1979), I: 304–06.

32. All quotations in this paragraphs are from Ann Douglas, *The Feminization of American Culture*, 218–20.

33. Ira D. Sankey, James McGranahan and George C. Stebbins, *Gospel Hymns, Nos. 1 to 6 Complete* (Chicago: Bigelow & Main, and Philadelphia: John Church, 1894), 511.

34. *Grove Dictionary of American Music*, s. v. "Hymnody."

35. For contemporary descriptions, see Eileen Southern, *The Music of Black Americans*, 3rd ed. (New York: W. W. Norton, 1997), 91–96; Stephen A. Marini, *Sacred Song in America: Religion, Music and Public Culture* (Urbana: Univ. of Illinois Press, 2003), 108, astutely observes that "the story of black church song is a compelling journey from West African roots through Evangelical Protestant hymns and slave spirituals to the gospel songs of the twentieth century.

36. Cited in Lawrence W. Levine, *Black Culture and Black Consciousness: Afro-American Folk Thought from Slavery to Freedom* (New York: Oxford University Press, 1977), 22, 39–44.

37. Lawrence W. Levine, *Black Culture and Black Consciousness*, 166.

38. John Ogasapian, *English Cathedral Music in New York: Edward Hodges of Trinity Church* (Richmond, Va.: The Organ Historical Society, 1994), 155.

39. Henry Lahee, *The Organ and Its Masters* (Boston: L. C. Page & Co., 1902), 279.

40. On the Trinity Church organ, see John Ogasapian, *Organ Building in New York City, 1700–1900* (Braintree: Organ Literature Foundation, 1977), 77–96.

41. The cathedral, exquisitely designed and beautifully furnished, is 188 feet long with a 109-foot transept span at the crossing: by no means small, but certainly not of European cathedral proportions. The instrument's effectiveness was hampered because it was simply too large. In 1925, it was finally rebuilt and drastically reduced in size. See Ogasapian, *Organ Building in New York City*, 172–74; 237–39.

42. William Osborne, *Clarence Eddy (1851–1937), Dean of American Organists* (Richmond: Organ Historical Society, 2000), 173–261; the book includes programs from his tours.

CHAPTER 5

1. Ethan Mordden, *Better Foot Forward. The History of American Musical Theatre* (New York: Grossman Publishers, 1976), 10–12; *New Grove Dictionary of American Music*, s.v. "Musical Theater"; Denny Martin Flinn, *Musical! A Grand Tour* (New York: Schirmer Books, 1997), 81–87; Katherine K. Preston, "American musical theatre before the twentieth century," in *The Cambridge Companion to the Musical*, ed. William A. Everett and Paul R. Laird (Cambridge: Cambridge University Press, 2002), 18–28.

2. Katherine K. Preston, "American musical theatre," 28.

3. Armond Fields and L. Marc Fields, *From the Bowery to Broadway: Lew Fields and the Roots of American Popular Theater* (New York: Oxford University Press, 1993), 206–07.

4. Katherine K. Preston, "American musical theatre," 18–25.

5. Ethan Mordden, *Better Foot Forward*, 12.

6. *American Music*, s.v. "Burlesque"; *Better Foot Forward*, 15–17; Joel Schrock, *The Gilded Age* (Westport, Conn.: Greenwood Press, 2004), 213.

7. For a recent edition see Richard Jackson, ed., *Early Burlesque in America: Evangeline (1877)*, vol. XIII of *Nineteenth-Century American Musical Theater*, gen. ed. Deane L. Root (New York : Garland Publishing, Inc., 1994).

8. *American Music*, s.v. "Vaudeville"; *The Gilded Age*, 214–16; *Musical!*, 120.

9. See Katherine K. Preston, ed., *Irish American Theater:'The Mulligan Guard's Ball' (1879) and 'Reilly and the Four Hundred' (1891)*, vol. X of *Nineteenth-Century American Musical Theater*, gen. ed. Deane L. Root (New York: Garland Publishing, Inc., 1994).

10. Gerald Bordman, *American Musical Theatre. A Chronicle*, 3rd ed. (New York: Oxford University Press, 2001), 45.

11. Katherine K. Preston, "Confronting the Stereotypes, Confounding Cultural Hierarchy: An Unexplored Web of American Musical Life, 1876–1880." Unpublished paper, given at the American Musicological Society in Washington, D.C., October 28, 2005.

12. All quotations in this paragraph are from Ethan Mordden, *Better Foot Forward*, 30–31.

13. The main sources for African American musical theater are Thomas L. Riis, *Just Before Jazz. Black Musical Theater in New York, 1890–1915* (Washington and London: Smithsonian Institution Press, 1989); Marva Griffin Carter, *"Swing Along": The Musical Life of Will Marion Cook* (New York and London: Oxford University Press, forthcoming); John Graziano, "Images of African Americans: African-American musical theatre, *Show Boat* and *Porgy and Bess*, in *The Cambridge Companion to the Musical*, ed. William A. Everett and Paul R. Laird (Cambridge: Cambridge University Press, 2002), 63–71; and Julian Mates, *America's Musical Stage. Two Hundred Years of Musical Theatre* (New York: Praeger, 1987), 174–77.

14. John Graziano, "Image of African Americans," 70; Thomas L. Riis, ed., *The Music and Scripts of 'In Dahomey,'* vol. 5 of *Music in the United States of America*, gen. ed. Richard Crawford (Madison, A-R Editions, 1996), xiii–lxxii; Marva Griffin Carter, "Removing the 'Minstrel Mask' in the Musicals of Will Marion Cook, *Musical Quarterly*, 84 no. 2 (2000): 206–20; Richard Crawford, *America's Musical Life. A History* (New York & London: W. W. Norton & Company, 2001), 535–36.

15. Richard Crawford, *America's Musical Life. A History*, 535.

16. Cited in Lawrence W. Levine, *Highbrow/Lowbrow* (Cambridge and London: Harvard University Press, 1988), 201.

17. Richard Crawford, *America's Musical Life: A History*, 294–95.

18. "The Tonic Sol-Fa System: Opinions of a Critic," *The Century Magazine* 35, No. 2 (December 1887): 318.

19. All quotes in this paragraph are from Joseph Musselman, *Music in the Cultured Generation: A Social History of Music in America, 1870–1900* (Evanston: Northwestern University Press, 1971): 169.

20. Ralph McVety Kent, "A Study of Oratorios and Sacred Cantatas Composed in America Before 1900" (Ph.D. diss., University of Iowa, 1954): 33–34.

21. Suzanne Gail Snyder, "The *Männerchor* Tradition in the United States: A Historical Analysis of Its Contribution to American Culture" (Ph.D., diss. University of Iowa, 1991), 426–551; 615–17.

22. Jacklin B. Stopp, "The Secular Cantata in the United States: 1850–1919," *Journal of Research in Music Education* 17, no. 4 (1969): 389–90; Jacklin Talmage Bolton, "Religious Influences on American Secular Cantatas, 1850–1930" (Ph.D. diss., University of Michigan, Ann Arbor, 1964), 447–64; George F. Root, *The Haymakers*, ed. Dennis R. Martin, vols. 9 and 10, *Recent Researches in American Music* (Madison: A-R Editions, Inc.), vii–x.

23. Any study of the American partsong must begin with Osborne's *American Singing Societies and Their Partsongs*, cited above. Other sources include *The New Grove Dictionary of American Music*, s.v. "Glee"; Arnold R. Thomas, "The Development of Male Glee Clubs in American Colleges and Universities" (Ed.D., diss., Columbia University, 1962); and B. E. Lindsay, "The English Glee in New England, 1815–1845" (Ph.D. diss., George Peabody College for Teachers, 1966). For a listing of partsongs by 10 of the most important composers, see Osborne, 69–92.

24. *American Memory* Site. Library of Congress Website. See also Osborne, *American Singing Societies*, 49–50.

25. For a modern edition of "In Absence" and "The Signal Resounds from Afar," see N. Lee Orr, ed., *Dudley Buck: American Victorian Choral Music*,' vol. 14 of *Music in the United States of America*, gen. ed. Richard Crawford (Madison, A-R Editions, 2005).

26. R. Allen Lott, *From Paris to Peoria. How European Piano Virtuosos Brought Classical Music to the American Heartland* (Oxford and New York: Oxford University Press, 2003), 174.

27. John Sullivan Dwight, *Dwight's Journal of Music* (October 30, 1875): 197.

28. Margaret Hindle Haze and Robert M. Hazen, *The Music Men. An Illustrated History of Brass Bands in America, 1800–1920* (Washington and London: Smithsonian Institution Press, 1987), 8.

29. *Dwight's Journal of Music* (April 16, 1853): 185.

30. *American Music*, s.v. "Bands."

31. Joel Schrock, *The Gilded Age* (Westport, Conn.: Greenwood Press, 2004), 197–98.

32. *American Music*, s.v. "Bands"; Crawford, *America's Musical Life*, 291–92.

CHAPTER 6

1. Richard Crawford, *America's Musical Life. A History*, 441; 471–91; Other important sources for the music of Tin Pan Alley include Nicholas E. Tawa, *The Way to Tin Pan Alley. American Popular Song, 1866–1910* (New York: Schirmer Books, Inc., 1990); David Ewen, *All the Years of American Popular Music* (Englewood Cliffs, N.J.: Prentice-Hall, Inc., 1977), 151–77; Russell Sanjek, *American Popular Music and Its Business. The First Four Hundred Years*, vol. 2 (New York and Oxford: Oxford University Press, 1988), 401–20; Charles Hamm, *Yesterdays. Popular Song in America* (New York, London: W. W. Norton & Company, 1983), 284–325.

2. Edward B. Marks, *They All Sang: From Tony Pastor to Rudy Vallee* (New York: The Viking Press, 1934), 3.

3. Charles K. Harris, *After the Ball: Forty Years of Melody* (New York: Frank-Maurice, 1926), 39–40.

4. Marks, *They All Sang*, 4.

5. Rudi Blesh and Harriet Janis, *They All Played Ragtime*, rev. ed. (New York: Oak Publications, 1971), 2. Other important sources for ragtime music include Ewen, *All the Years of American Popular Music*, 159–72; Jeffrey MaGee, "Ragtime and Early Jazz," in *The Cambridge History of American Music*, ed. David Nicholls (Cambridge: Cambridge University Press, 1998), 388–403; Gilbert Chase, *America's Music from the Pilgrims to the Present*, rev. 3rd ed. (Urbana and Chicago, University of Illinois Press, 1992), 413–28; Eileen Southern, *The Music of Black Americans*, 314–32: Edward Berlin, *Ragtime. A Musical and Cultural History* (Berkeley, Los Angeles, London: University of California Press, 1980); Crawford, *America's Musical Life. A History*, 524–46; *New Grove Dictionary of American Music*, s. v. "Ragtime." Sanjek, *American Popular Music and Its Business*, 290–302.

6. Blesh, *They All Played Ragtime*, 39–40.

7. Scott Joplin, *Ecole du ragtime* [school of Ragtime] (Paris: A. Zurfluh, 1995), 1–2.

8. Crawford, *America's Musical Life. A History*, 541.

9. ———, *America's Musical Life. A History*, 541–542.

10. ———, *America's Musical Life. A History*, 543.

11. Southern, *The Music of Black Americans*, 332.

12. ———, *The Music of Black Americans*, 332.

13. Sanjek, *American Popular Music and Its Business*, 411.

CHAPTER 7

1. *The Writing of Fiction* (New York: Scribner's, 1925), 14, 17.

2. All quotations in this paragraph are from W. L. Hubbard, ed., *The American History and Encyclopedia of Music*, vol. 8 (Toledo and New York, Irving Squire, 1908), 13.

3. Citied in Horowitz, *Classical Music in America* (New York: W. W. Norton & Company, 2005), 256.

4. Lewis A. Erenberg, *Steppin' Out: New York Nightlife and the Transformation of American Culture, 1890–1930* (Westport, Conn.: Greenwood Press, 1981), 153.

5. ———, *Steppin' Out,* 150, 146.
6. ———, *Steppin' Out,* 146, 150–52.
7. ———, *Steppin' Out,* 147.
8. *Along This Way* (New York: Viking Press, 1968), 328.

Bibliography

Ahlquist, Karen. *Democracy at the Opera: Music, Theater and Culture in New York City, 1815–1860.* Urbana: University of Illinois Press, 1997.

Allen, William Francis, Charles Picard Ware, and Lucy McKim Garrison, *Slave Songs of the United States.* New York: A. Simpson & Co., 1867.

American Musical Directory, The. New York: Thomas Hutchinson, 1861.

Ammer, Christine. *Unsung: A History of Women in American Music.* Westport: Greenwood Press, 1980; revised and expanded edition Portland, Oregon: Amadeus Press, 2001.

Ayars, Christine Merrick. *Contributions to the Art of Music in America by the Music Industries of Boston, 1640 to 1936.* New York: H. W. Wilson Co., 1936; reprinted New York: Johnson Reprints, 1969.

Beard, Patricia. *After the Ball.* New York: Harper Collins, 2003.

Beckerman, Michael B. *New Worlds of Dvorak: Searching in America for the Composer's Inner Life.* New York: W. W. Norton Co., 2003.

Berlin, Edward A. *King of Ragtime: Scott Joplin and His Era.* New York: Oxford University Press, 1994.

———. *Ragtime: A Musical and Cultural History.* Berkeley and Los Angeles: University of California Press, 1980.

Block, Adrienne Fried. *Amy Beach, Passionate Victorian.* New York: Oxford University Press, 1998.

———. "Dvorak, Beach, and American Music." In *A Celebration of American Music: Words and Music in Honor of H. Wiley Hitchcock*, eds. Richard Crawford, R. Allen Lott, and Carol Oja. Ann Arbor: University of Michigan Press, 1990.

Bordman, Gerald. *American Operetta, From* H.M.S. Pinafore *to* Sweeney Todd. New York: Oxford University Press, 1981.

Boyer, Horace Clarence. *How Sweet the Sound: The Golden Age of Gospel.* Washington: Elliott and Clark, 1995.

Brancaleone, Francis. "Edward MacDowell and Indian Motives." *American Music* 7:4 (Winter 1989): 359–381.

Briggs, John. *Requiem for a Yellow Brick Brewery: A History of the Metropolitan Opera.* Boston: Little, Brown and Co., 1969.

Bronner, Simon J., ed. *Consuming Visions: Accumulation and Display of Goods in America, 1880–1920.* New York: W. W. Norton Co, 1989.

Bruhn, Christopher. "Taking the Private Public: Amateur Music-Making and the Musical Audience in 1860s New York." *American Music* 21:3 (Fall 2003): 260–90.

Buck, Dudley. *Illustrations in Choir Accompaniment.* New York: G. Schirmer, 1877.

Burkholder, J. Peter, ed. *Charles Ives and His World.* Princeton: Princeton University Press, 1996.

———. *Charles Ives: The Ideas Behind His Music.* New Haven: Yale University Press, 1985.

Butterworth, Neil. *The American Symphony.* Aldershott: Ashgate Publishing, 1998.

Chmaj, Betty, "Fry versus Dwight: American Music's Debate Over Nationality." *American Music* 3:1 (Spring 1985): 63–84.

Collins, Theresa M. *Otto Kahn: Art, Money and Modern Time.* Chapel Hill: University of North Carolina Press, 2002.

Cone, John Frederick. *Adelina Patti, Queen of Hearts.* Portland, Oregon: Amadeus Press, 1993.

———. *Oscar Hammerstein's Manhattan Opera Company.* Norman: University of Oklahoma Press, 1966.

Cooke, George Willis. *John Sullivan Dwight: Brook-Farmer, Editor and Critic of Music.* Boston: Small, Maynard & Co., 1898; reprinted, New York: Da Capo Press, 1969.

Cornelius, Stephen H. *Music of the Civil War Era.* Westport, Conn.: Greenwood Press, 2004.

Couvares, Francis G. *The Remaking of Pittsburgh: Class and Culture in an Industrializing City, 1877–1919.* Albany: State University of New York Press, 1984.

Cowell, Henry and Sidney. *Charles Ives and His Music.* New York: Oxford University Press, 1955.

Crawford, Richard. *The American Musical Landscape.* Berkeley and Los Angeles: University of California Press, 1993.

———. *America's Musical Life: A History.* New York: W. W. Norton, 2001.

Crawford, Richard, R. Allen Lott, and Carol Oja, eds. *A Celebration of American Music: Words and Music in Honor of H. Wiley Hitchcock.* Ann Arbor: University of Michigan Press, 1990.

Damian, Ronald. "A Historical Study of the Cæcilian Movement in the United States." PhD diss., The Catholic University, 1984.

Davis, Ronald L. *A History of Music in American Life, Vol. 2: The Gilded Years, 1865–1920.* Huntington, N.Y.: Robert Krieger Publishing, 1980.

Davison, Archibald T. *Church Music, Illusion and Reality*. Cambridge: Harvard University Press, 1966.

Dizikes, John. *Opera in America: A Cultural History*. New Haven: Yale University Press, 1993.

Dwight's Journal of Music. Boston, 1852–1881; reprinted New York: Arno Press, 1968.

Eisler, Paul E. *The Metropolitan Opera: The First Twenty-Five Years*. Croton-on-Hudson, N.Y.: North River Press, 1984.

Ellinwood, Leonard. *A History of American Church Music*. New York: Morehouse-Gorham, 1953; reprinted, New York: Da Capo Press, 1970.

Fiedler, Johanna. *Molto Agitato: The Mayhem Behind the Music at the Metropolitan Opera*. New York: Doubleday Anchor, 2001.

Finson, Jon W. *The Voices That Are Gone: Themes in Nineteenth-Century Popular Song*. New York: Oxford University Press, 1994.

Fitzlyon, April. *Maria Malibran, Diva of the Romantic Age*. London: Souvenir Press, 1987.

Foote, Arthur. *An Autobiography*. Norwood: Plympton Press, 1946.

———. "A Bostonian Remembers." *Musical Quarterly* 23 (1937): 37–44.

Fostle, D. W. *The Steinway Saga*. New York: Charles Scribner's Sons, 1995.

Gatti-Casazza, Giulio. *Memories of the Opera*. New York: Vienna House, 1973.

Gay, Ralph Gerald. "A Study of the American Liturgical Revival." PhD diss., Emory University, 1977.

Gipson, Richard McCandless. *The Life of Emma Thursby (1845–1931)*. New York: The New-York Historical Society, 1940.

Glackens, Ira. *Yankee Diva: Lillian Nordica and the Golden Days of Opera*. New York: Coleridge Press, 1963.

Glahn, Denise von. *The Sounds of Place: Music and the American Cultural Landscape*. Boston: Northeastern University Press, 2003.

Good, Edwin M. "William Steinway and Music in New York." *Music and Culture in America, 1861–1918*, ed. Michael Saffle. New York: Garland Publishing, 1998.

Grant, Mark N. *Maestros of the Pen: A History of Classical Music Criticism in America*. Boston: Northeastern University Press, 1998.

Graziano, John. "Jullien and His Music for the Million." In *A Celebration of American Music: Words and Music in Honor of H. Wiley Hitchcock*, ed. Richard Crawford, R. Allen Lott, and Carol Oja. Ann Arbor: University of Michigan Press, 1990.

Green, Martin. *The Problem of Boston*. New York: W. W. Norton Co., 1966.

Hamm, Charles. *Music in the New World*. New York: W. W. Norton Co., 1983.

———. *Yesterdays: Popular Song in America*. New York: W. W. Norton, 1979.

Hart, Philip. *Orpheus in the New World: The Symphony Orchestra as an American Cultural Institution*. New York: W. W. Norton Co., 1973.

Hitchcock, H. Wiley. *Music in the United States: A Historical Introduction*, 4th ed. Englewood Cliffs: Prentice Hall, 1999.

Hodges, Edward. "Choristers." *New York Musical World* 16:294 (November 22, 1856): 627.

Holbrook, Stewart H. *The Age of Moguls*. Garden City: Doubleday, 1954.

Homberger, Eric. *Mrs. Astor's New York: Money and Social Power in a Gilded Age*. New Haven: Yale University Press, 2002.

Horowitz, Joseph. "Dvorák and Boston." *American Music* 19:1 (Spring 2001): 3–17.

———. *Dvorak in America*. Chicago: Cricket Books, 2003.

———. *The Post Classical Predicament: Essays on Music and Society*. Boston: Northeastern University Press, 1995.

———. "Reclaiming the Past: Musical Boston Reconsidered." *American Music* 19:1 (Spring 2001): 18–38.

———. "'Sermons in Tones': Sacralization as a Theme in American Classical Music." *American Music* 16:3 (Fall 1998): 311–40.

———. *Wagner Nights*. Berkeley and Los Angeles: University of California Press, 1994.

Howe, Mark A. De Wolfe. *The Boston Symphony Orchestra: An Historical Sketch*. Boston: Houghton Mifflin, 1914.

Hubbard, W. L. *History of American Music*. New York: Irving Squire, 1908.

Hughes, Rupert and Arthur Elson. *American Composers*. Boston: Page Co., 1915; reprinted New York: AMS Press, 1974.

Jaher, Frederic Cople. *The Urban Establishment: Upper Strata in Boston, New York, Charleston, Chicago and Los Angeles*. Urbana: University of Illinois Press, 1982.

Johnson, H. Earle. *Symphony Hall, Boston*. Boston: Little, Brown, 1950.

Josephson, Matthew. *The Robber Barons*. New York: Harcourt Brace, 1934.

Kaatrud, Paul Gaarder. "Revivalism and the Popular Spiritual Song in Mid-Nineteenth Century America: 1830–1870." PhD diss., University of Minnesota, 1977.

Kearns, William K. *Horatio Parker (1863–1919), His Life, Music and Ideas*. Metuchen: Scarecrow Press, 1990.

Knight, Ellen. *Charles Martin Loeffler: A Life Apart in American Music*. Urbana: University of Illinois Press, 1993.

Kobler, John. *Otto the Magnificent: The Life of Otto Kahn*. New York: Charles Scribner's Sons, 1988.

Kolodin, Irving. *The Metropolitan Opera, 1883–1966: A Candid History*. New York: Alfred A. Knopf, 1966.

Krehbiel, Henry. *How to Listen to Music*. New York: Scribner's, 1896.

Lamb, Andrew. *150 Years of Popular Musical Theatre*. New Haven: Yale University Press, 2000.

Lawrence, Vera Brodsky. *Strong on Music: The New York Music Scene in the Days of George Templeton Strong. 1: Resonances, 1831–1849*. New York: Oxford University Press, 1988.

———. *Strong on Music: The New York Musical Scene in the Days of George Templeton Strong. 2: Reverberations, 1850–1856*. Chicago: University of Chicago Press, 1995.

———. *Strong on Music: The New York Musical Scene in the Days of George Templeton Strong. 3: Repercussions, 1857–1862*. Chicago: University of Chicago Press, 1999.

———. "William Henry Fry's Messianic Yearnings: The Eleven Lectures, 1852–53." *American Music* 7:4 (Winter 1989): 382–411.

Ledbetter, Steven. "Higginson and Chadwick: Non-Brahmins in Boston." *American Music* 19:1 (Spring 2001): 51–63.

Levine, Lawrence W. *Black Culture and Black Consciousness: Afro-American Folk Thought from Slavery to Freedom.* New York: Oxford University Press, 1977.

———. *Highbrow, Lowbrow: The Emergence of Cultural Hierarchy in America.* Cambridge: Harvard University Press, 1988.

Levy, Alan Howard. *Edward MacDowell: An American Master.* Lanham, Md.: Scarecrow Press, 1998.

———. *Musical Nationalism: American Composers' Search for Identity.* Westport: Greenwood Press, 1980.

Lieberman, Richard K. *Steinway and Sons.* New Haven: Yale University Press, 1995.

Locke, Ralph P. and Cyrilla Barr, eds. *Cultivating Music in America: Women Patrons and Activists since 1960.* Berkeley and Los Angeles: University of California Press, 1997.

Loesser, Arthur. *Men, Women, and Pianos.* New York: Simon and Schuster, 1954.

Lott, R. Allen. *From Paris to Peoria. How European Piano Virtuosos Brought Classical Music to the American Heartland.* Oxford and New York: Oxford University Press, 2003.

Maritzek, Max, *Revelations of an Opera Manager in Nineteenth-Century America [Crotchets and Quavers* (1855), *Sharps and Flats* (1890)]. New York: Dover, 1968.

Martin, George. *The Damrosch Dynasty: America's First Family of Music.* Boston: Houghton Mifflin, 1983.

Mason, William. *Memories of a Musical Life.* New York: The Century Co., 1901.

Mathews, William Smythe Babcock and Glanville Howe. *A Hundred Years of Music in America.* Chicago: G. L. Howe, 1889; reprinted New York: AMS Press, 1970.

McConachie, Bruce A. "New York Opera Going, 1805–1850: Creating an Elite Social Ritual." *American Music* 6:2 (Summer 1988): 181–92.

McDaniel, Stanley Robert. "Church Song and the Cultivated Tradition in New England and New York." DMA diss., University of Southern California, 1983.

Menand, Louis. *The Metaphysical Club: A Story of Ideas in America.* New York: Farrar, Strauss and Giroux, 2001.

Messiter, Arthur H. *A History of the Choir and Music of Trinity Church, New York.* New York: Edwin S. Gorham, 1906.

Mussulman, Joseph A. *Music in the Cultured Generation: A Social History of Music in America, 1870–1900.* Evanston: Northwestern University Press, 1971.

Nelson, E. Clifford. *The Lutherans in North America.* Philadelphia: Fortress Press, 1980.

Nevins, Allan, ed. *The Diary of Philip Hone.* New York: Dodd, Mead and Co., 1927.

Nicholls, David, ed. *The Cambridge History of American Music.* London: Cambridge University Press, 1998.

Ochse, Orpha. *The History of the Organ in the United States.* Bloomington: Indiana University Press, 1975.

Odell, George C. D. *Annals of the New York Stage.* 12 Volumes. New York: Columbia
       University Press, 1927; reprinted New York: Arno Press, 1968.
Ogasapian, John. *English Cathedral Music in New York: Edward Hodges of Trinity Church.*
       Richmond: Organ Historical Society, 1994.
———. *Music of the Colonial and Revolutionary Era.* Westport: Greenwood Press, 2004.
———. *Organ Building in New York City, 1700–1900.* Braintree, Mass.: Organ Literature
       Foundation, 1977.
———. "The Restoration of Sacred Music in Romantic Germany." *Journal of Church
       Music* 30:3 (March, 1988): 9–12, 30.
Oliver, Paul, Max Harrison, and William Bolcum. *The New Grove Gospel, Blues and
       Jazz.* New York: W. W. Norton, 1986.
Olmstead, Andrea. *Juilliard: A History.* Urbana: University of Illinois Press, 1999.
Orr, N. Lee. "Dudley Buck: Leader of a Forgotten Tradition," *The Tracker* 38:3 (1994):
       10–21.
Osborne, William. *Clarence Eddy (1851–1937), Dean of American Organists.* Richmond:
       Organ Historical Society, 2000.
Owen, Barbara. *The Organ in New England.* Raleigh: Sunbury Press, 1979.
*Parish of the Advent in the City of Boston (1844–1944), The: A History of One Hundred
       Years.* Boston: Parish of the Advent, 1944.
Patterson, Jerry E. *The First Four Hundred: Mrs. Astor's New York in the Gilded Age.* New
       York: Rizzoli International, 2000.
Perlis, Vivian. *Charles Ives Remembered: An Oral History.* New Haven: Yale University
       Press, 1974.
Pisani, Michael V. "From Hiawatha to Wa-Wan: Musical Boston and the Uses of Native
       American Lore." *American Music* 19:1 (Spring 2001): 39–50.
Pleasants, Henry. *The Great Singers from the Dawn of Opera to our Time.* New York:
       Simon and Schuster, 1966.
Preston, Katherine K. "Between the Cracks: The Performance of English Opera in Late
       Nineteenth-Century America." *American Music* 21:3 (Fall 2003): 349–74.
———. *Opera on the Road: Traveling Opera Troupes in the United States, 1885–1880.*
       Urbana: University of Illinois Press, 2001.
Rainbow, Bernarr. *The Choral Revival in the Anglican Church.* London: Oxford University
       Press, 1970.
Rasmussen, Jane. *Musical Taste as a Religious Question in Nineteenth-Century America.*
       Lewiston, N.Y.: Edwin Mellen Press, 1986.
Roell, Craig. *The Piano in America, 1890–1940.* Chapel Hill: University of North Caro-
       lina Press, 1989.
Rubin, Emanuel. "Jeanette Meyer Thurber (1850–1946): Music for a Democracy." In
       Cultivating Music in America: Women Patrons and Activists Since 1860, ed.
       Ralph P. Locke and Cyrilla Barr. Berkeley and Los Angeles: University of
       California Press, 1997.
Russell, Charles Edward. *The American Orchestra and Theodore Thomas.* New York:
       Doubleday, 1927; reprinted Westport: Greenwood Press, 1971.
Saarinen, Aline B. *The Proud Possessors: The Lives, Times and Tastes of Some Adventurous
       Art Collectors.* New York: Random House, 1958.

Sablosky, Irving. *American Music*. Chicago: University of Chicago Press, 1969.

———. *What They Heard: Music in America, 1852–1881, from the Pages of Dwight's Journal of Music*. Baton Rouge: Louisiana State University Press, 1986.

Saffle, Michael, ed. *Music and Culture in America, 1861–1918*. New York: Garland Publishers 1998.

Sanjek, Russell. *American Popular Music and Its Business. The First Four Hundred Years*, vol. 2. New York and Oxford: Oxford University Press, 1988.

Schabas, Ezra. *Theodore Thomas, America's Conductor and Builder of Orchestras, 1835–1905*. Urbana: University of Illinois Press, 1989.

Schickel, Richard. *The World of Carnegie Hall*. New York: Julian Messner, 1960.

Schmidt, John C. *The Life and Works of John Knowles Paine*. Ann Arbor, Mich.: UMI Research Press, 1980.

Schoenberg, Harold. *The Great Conductors*. New York: Simon and Schuster, 1967.

———. *The Great Pianists from Mozart to the Present*. New York: Simon and Schuster, 1967.

Schwab, Arnold T. *James Gibbons Huneker, Critic of the Seven Arts*. Palo Alto: Stanford University Press, 1963.

Shand-Tucci, Douglass. *The Art of Scandal: The Life and Times of Isabella Stuart Gardiner*. New York: Harper Collins, 1998.

Shanet, Howard. *Philharmonic: A History of New York's Orchestra*. New York: Doubleday, 1975.

Shaw, Watkins. *The Succession of Organists*. Oxford: Clarendon Press, 1991.

Sheean, Vincent. *Oscar Hammerstein I: The Life and Exploits of an Impresario*. New York: Simon and Schuster, 1956.

Shrock, Joel. *The Gilded Age*. Westport: Greenwood Press, 2004.

Sizer, Sandra. *Gospel Hymns and Social Religion*. Philadelphia: Temple University Press, 1978.

Smith, Catherine Parsons. "Inventing Tradition: Symphony and Opera in Progressive-Era Los Angeles." In *Music and Culture in America, 1861–1918*, ed. Michael Saffle. New York: Garland Publishing, 1998.

Snyder, Robert W. *The Voice of the City: Vaudeville and Popular Culture in New York*. New York: Oxford University Press, 1989.

Southern, Eileen. *The Music of Black Americans: A History*, 3rd ed. New York: W. W. Norton Co., 1997.

Stoner, Thomas. "The New Gospel of Music: Arthur Farwell's Vision of Democratic Music in America." *America Music* 9:2 (Summer 1991): 183–208.

Stowe, David W. *How Sweet the Sound: Music in the Spiritual Lives of Americans*. Cambridge: Harvard University Press, 2004.

Swafford, Jan. *Charles Ives: A Life With Music*. New York: W. W. Norton Co., 1996.

Tawa, Nicholas. *Arthur Foote: A Musician in the Frame of Time and Place*. Lanham: Scarecrow Press, 1997.

———. *The Coming of Age of American Art Music: New England's Classical Romanticists*. Westport: Greenwood Press, 1991.

———. *From Psalm to Symphony: A History of Music in New England*. Boston: Northwestern University Press, 2001.

———. *Sweet Songs for Gentle Americans: The Parlor Song in America, 1790–1860.* Bowling Green: Bowling Green University Popular Press, 1980.

Temperley, Nicholas. *The Music of the English Parish Church.* London: Cambridge University Press, 1979.

Tharp, Louise Hall. *Mrs. Jack: A Biography of Isabella Stuart Gardiner.* Boston: Little Brown, 1965.

Thaxter, Rosamond. *Sandpiper: The Life and Letters of Celia Thaxter.* Portsmouth: Peter Randall, 1999.

Tibbets, John C. *Dvorak in America, 1892–1895.* Portland, Ore.: Amadeus Press, 1993.

Upton, George P., ed. *Theodore Thomas: A Musical Autobiography.* Chicago: A. C. McClurg, 1905; reprinted New York: Da Capo Press, 1964.

Upton, William Treat. *William Henry Fry, American Journalist and Composer-Critic.* New York: Thomas Y. Crowell, 1954; reprinted New York: Da Capo Press, 1974.

Urrows, David Francis. "Apollo in Athens: Otto Dresel and Boston, 1850–1890." *American Music* 12:4 (Winter 1994): 345–88.

Ward, Andrew. *Dark Midnight When I Rise: The Story of the Fisk Jubilee Singers.* New York: Farrar, Strauss and Giroux, 2000.

Weinandt, Elwyn A., and Robert H. Young, *The Anthem in England and America.* New York: The Free Press, 1970.

Yellin, Victor Fell. *Chadwick: Yankee Composer.* Washington: Smithsonian Institution Press, 1990.

Yoffe, Elkhonon. *Tchaikovsky in America: The Composer's Visit in 1891.* Translated by Lidya Yoffe. New York: Oxford University Press, 1986.

Index

About the Authors

JOHN OGASAPIAN was a professor of music history at the University of Massachusetts, Lowell, and author of *Music of the Colonial and Revolutionary Era*.

N. LEE ORR is a professor of music and the coordinator of music history and literature at Georgia State University.